Let me tell you this: faith comes and goes. It rises and falls like the tides of an invisible ocean. If it is presumptuous to think that faith will stay with you forever, it is just as presumptuous to think that unbelief will.

— *Flannery O'Connor, in a letter*

Not Sure

A Pastor's Journey
from Faith
to Doubt

John Suk

William B. Eerdmans Publishing Company

Grand Rapids, Michigan / Cambridge, U.K.

Published 2011 by
Wm. B. Eerdmans Publishing Co.
2140 Oak Industrial Drive N.E., Grand Rapids, Michigan 49505 /
P.O. Box 163, Cambridge CB3 9PU U.K.

Printed in the United States of America

17 16 15 14 13 12 11   7 6 5 4 3 2 1

Library of Congress Cataloging-in-Publication Data

Suk, John D., 1956-
Not sure: a pastor's journey from faith to doubt / John Suk.
p.   cm.
ISBN 978-0-8028-6650-9 (pbk.: alk. paper)
1. Suk, John D., 1956-
2. Christian Reformed Church — Clergy — Biography.
3. Agnostics — United States — Biography.
4. Faith. I. Title.

BX6843.S85A3 2011
285.7′31092 — dc23
[B]
2011016840

www.eerdmans.com

Contents

Foreword, by Nicholas Wolterstorff   vii

Introduction   1

1. Oral Faith: Enchanted and Childlike   9

2. Literate Faith   31

3. Postmodern Faith: Loss and Doubt   59

4. Oral Again: Digital Faith   83

5. So, What Is Faith, Really?   121

6. Faith Is Not a Personal Relationship with Jesus   140

7. Faith Has No Cash Value   158

8. The Trouble with Doctrine, Mores, and Tribes   170

9. Greater Than My Heart   198

Index   208

Foreword

This book is not about loss of faith. It is not a story that begins with faith and ends with unbelief. It's a story about changes in the author's Christian faith, from the undoubting and unwavering faith of a child, through a bout with wracking doubt, to the faith of a mature adult who is able to say about many of his former certainties that he is no longer sure.

This story is interwoven with the telling of another story, fascinating and deeply informed, about changes in the mentality of the West and changes in the character of Christian faith corresponding to those changes. The author sees changes in his own faith as mirroring those historical changes. Phylogeny repeats ontogeny.

As a child he believed in a storied world, full of heroes, enchanted, with no wall separating the sacred from the secular. This was the faith of most people in oral, preliterate cultures. The wide availability of print in the early modern period, and the spread of literacy throughout the population, produced a profound change in the mentality of people in general and in the nature of Christian faith in particular. Now system, doctrine, rational argumentation became more important than story in the faith of many. The author narrates, both movingly and humorously, how he too became infatuated with theology and theological argumentation in his college days, and remained infatuated for several decades thereafter.

Eventually doubts began to set in. How could he be so sure in the face of others who were equally sure? And where was love, charity? The author's introduction to postmodernism proved to be a decisive experience. He was not persuaded by the relativism of the post-modern writers. But he learned to discern power where previously he had never noticed it; and a good many of his old certainties were shaken. The biblical text is open to a greater diversity of interpretations than he had previously conceded. His faith, and his understanding of faith, took yet a new form. Christian faith, at its core, is not belief in a set of doctrines but the way of life taught by Christ and grounded in trust.

The author's historical sketch concludes with his discussion of what he calls "the new orality" and "digital faith." He is sharply critical of many manifestations of this development, in particular of its mantra of "a personal relationship with Jesus" and of its selling of faith on the ground that it will yield health and wealth.

It's a rich, eloquent, beautifully written book. The author's story of his own faith, from the undoubting faith of the child, to the confident certainty of early adulthood, through a wracking bout with doubt, to a trust that lives with doubt, is deeply personal and unwaveringly honest. His sharp critique of the elevation of doctrine to central position in his own religious tradition is brave but loving. And his tracing of changes in the mentality of the West, the change from oral culture to literate culture and back to oral culture in a new digital form, is fresh and illuminating. Seldom has personal story been so imaginatively interwoven with cultural history, analysis, and critique.

NICHOLAS WOLTERSTORFF

Introduction

Between August 2002 and July 2003, my wife, Irene, and I toured North America in our recreational vehicle, which we named "The Bananer" after a spoof version of the church magazine I had edited for the previous ten years — *The Banner* (the official magazine publication of the Christian Reformed Church). Like the spoof, our year away was supposed to be mostly fun, but with a serious edge.

I was ready for a change of pace. As editor of a church weekly, I had been a denominational lightning rod, and ten years of high-voltage strikes had left me spiritually frayed, if not actually burned out. We planned our trip as an opportunity not only to quietly find rest and relaxation, but also to dream some dreams about what might be next. What I did not expect was the crisis of faith that engulfed me that year.

In hindsight, I realize that the crisis had actually been brewing for years, and I had simply gotten into the habit of burying it. As the editor of *The Banner*, I was one of the most visible leaders in the Christian Reformed denomination. As such I had responsibilities. I never believed that, as editor of the magazine, I should be a loose cannon. I had been appointed to nurture the church. Personally, however, over the course of those ten years I changed my mind more often and more radically than I was able to express publicly. This led to spiritual and intellectual tension. But the pressure I felt not to shock the church, combined with the busyness of work and family life, led me to mostly ignore that tension. As it turned out, I finished my time at *The Banner* just before the pressures of negotiating the internal dissonance between me and my church would have erupted.

I can still remember the exact moment that the spiritual issues I had been working through, mostly unconsciously, surfaced. It was about three weeks into our road trip. We were camped at North Rustico Beach on Prince Edward Island. I was on an early morning walk by myself. My head was down because the wind was blowing so hard that grains of sand were stinging my face. Large swells crashed onto the shore, and overnight they had left large piles of seaweed and even the occasional lobster trap behind. At one point the beach was split in two by a small stream flowing out from under a shingled bluff, through the sand and wreckage to the sea. As I stopped to look — from shingles to beach to sea billows — it seemed like the whole ocean was marching home to its source.

And suddenly, at that moment, I realized that, in terms of faith, I wanted to come home, too: that is, I wanted to be taken back to the place where, as a child, I could rest and find solace in my faith. But it also struck me at that moment that I would never again find it. How it was that everything I had for years pushed down beneath my consciousness erupted just then, I'm not sure. But I sat down and wept. After being raised in a deeply committed and loving Christian family; after attending Christian day schools, college, and seminary; after serving eight years as a church pastor and ten more as editor of the denominational magazine — after all this, I realized that my faith-as-usual had little currency. Looking out over the roiling ocean and feeling it deep inside, I realized that perhaps my upbringing and early career choices had made me into an accidental pastor. Maybe it was time to start over, maybe even without faith. I felt like a mess.

Six years after that walk along the beach — three spent teaching at a seminary in the Philippines and three more as president of a Christian graduate school of philosophy — I am still sometimes swamped by doubt and uncertainty. I would love to revel in the old, old story that I was taught as a child; I want to dream the dreams I had for the kingdom when I was a young pastor just out of seminary; I want to worship with songs that I sing from the roots of my being. But, faith-wise, all I can honestly do most days is put one foot in front of the other. I have lived for long periods when my faith has been mostly effort and not much consolation, and my doubts are often weighty and depressing.

When I was struggling at *The Banner* and didn't even really know it, Lewis Smedes, a professor of ethics at Fuller Seminary and former beloved Calvin College professor, read it between the lines of my editorials. He sought me out, asked me about it, and offered me a listening ear — as well as friendship. In the last book he wrote, before his untimely death, Smedes says: "Sometimes I hang on to faith by my fingernails; when the dream of a new world of Jesus' peace and love is more than two thousand years old and still shows no clear sign of coming true, anybody's faith is bound to turn to doubt."[1] I now know what Smedes meant. My life feels like a marathon, with doubt at one shoulder and faith on the other.

At the same time, I've discovered, much to my surprise — or at least to the surprise of the eager and naive young pastor I once was — that doubt isn't all bad. I first realized this halfway through our RV trip, just when we were ready to turn the "Bannaner" northward and head back home. We were camped on the top of a high hill overlooking Escondido, California. Off to one side of the hill I could see Dixon Lake, a reservoir for San Diego. About a thousand feet below our site and a mile away was the city. The slope down was a mix of cliffs and narrow ledges, with no trees to speak of — mostly chamise, scrub oak, and black sage.

It's a picture that demands a second look. Take it, and you're sure to see a wren in the underbrush or a red-tailed hawk sailing by. Lower down, in Escondido itself, there's a single farm holding out against urban sprawl, mostly brown dirt and weeds where the tractor yard used to be. At night the scene is a string of lights: cars driving north on Interstate 15, an ambulance racing to the hospital, and street lights like rings of pearls snaking up the hillsides till they're lost in the arching curve of some canyon.

1. Lewis Smedes, *My God and I: A Spiritual Memoir* (Grand Rapids: Eerdmans, 2003), p. 175.

Introduction

The second look is usually richer and deeper than the first, full of small surprises. Doubt is like that. Doubt has turned me back to theology and Scripture with attention to detail that I haven't known since studying for seminary exams. Doubt reveals texts I used to skip over because they were obtuse, difficult, or didn't easily fit the picture I expected to see. Does God love enemies just as Jesus instructs us to love ours? (Luke 6:27) Does God, in his love for all, really keep no record of wrongs? (1 Cor. 13:5)[2] Why would we lend without expecting to get anything back? Well, says Jesus, because God the father is "kind to the ungrateful and the wicked" (Luke 6:35). How kind? I used to presume what I had been taught from day one, namely, that God damned the ungrateful and wicked. But, at second glance, such presumptions are obviously laden with values and best guesses that I picked up from others — and that I am only slowly coming to grips with.

The second look that doubt invites is richer but not always comfortable. Doubt is like a new set of glasses: you see more, but it also hurts. For example, on the drive home from the optometrist after I had picked up a new set of glasses in Escondido, I could tell the difference between an Ontario and California license plate. I could see the scowl on the face of a driver waiting to turn left against the traffic. First Presbyterian Church — which always seemed an odd name out here in the suburbs — turned out to be First Pentecostal. But by the time I had driven the four miles between the optometrist and our RV, my new glasses had also given me a splitting headache, as my eyes adjusted to what they were seeing. Whatever it may be good for in seeing things anew, doubt is also a headache. As much as I have learned from the second look, it also rocks my world. I second-guess my return to parish ministry. I worry about whether or not I have the chutzpah, anymore, to speak with confidence about the intersection of the divine and the common. I wonder whether an emphasis on grace to the exclusion of judgment will eventually get me into trouble. Giving up a career that I have been successful at, that I spent four years of

2. This is the NIV's translation, and is more literal than the NRSV's. See, for example, Gordon Fee, *The First Epistle to the Corinthians*, New International Commentary on the New Testament (Grand Rapids: Eerdmans, 1987), p. 639.

4

postgraduate study to get ready for — and that offers me a great pension so long as I stick with it — would be tough. Besides, I love my parishioners. But doubt reveals to me that all my life I have romanced a woman — faith — whom I cannot have.

Doubt has also put enormous stress on my marriage. I'm not sure what, exactly, has gotten Irene and me through the worst of it. Her long-suffering patience has helped a lot, as have her insights as a marriage counselor. My doubts have made us both aware of just how formative and comfortable our church membership has always been, and how difficult it is to reconsider it for something new and uncertain. The worship and the committees, the family devotions and Sunday coffee klatches, the shared commitment to Christian education, parachurch organizations, and a community of friends — all these make for a cozy, ordered way of life. Question any of the planks that everything else stands on, though, and you are on shaky ground. People — whether elders and deacons, friends or family — don't know what to make of it. We have found that in marriage we have had to find a new equilibrium.

Doubt has also led me to reflect on my relationship with my children. They seem to have inherited my two left feet when it comes to faith. William and David are deeply spiritual and very knowledgeable about Christianity and the church they grew up in. In fact, they have mostly good memories of church and family devotions and pastors. Their university classmates used to kid them sometimes about being Calvinists. But what they do best — like me and to the consternation of my wife — is doubt, especially about the institutional manifestations of a faith that they are having a hard time hanging onto. In our faith tradition, a lot rides on how your kids turn out. That is, Christian Reformed people have been socialized to think that passing on the faith to their children is just about the most important thing going. And when people take the measure of each other in our communion, they do so, in part, by checking out where the kids are and how the parents have done by them. For both Irene and me, my doubt, as it gets mirrored in our sons' lives, is a very emotional issue — even if we have figured out, intellectually, how to deal with it.

In *Life of Pi*, Yann Martel says that while doubt may be appropriate for a season, "to choose doubt as a philosophy of life is akin to choosing immobility as a means of transportation."[3] I'm not so sure it is as simple as that. Doubt has advantages associated with that second look: a "hermeneutic of suspicion" is what some theologians call it. But doubt is not necessarily a choice. I have not chosen doubt as a way to strike back at former colleagues or verities or at institutions where I have worked. No, doubt is a virus: you catch it without knowing where you caught it. There are very few, if any, effective treatments, and it can be painful and debilitating. Doubt may go into remission, but it is also chronic and may flare up anytime. As Voltaire famously put it, "Doubt is not a pleasant condition, but certainty is absurd."

Doubt is always a stranger; therefore, as a good Christian, I must always work to be its gracious host. If I become too angry or impatient or upset at doubt, I spoil the visit and think less of myself. But in the end, doubt usually overstays its welcome anyway, no matter how I treat it. So I try to make the best of it.

This book is for the person of faith who struggles, for the person who is not sure, for one whom Leslie Weatherhead once called a "Christian agnostic":

> [a] person who is immensely attracted by Christ and who seeks to show his spirit, to meet the challenges, hardships and sorrows of life in the light of that spirit, but who, though he is sure of many Christian truths, feels that he cannot honestly and conscientiously "sign on the dotted line" that he believes certain theological ideas about which some branches of the church dogmatize; churches from which he feels excluded because he cannot "believe." His intellectual integrity makes him say about many things, "It may be so. I do not know."[4]

I am a Christian agnostic in this sense, and my book, like Weatherhead's, will be an extended reflection on why I am a Christian agnostic — and what I make of it. This book is not an exercise in what theo-

---

3. Yann Martel, *Life of Pi* (New York: Harcourt, 2001), p. 28.

4. Leslie D. Weatherhead, *The Christian Agnostic* (Nashville: Abingdon, 1965), p. 15.

logians call apologetics. I will not try to convince readers to believe despite their doubts, or to throw faith to the winds. What I will do, however, is try to come to grips with my doubt by laying bare its sources, sources from both the wider culture we live in and my own personal experience. Ultimately, I want to share with the reader the quiet place where I have found a measure of peace when it comes to faith, even while doubt still plays an important role in my life.

I tend to look for the big picture. When I sat, overwhelmed, on the beach at North Rustico, the ocean's vastness suggested to me that, even if I wished to go home to the comforts of childlike faith, my issues were too deep and ancient to do so. This book, too, will take the larger, longer view. To get at some of the deeper issues that relate to my faith and doubt, I'll explore the role that faith has played in human culture through the ages. In the course of the first four chapters, bringing us to the present, I'll explore how "faith" has never been one clearly definable thing. In the fifth chapter, I will sketch a picture of the kind of faith and doubt I can live with. The rest of the book will build on that story of both personal and cultural faith by exploring some contemporary misconceptions about faith that have not helped me in my own journey. These include the notion that faith is having a personal relationship with Jesus, that faith has cash value, and that faith is about obedience and doctrine. Finally, I will wrap up the book by suggesting what I hope is a plausible way forward for Christian agnostics like me: a way forward that is deeply spiritual, that trades in the great values of Scripture, especially love, and that helps us live an authentic and happy life in today's world.

One feature of this book requires a brief word of explanation. As the book unfolds, I compare and contrast the various stages of the history of Western faith with my own faith development as an individual. In some ways, this plan for the book reminds me of an old, mostly discounted, evolutionary theory known as "ontogeny recapitulates phylogeny." According to this theory, the stages of growth any one human fetus goes through in the womb (ontogeny) actually mirror (recapitulate) the stages of evolution (phylogeny). That is, in its earliest stages of growth, the human fetus physically looks like and has the features of earlier forms of life. Thus, the fetus starts off as a single cell, like the earliest life. The fetal cell splits and becomes more complex multicellular life, just as primitive microorganisms evolved. The fetus then develops a backbone. Like a fish, it develops what look like gills; the gills give way to land-animal lungs. Legs and feet grow from the body's trunk; the brain, first tiny, grows; the tail, once prominent, disappears. And so on until you get a human fetus, the pinnacle of evolution.

This theory has a lot of problems, not the least of which is the underlying egotistical presumption that all of evolution somehow had the goal of achieving human life. A similar conceit could easily be attributed to me: that is, at first glance it may seem that I'm describing how the history of Western faith somehow produced me. But that is not, in fact, what I am arguing. The comparison is strictly illustrative, and no necessity or divine plan is attached to it. In the end, I see my faith development — and probably that of many readers — as simply being illuminated, at various points, by the story of Western faith in general. In any case, I also show how, in the end, my faith has taken a sharp left turn from the general pattern in the West. In other words, the analogy works — but only to a point.

So I think the two stories — my own story of doubt and faith, and the faith story of Western civilization — illuminate each other without being the explanation for each other. I think that the reader, in comparing and contrasting, will learn not only something about my struggles with faith and doubt, but also something about how the world of faith as we know it today came to be, at least in part.

Finally, I hope that readers, by the end of the book, will be more relaxed about both their faith and doubt, and will be ready to engage both faith and doubt with deeper self-understanding — perhaps even with a sense of adventure.

chapter 1

Oral Faith: Enchanted and Childlike

Introduction

For three years after my stint as editor of the Christian Reformed Church magazine, *The Banner*, my wife and I lived in the Philippines, where I taught at Asian Theological Seminary in Manila. It was good to be out of the denominational glare, and I loved teaching. While we were there, Irene and I visited the ancient Banaue Rice Terraces in Ifugao Province, about two hundred miles north of Manila.

The rice terraces are old, but 2500 years ago they did not yet exist. If I had been able to look over the Banaue Valley back then, I would have seen craggy mountain tops covered by rain forest descending into steep gorges all the way down to rocky valley bottoms, landscape typical of the Philippine Cordilleras. However, a thousand years later, standing and viewing at that very same spot would have been a revelation. For by that time, where once everything was untamed rock and forest, there were thousands of square miles of cropland. Using only simple tools, the Ifugaoans cut flat terraces into the sides of the steep mountains and constructed a complex irrigation system to bring water from the upland jungles down to the fields. To this day rice and vegetables are grown in many of those terraced fields.

The contrast between the original mountainside and later terraced landscape would have been dramatic: before — all rock and crags and wild creeper; after — all steps, walls, paths, and level places full of uniform green. But now, in the twenty-first century, things have changed once again. The mountaintop jungles, often lost in clouds, are still there, as well as the cool alpine breezes. But many terraces are no longer planted in rice; now overgrown, they are patchy green as the native plants have taken over. Bare slopes of dirt often mark the vertical distance between terraces, a sign that they are eroding. The terraces look romantic — the eighth wonder of the world, according to Filipinos — but climbing up and down the mountainsides to fields that are inaccessible to modern tractors and combines makes for a difficult life. Young Ifugaoans are opting for city jobs instead of terrace farming. It is hard to blame them.

Faith is like that Banaue mountainside. Over thousands of years, there is something about the landscape of the Christian faith that is constant and unchanging, like the mountain setting of the Banaue Rice Terraces. This unchanging thing might be God, or perhaps human nature, or both. At the same time, over thousands of years, as people take up faith, wear it out, and pass it on to their children, the nature of faith is also transformed in ways that make it almost unrecognizable from one era or culture to the next.

Awareness of the evolution of faith informs my current faith and doubt. For what if the faith I agonize over now is something radically different from what my ancestors wrestled with? That there is such evolution is certain. We can track it even within the pages of the Bible. Reading the Old Testament from beginning to end, for example, one soon realizes that Abraham's faith, compared to that of worshipers in King Solomon's temple, compared to that of Pharisees and Sadducees of Jesus' day, compared to that of the apostle Paul — all differed significantly despite some continuity. Over time, the religion of Yahweh evolved as circumstances changed and the understanding of Yahweh grew.

In the next four chapters I want to explore how the Christian faith, like the Banaue landscape, has evolved over the past two thousand years, since the end of the biblical record. In this chapter I'll start by describing the faith of people in Europe during the medieval era. In the next chapter I will examine how several factors radically transformed the nature of faith, beginning in the sixteenth and seventeenth centuries, and moving toward the eighteenth century, the era roughly corresponding to what is often called the Enlightenment. Then, in chapters 3 and 4, I'll explore how the popular experience of faith has been transformed again over the past hundred years by two intellectual sea changes, one known as postmodernism and the other known as secondary orality, or the secondary oral tradition.

Rather than simply analyze what scholars in each era made of that faith, my focus will be on how people actually experienced and lived faith. I'll also reflect on how each of the different kinds of faith I'll be describing have something in common with faith as I've thought about it and experienced it over my own lifetime. We'll discover that, as at Banaue, there are continuities and differences. We start with the medieval landscape.

The Medieval Landscape

From the fall of the Roman Empire in the fifth century, until some time after the invention of the printing press, the European peasants' faith and material condition was never exactly the same from one place or time to another. Over the time that we are investigating, languages slowly evolved; large groups of people moved from one part of Europe to another; plagues killed up to a third of the population with each epidemic; and a series of political regimes succeeded each other.

Still, in the midst of all these huge changes, much was also constant for the European peasant. Life was hard. Few have described it as simply and depressingly as Thomas Hobbes did in 1651: the lot of the peasant, said Hobbes, was "[n]o arts; no letters; no society; and which is worst of all, continual fear, and danger of violent death: and the life of man, solitary, poor, nasty, brutish and short."[1] One fascinating aspect of Hobbes's description is the identification of illiteracy with poverty. Although he does not explain the exact nature of their

1. Quoted in Gregory Clark, *Farewell to Alms: A Brief Economic History of the World* (Princeton, NJ: Princeton University Press, 2007), p. 19.

relationship, Hobbes apparently thought they needed to be mentioned in the same breath.

Gerson, a medieval theologian and chronicler, describes life in about 1400 in a speech he delivered to the queen of France:

> The poor man will not have bread to eat, except perhaps a handful of rye or barley; his poor wife will lie in and they will have four or six little ones about the hearth . . . they will ask for bread, they will scream, mad with hunger. The poor mother will have but a very little salted bread to stuff between their teeth. Now such misery ought to suffice; but no; — the plunderers [the church and feudal lords] will come, who will seek everything.[2]

J. A. MacCulloch adds that "war brought wretchedness in its train . . . hunger and disease and cold were too well known. Famine and plague, with their trains of death. . . . If men's bodies suffered much from disease, their minds were darkened by superstitions."[3]

Not all scholars speak so disparagingly of ancient superstition while presuming on modern enlightenment. What was the world of faith and religion really like back then, and for most of the church's history — at least in Europe?

An Enchanted World

From the perspective of most people of that time, the world was enchanted. All of life — worship and work in the fields, the parish church and the family home — was cut from one cloth. There was no division in that cloth between the world of spirits and that of bread and butter. Some scholars have called this a "porous" world. People lived and acted as if the physical and spiritual realms completely interpenetrated each other.

2. Quoted in Johan Huizinga, *The Autumn of the Middle Ages*, trans. Rodney J. Payton and Ulrich Mammitzsch (Chicago: University of Chicago Press, 1996; first published, 1921), p. 66.

3. J. A. MacCulloch, *Medieval Faith and Fable* (London: George G. Harrap, 1932), p. 6.

Charles Taylor describes the enchanted world as one where all members had a naïve — that is, uncritical — acceptance of a worldview that embraced spirits, demons, and charged moral forces as the stuff of everyday life.[4] Taylor describes a Hieronymus Bosch painting, for example, this way:

> Those nightmare scenarios of possession, of evil spirits, of captivation in monstrous animal forms; . . . these were not "theories" in any sense in the lived experience of many people in that age. They were objects of real fear, of such compelling fear, that it wasn't possible to entertain seriously the idea that *they might be unreal.* You or people you knew experienced them. And perhaps no one in your milieu ever got around even to suggesting their unreality. (p. 11, emphasis added)

Mysterious spiritual power lay just around every corner — in streams and stones, in the weather and stars. In this world, saints, their relics, sacred places such as a shrine where the Virgin Mary had last been seen locally, or a small chapel dedicated to an image of the sacred heart — all of these had power to make your day or undo it, perhaps even make your destiny or undo it. The enchanted world was full of trouble and danger. Taylor says that people walked through it much like people today might walk through a dangerous, crime-ridden neighborhood (p. 37).[5] People did not know when they might come into the field of some malevolent power; nor did they have a clear sense about how they might influence such powers. But — and

4. Charles Taylor, *A Secular Age* (Cambridge, MA: Belknap Press, 2007), pp. 25-26 (hereafter, page references to this work appear in parentheses in the text). Taylor notes that the phrase "enchanted world" is used as the (positive) negation of Weber's description of the modern world as "disenchanted." Another helpful work about the concepts of enchantment and disenchantment, as well as the related concepts of an axial and postaxial age, is Marchel Gauchet, *The Disenchantment of the World: A Political History of Religion,* trans. Oscar Burge, New French Thought series (Princeton, NJ: Princeton University Press, 1997).

5. Thus, for medieval people living in an enchanted world, meaning, purpose, and truth were all givens. There was no need for people to search these things out. See also Gauchet, *Disenchantment of the World,* p. 47.

perhaps this is the most important thing — Christians in the enchanted world took comfort and hope from the conviction that their
God was the final arbiter and guarantor of good in this world. He
watched over, ordered, restrained, and animated both the physical and
spiritual realms, without prejudice.

The vast majority of people did not theorize — or theologize —
about God's existence; they simply lived it, "as immediate reality, like
stones, rivers and mountains" (p. 12). Taylor also makes the point that
things like good weather or a bountiful harvest were thought to de-
pend on everyone in the community acting in concert with respect to
the ritual demands that would influence events in a positive way. This
put tremendous pressure on everyone to hold to the worldview consensus (p. 42).

However, just because people who were alive at that time could
hardly think of faith apart from the rest of reality that surrounded
them does not mean that their faith is invisible to our probes, as Marshall McLuhan would have said. It was. And when we examine this
ancient faith, we discover that it had a richness and uniqueness that is
all but lost on us today.

Oral Faith

The enchanted worldview was pervasive in the West for a millennium,
and probably for most of human history for millennia before. A version of this worldview was also the reality Israel lived with during the
centuries that the Old Testament came together and when Jesus lived.
Many factors led to the eventual abandonment of this worldview, and
we'll examine some of those in the next chapter. But first, even if the
person living in an enchanted world had a hard time separating out
faith from life, we can, from the perspective of a few hundred years,
say a few analytical things about what the faith of most people in that
era looks like to us. And those things, by way of contrast, may illuminate both the fact that we have faith — as we experience it today —
along with its attendant doubts.

The first thing to say about that enchanted faith is that it was, for most people, an oral faith. The vast majority of Europeans could neither read nor write until sometime in the seventeenth or eighteenth century. Not many scholars have reflected on what oral-only faith would have meant for Christian experience during this time. Perhaps this is because there always existed within Europe an educated elite who carried on philosophical and theological discussions that continue to fascinate and shape contemporary scholarly reflection — much more than whatever it was the peasants were thinking about. The absence of widespread literacy during this time also means that there is very little writing by people of that time for contemporary scholars to study. What we do know about medieval peasant life we have to infer from contemporaneous and often contemptuous accounts by the educated rich or the clergy.

At the same time, the oral tradition among Christians had to be important because of Christianity's very nature as a religion of the Word. The question of how people who could neither read nor write could nonetheless be people of the Word — a written Word — seems natural. They must be able to be, otherwise why would Christians, starting with Jesus, idealize the faith of children? Certainly, I believed with more conviction when I couldn't read or write than I do now. Still, so much of the Christian tradition is doctrine and confession, Scripture study and reflection, all bound into how-to and devotional books, that one has to ask what difference literacy makes.

The oral tradition and literacy are actually different kinds of what American philosopher Kenneth Burke calls "equipment for living."[6] Depending on the equipment you have, you are suited to accomplish some things with ease, while prevented from accomplishing others. Consider this analogy. My wife and I like to hike into the wilderness for a few days at a time carrying everything we are going to need in our packs: tent, sleeping bags, food, stove, and water. Backpacking allows us to break out of our dull routines and get into nature, which is a great gift. But backpacking also constrains us. Out in the woods we can't order pizza, drink cold beer, or play a Dylana Jenson violin performance on the stereo.

6. Kenneth Burke, *The Philosophy of Literary Form: Studies in Symbolic Action* (Berkeley: University of California Press, 1973 [1941]), p. 293.

That's how it is with orality, too. It gives gifts. For example, the oral tradition encourages the development of great storytelling and listening gifts. Orality frees people from having to spend years learning their ABC's in school. Orality ties people to their local scene and often creates a warm link between them and the land. But the oral tradition, like backpacking, also constrains people. Orality limits the amount of information people have at hand, since that information consists only of what you or whoever is with you has memorized. When in church, oral people cannot scan the back of hymnals for detailed explanations of the Apostles' Creed or read the Heidelberg Catechism's summary of what it is they believe. The oral tradition also doesn't equip you to think in great detail about long chains of abstract reasoning, since having a pencil and paper in hand, or a book, are a necessary aid for most people following that sort of calculation. People in oral societies generally don't subscribe to underground journals from the other end of the continent, so the oral tradition constrains one's opportunities to hear new ideas.

Thus, besides being enchanted, what would oral faith in an oral world look like?

1. Conservative

In orality, conservatism is a function of not wanting to give up — or not even being able to imagine giving up — a skill or thought or structure that one had invested a great deal of time in learning. Imagine growing up as the son of a shoemaker. As a child, you would spend years learning how to acquire leather, learning what cuts worked best for different tasks, and how to prepare the leather for use. You would learn how to use the awl, and sew, and size shoes or boots. You would also have learned all this not from books or in a classroom, but probably from a parent or perhaps a neighbor you apprenticed with. Having invested so much time and effort in becoming a shoemaker, you would not be likely to ever give up all this knowledge to learn a new trade.

So change, and the investment in time and intellectual resources it would take to master change, was looked on with deep suspicion. This suspicion helped ensure uncommon stability over long periods of time in both the political and religious realms, even in the face of incredible physical instability when it came to food, disease, weather, and other "acts of God." While kings and popes might come and go, or even reign in competition with each other, the structure and the enchanted world they were part of stood the test of time. Walter Ong explains this conservativism: "Knowledge is hard to come by and precious, and society regards highly those wise old men and women who specialize in conserving it, who know and can tell the stories of the days of old."[7]

As a result of this conservatism, ancient pagan religious practices were stamped out in Europe only with great difficulty. Tribes of Europeans came under Christian influence when their tribal leader converted — often for political reasons. However, when a prince was converted, the tribal nature of his society demanded tribal conversion. These tribal *pagani* rarely understood what this new religion meant. They were poorly instructed, and they could not read to catch up. Good political conversions made for poor spiritual ones. So these new converts and their clans clung to their ancient customs and beliefs, to the rites of seedtime and harvest, and to the venerations of their sacred trees and springs. "On the estates of the holy monks of St. Germain you would have found the country people saying charms which were hoary with age. . . . Christianity has colored these charms, but it has not effaced their heathen origin."[8]

2. Simple

I've already noted that when you only know what you can remember, you don't add to that knowledge unnecessary detail. That is also true in religious matters. The content of popular Christian faith was

---

7. Walter Ong, *Orality and Literacy: The Technologizing of the Word* (London: Routledge, 1988), p. 41.

8. Eileen Power, *Medieval People* (New York: Barnes and Noble Books, 1963), p. 27.

marked by bare simplicity. Whatever Anselm or Aquinas might have argued with respect to original sin or the nature of the atonement in one of Europe's very few universities, such matters would have been far too complex for most people to understand. That is why Augustine taught that preachers should "leave difficult concepts to written books."[9]

When preachers followed Augustine's suggestion, they produced predictable sermons that focused on the bare essentials of faith.

> Most non-polemical sermons which survive seem linked to the church's confessional and penitential functions, concerned with the Christian brotherhood and the demands of caritas. They therefore define sins, castigate the sinful, call for repentance, urge penance and a return to something like pristine innocence by the rejection of sin, and offer hope of salvation. . . . Discipline and devotion are to the fore, rather than theology. The bases are the Ten Commandments and the lives of saints.[10]

We shall return to the emphasis on *caritas* (loving others) in future chapters. The widespread and enduring emphasis on simplicity in doctrinal matters is confirmed by instructions promulgated by the Synod of Orleans in 797, which also insisted that sermons should emphasize the Apostles' Creed and the Lord's Prayer — "since these provided the key to salvation."[11]

For most people in the enchanted era, the Christian life could not have been centered on one's knowledge of Scripture. They did not read a passage for devotions before the start of the day! Biblical knowledge consisted of the stories about creation, the Fall, and re-

9. Augustine, *On Christian Doctrine* 4:23, trans. D. W. Roberts, Jr., Macmillan Library of Liberal Arts (New York: Macmillan, 1958).

10. R. N. Swanson, *Religion and Devotion in Europe, c. 1215–c. 1515*, Cambridge Medieval Textbooks (Cambridge: Cambridge University Press, 1995), p. 66.

11. Thomas L. Amos, "Preaching and the Sermon in the Carolingian World," in *De Ore Domini: Preacher and Word in the Middle Ages*, ed. Thomas Amos, Eugene A. Green, Beverly Mayne Kienzle, Studies in Medieval Culture 27 (Kalamazoo, MI: Medieval Institute Publications, 1989), p. 45.

demption, with a few other narrative favorites thrown in: the Flood, the Exodus, and King David. A little of Israel's prophets, less of Paul. Faith in the enchanted era was a kind of folk wisdom about how the world, including its spiritual aspect, worked. While some basic doctrine was taught, faith certainly was not thought of as giving assent to such doctrines.

3. Agonistic

The oral world adored stories about outsize heroes who battled in the heavens and on earth. Such stories reflected the enchanted worldview that the listeners felt themselves to be part of. Not only were such stories dramatic; they were thus also memorable. Oral culture is agonistic, that is, focused on the heroic (from the Greek word *agon* ("hero").

Consider these few lines from the medieval saga *Beowulf* (recently made into a movie starring Angelina Jolie). Although awkward in diction and vocabulary compared to our everyday language, it is well worth trying to read these lines aloud and imagining the scenes as described. In this section the evil monster Grendel comes upon a large group of heroic men, including Beowulf, who are asleep in a large mansion. Naturally, Grendel is hungry.

> Then from the moorland, by misty crags,
> with God's wrath laden, Grendel came. . . .
> To the house the warrior walked apace,
> parted from peace; the portal opened,
> though with forged bolts fast, when his fists had struck it,
> and baleful he burst in his blatant rage,
> the house's mouth. . . .
> He spied in hall the hero-band,
> kin and clansmen clustered asleep,
> hardy liegemen. Then laughed his heart;
> for the monster was minded, ere morn should dawn,
> savage, to sever the soul of each,

life from body, since lusty banquet
waited his will! . . .
Straightway he seized a sleeping warrior
for the first, and tore him fiercely asunder,
the bone-frame bit, drank blood in streams,
swallowed him piecemeal.[12]

This story has an almost comic-book feel to it. Despite what seems to us dated language, *Beowulf* sounds like a superhero saga ("Take this!" Bam! "Take that!" Bang!). Oral literature, from the Babylonian *Enuma Elish* creation story (a version of which the book of Genesis satirizes) to Homer's *Iliad* to Old Testament stories like those of Sodom and Gomorrah or David and Goliath, always has this heroic aura. Walter Ong calls such works "agonistically toned," because, he says, "[o]ral memory works effectively with 'heavy' characters, persons whose deeds are monumental, memorable and commonly public . . . to organize experience in some sort of permanently memorable form."[13] Ong means that oral memory works best with gory battles, lots of blood, and giants.

So action-oriented stories would have been much more important to oral Christianity than theological doctrine would have been. One such favorite story (which I will return to in the next chapter) was that of Jesus' surprising and violent victory over Satan, after his death, when he descended into hell. As told in oral times, this is a story of Jesus tricking Satan by dying to get into hell, a story of great conflict in the deepest dungeons, and of Jesus' heroic victory over incredible odds — much more interesting and thus more memorable than an atonement-oriented legal account of a transaction Jesus carried out by offering up his life as a payment for sin. Beyond this heroic account, one can generally characterize that era's church teaching about Jesus as the *Pantokrator*, the all-powerful one, "solemn and just, tranquil in his triumph because he has changed the world for-

12. http://classiclit.about.com/library/bl-etexts/beowulf/bl-beowulf-all.htm.
13. Ong, *Orality and Literacy*, p. 70; see also John Suk, "Why Jedi Knights Rule: How Reading and Writing Still Matter," *Perspectives: A Journal of Reformed Thought* 19 (January 2004).

ever, and very male."[14] Today, far from being the mighty ruler of all, nearly inaccessible in the reflected glory of God, by whose side he stands, Jesus is much closer to us: he is a friend with whom we have a "personal relationship."

The agonistic stories that spoke to the shape of the enchanted world that medieval peasants lived in included many more than those in the Bible. Stories of saints burned at the stake, whose remains were kept in reliquaries, or who worked miracles from graves that were the shrines of pilgrimages, were also part of the agonistic nature of religion in this era. In sum, agonistic faith in its enchanted and oral context was a story that people told each other and delighted in. Faith was knowing the story because you listened to it and had assimilated it rather than accepting the story's truth because you found it convincing.

4. Memorable

The other side of this equation was that the best teachers and preachers, like the minstrels who told the story of Beowulf, had to be memorable to succeed. They used a variety of strategies besides that of using agonistic characters such as Beowulf in their stories. Ong mentions several of them in his *Orality and Literacy*. First of all, memorable oral sermons would be formulaic: they would be told

> in heavily rhythmic, balanced patterns, in repetitions or antitheses, in alliterations and assonances, in epithetic and other formulary expressions, in standard thematic settings (the assembly, the meal, the duel, the hero's "helper," and so on), in proverbs which are constantly heard by everyone so that they come to mind readily and which themselves are patterned for retention and ready recall, or in other mnemonic form.[15]

14. Margaret Visser, *The Geometry of Love: Space, Time, Mystery, and Meaning in an Ordinary Church* (New York: North Point Press, 2000), p. 14. The classic statement about the changing perception of Jesus through the ages is Jaroslav Pelikan, *Jesus Through the Centuries: His Place in the History of Culture* (New Haven: Yale University Press, 1985).

15. Ong, *Orality and Literacy*, p. 34.

For example, Greek epics were always written in hexameter verse. In Hebrew poetry such as the Psalms, each line is restated, in parallel fashion, at least once, sometimes twice, both to fix it in memory and to allow for subtle underscoring of sense. A whole range of standardized word pairs is consistently used in the first and second lines (and even in the third) in order to aid memory. "Happy are those who do not follow the advice of the wicked, or take the path that sinners tread, or sit in the seat of scoffers" (Ps. 1:1).

Language also tended toward colorful adjectives to help fix characters in the mind's eye. In *Beowulf,* for example, the monster isn't just Grendel, but "God-cursed Grendel." Similarly, in the seventh-century Anglo-Saxon poem "Dream of the Rood [Cross]," within the first few lines the cross of Jesus is described as the "beauteous tree," "victor-tree," "cross of glory," and "forest tree."[16] Poetic devices were used to fix concepts in memory as well. Eric Havelock speaks of "poetized speech" that was "managed by memory specialists such as oral poets or wisemen . . . [to] serve as an oral encyclopedia, that is, a storehouse of important cultural information."[17] Oral strategy also leans on repetition to help people remember. Their bards said things over and over again. "Redundancy, repetition of the just-said, keeps both speaker and hearer surely on the track."[18] They also had lists to aid in repetition and memorization, often using mnemonic devices to help people remember the lists. Typically, John Drury, a fifteenth-century schoolmaster, enumerated what the laity needed to know to make Lenten penance: the three demands of penance, the Ten Commandments, the seven deadly sins, the seven virtues, the five senses as means of sinning, the five towers or five gates to save or lose your soul, seven corporal acts of mercy, seven acts of spiritual comfort, seven sacraments, seven theological virtues.[19]

In case anyone thinks that this kind of memorable patterning made

---

16. *The Dream of the Rood,* trans. Charles W. Kennedy, Old English Series (Cambridge, ON: In Parentheses Publications, 2000), p. 2.

17. David Olson, *The World on Paper: The Conceptual and Cognitive Implications of Writing and Reading* (Cambridge: Cambridge University Press, 1994), p. 101.

18. Ong, *Orality and Literacy,* p. 40.

19. Swanson, *Religion and Devotion,* pp. 27-30.

ancient preaching for oral audiences wooden and unappealing, they would be wrong. No age has ever had a shortage of poor preachers, of course. But the best medieval preachers could keep oral audiences in their thrall for hours, and even days, telling stories of agonistic heroes using all the tricks of the storytelling trade. Johan Huizinga describes — albeit in prejudicial terms — how such preachers did that.

> We, readers of newspapers, can hardly imagine anymore the tre- mendous impact of the spoken word on naïve and ignorant minds. The popular preacher Brother Richard, who may have served Jeanne d' Arc as father confessor, preached in Paris in 1429 for ten days running. He spoke from five until ten or eleven o'clock in the morning. . . . When he informed his audience after his tenth sermon that it would have to be his last . . . the people, great and small, "wept from the bottom of their hearts as if they were watching their best friends being put into the ground, and so did he."

Keeping in mind how faith was shared using agonistically toned stories, and how intense the experience these preachers could in- duce — Huizinga's stories could be endlessly reproduced here — one should think of enchanted faith not only as pretty scary (walk- ing through that dark neighborhood) but also intense, alive, charged with emotion and feeling. "Every experience had that degree of di- rectness and absoluteness that joy and sadness still have in the mind of a child," says Huizinga. "Evil is powerful, the devil covers a dark- ened earth with his black wings. And soon the end of the world is expected."[20]

5. Complex Teaching Strategies

The medieval church became expert at sharpening and informing the faith of illiterate Christians apart from the use of written texts

20. Huizinga, *Autumn of the Middle Ages*, pp. 4-5, 1, 29.

through the use of alternatives, everything from paintings to statuary, from liturgies to crusades — to name just a few strategies. "Action was more important than belief, cult and liturgy far more important than confession. In brief, religion both for lay masses and the vast majority of clerics was physical, not intellectual; danced, not believed."[21] The church also taught laity through the use of drama, for example, mystery and passion plays. Traveling groups of actors would bring these plays from village to village. The plays themselves would be about biblical stories, such as Jesus' birth and death, and they would use fanciful stock characters to teach morality.

The church also invested heavily in visual arts. Pope Gregory the Great wrote that "painting should be used in churches, that those who do not know letters at least by looking at the walls may read those [things] which they are not able to read in books."[22] Thus, in the windows of the cathedrals, the statuary and paintings portrayed the Stations of the Cross, and every church was full of messages that helped fix the stories and truths of Christianity in the minds and hearts of the worshipers. Margaret Visser says of the small, ancient Roman church of *Sant' Agnese fuori le Mura* (Saint Agnes Outside the Walls) that it "vibrates with intentionality. It is meaningful — absolutely nothing in it is without significance."

> [T]his building has been made in order to communicate with the people in it. A church is no place to practice aesthetic distance, to erase content and simply appreciate form. The building is trying to speak; not listening to what it has to say is a form of barbarous inattention, like admiring a musical instrument while caring nothing for music. The building "refers" to things beyond itself, and it deliberately intends to be a setting where spiritual knowledge receives explicit recognition and focal attention.[23]

21. Patrick J. Geary, "The Ninth-Century Relic Trade: A Response to Popular Piety?" in *Religion and the People, 800-1700*, ed. James Obelkevich (Chapel Hill: University of North Carolina Press, 1979), pp. 8-9.

22. Quoted in Mary J. Carruthers, *The Book of Memory* (Cambridge: Cambridge University Press, 1990), pp. 340-41.

23. Margaret Visser, *Geometry of Love*, pp. 13-14.

The church, like everything else, is enchanted. In the same vein, a profusion of sacraments — really, the dramas acted out before the congregation, the reliquaries, rosaries, shrines, pilgrimages, and even crusades — all had a role to play in making the content of the faith come alive for illiterate peasants. All of these were aids to memory, which is something that modern people like us, who are often taken aback by the beauty of many of these artifacts, often forget.[24]

6. Focus on Moral Action

I have noted above that one of the consequences of the necessity for simplicity in doctrinal matters was a focus on morality: the demands of *caritas*, the keeping of the commandments, and obedience to the powers that be. It has to be said of enchanted faith that such faith could not be separated from works. To be a Christian was not a matter of committing to the right propositions versus rejecting others. Rather, it was a matter of fulfilling one's obligations — ritual, tax, community, superstitious, and familial — obediently. The focus on moral obligation may go some way toward explaining why confession and penance became an important part of one's relationship to the church and to God. In the next section we'll discover, for example, that the Lateran Council's emphasis on confession was one of the strands that led to a greater interiority of faith.

Summarizing Enchanted Faith

For most of Western history since the fall of Rome — and perhaps much further back than that — faith was something very different

---

24. Margaret Visser's *Geometry of Love* is a moving book-length tour of an early medieval church just outside of Rome. The tour enumerates the many didactic yet aesthetically satisfying aspects of the church's design and decoration. Similarly, Hans Belting, *Likeness and Presence: A History of the Image Before the Era of Art* (Chicago: University of Chicago Press, 1994), offers a fascinating account of how icons functioned — among many other things — to inculcate faith, especially in the Eastern church.

from what we are used to thinking of it as. Today we do not live in an enchanted world, but a world of natural processes that we try to describe scientifically. While devoted Christians may pray to God for rain, or for a child, very few of those people would think, for even a minute, that God would find a way for providing such things apart from natural processes. The space that we afford to faith has become much smaller in some ways. Faith is for Sunday observance, and it is a personal decision and relationship: that is, it may inform one's moral aspirations, but it has little to do with streams, stars, sprites, or spirits. At the same time, faith has an intellectual depth dimension that is at least *available* to those who are interested, a dimension that was available to only a very few people for most of Western history. In a way, the spiritual realm that faith observes has moved from the whole cosmos to a corner of our hearts and psyches — where it remains deeply lodged.

What our examination of this ancient faith cannot easily ascertain is whether or not such faith inspired or created fear, that is, whether it was a source of comfort, moral commitment, and hope — or not. It embraces a conception of the cosmos that is so out of touch with modern perception that it is hard to relate to. Perhaps it is impossible to relate to. The enchanted world was really a different spiritual paradigm. As Thomas Kuhn famously said, communication between paradigms is incommensurate — that is, pretty much impossible.

And yet there is something about the enchanted worldview that is very appealing. Whereas the physical difficulty of peasant life described earlier in this chapter repels me, the sense that one could live in immediate contact with the spiritual realm — and especially the best of the spiritual realm — is appealing to someone who does not have any unquestionable experience of the divine, like me. The aesthetic dimension of spirituality — painting, drama, and the well-told tale — are also very attractive. The need for simplicity forced spiritual leaders to narrow the focus of the faith to essentials: among those was *caritas*, a life of love, and moral uprightness. An approach to faith based on these paths seems very difficult today, at least for those of us still deeply grounded in the propositional, dogmatic understanding of faith we learned in seminary.

Or is it? There is also something about this ancient way of being that resonates with personal memories I have of growing up.

Before I Believed

Once upon a time — long before the doubt I have described in the introduction — I believed, plain and simple. When I was a child, faith was so easy, so much a part of the fabric of my life, that I could hardly have separated it out to give it a name. I prayed as inevitably as I went to bed. I was bound for heaven just as surely as Mom bundled me up for school on winter mornings. God was perched on the headboard just as surely as my brother was in the next bed. Maybe this lack of effort when it comes to faith is what Jesus was talking about when he said that we should receive the kingdom of God as children do (Mark 10:13-16). I received the faith via prayer and church, via Bible reading at dinnertime and Sunday school; I received it all with empty hands raised up. Children are like that. They accept even the most amazing gifts without ever worrying about how this could be or whether it is deserved.

As I look back on it, faith was part of how things were, as inevitable as the backyard swing set becoming my rocket ship to the moon. My entire childhood was hemmed in with such gifts. My father and mother were Dutch immigrants to Canada, having arrived there not quite ten years after World War II. They loved each other. They laughed a lot. They were serious about church and Christian school, but not so serious that they took all the fun out of it. We would go to a cottage every year and picnic every summer weekend.

My parents were not legalists. They did not often lecture us kids about hell or threaten us with God's judgment. The prayers we said at meals were serious ones that spoke to God about what was really going on in our lives and the world. Church and faith were important, but so were other things — like the Maple Leafs on Saturday night or the space race. Buying gas on Sundays, if it had somehow been forgotten on Saturday, was okay. Riding bikes or running through the sprinklers on Sundays was also fine — much to the astonishment of our Sabbatarian American relatives who visited us from time to time. Skipping the reading of Scripture after a meal if we were in a big hurry, or attending a Presbyterian church while on vacation, or going to a movie if it was uplifting — these all were also okay if done in moderation.

I was happy. I remember waking up earlier on weekends than my parents did. The rule was that I had to stay in my bedroom until they were also up. So, on winter mornings, I used to wrap a blanket around myself, climb onto my bedroom windowsill, and hum hymns to myself as I watched the sun rise. At first, everything was dark. Slowly but surely, though, I could make out the high red tower over the Loblaw's store behind the empty lot across the street. Next, tree branches across the street became visible against the brightening horizon. Eventually, enough sunshine would reach down to the sidewalk so that I could see the paperboy walking in and out of the shadows. Only then would I finally hear my parents talking in their bedroom, because on Saturdays they woke to the light of the rising sun rather than to the clang of the alarm clock.

My parents gave gifts, including faith, which was like the sun that lit my street. I was happy, but I understand that this happiness was a very personal thing, not something I can easily generalize from to all readers of this book. At the same time, when I think of faith, it is always rooted in the glow that those days still have for me.

Our church was Christian Reformed, which really amounts to conservative Dutch Presbyterians. Our congregation was composed of immigrants like us. My parents said that we went to that church because we specifically believed what it taught. In fact, we actually went because our tribe did. We thought of ourselves as a holy nation, a royal priesthood, "in the world, but not of the world," just as another group of Dutch Calvinist immigrants, the Boers of South Africa, had thought of themselves a hundred years earlier. As parochial and wrong-headed as that sounds now, it seemed fine back then, at least in my little corner of the world, because it was warm and safe, exciting and alive. Not perfect, but as good as one can hope for.

I do not remember ever not having a Sunday suit and Sunday shoes to polish on Saturday nights. We went to church twice on Sundays. My family sat behind Uncle John and my grandparents, Opa and Oma, over on the east side of the sanctuary, a row behind the middle exit. We arrived early, the better to watch everyone else arrive. After church all the uncles, aunts, and cousins got together at Opa and Oma's to smoke cigarettes and cigars, have soup and buns, and talk about church and politics and people. Afterwards, during the evening service I'd cuddle up against my mother's shoulder and fall asleep.

By the time the collection plate came around, it was almost time to go home. I sometimes put the envelope with our tithe in the plate. In addition to the church tithe, more money went into the collection plate for Christian organizations: a labor union, a political movement, a hospital, and even a graduate school (of which I would later become the president briefly). Every meal at home began and ended with prayer. We watched our language. Dad and Mom never criticized the church or the pastor in front of us kids. We memorized Bible texts and catechism passages. And television was closely monitored: Walt Disney entertainment was fine, but the Three Stooges were out because they were violent and used bad language.

Weekdays I went to Calvin Memorial Christian School with all my church friends. We learned reading, writing, arithmetic, and Bible stories from young teachers, all of them recent graduates of Calvin College, our denomination's very own college in Grand Rapids, Michigan (where I would later teach from time to time). Three words were drilled into us to explain what the Bible was all about long before we had the intellectual tools to know what they meant: Creation, Fall, Redemption. Christian Reformed people took their theology seriously. Everything in the Bible fit into this three-word schema, and if it didn't, we either had a very complicated and interesting reason to explain how it really did fit despite appearances, or we unconsciously chose not to see the problem.

When I fell in love with God, faith was whole — like that. And when Europe fell in love with the God of Israel, faith was whole, too, even if that faith was also substantively different from my childlike faith. It is almost as if I had, as a child, many of the advantages of enchanted faith without the disadvantages of living in medieval Europe. When I could not read or write, I nevertheless reveled in the heroic adventures of Daniel in the lions' den and David and Goliath. I didn't trouble myself about Jesus being one person with two natures whose presence at the Lord's Super was because of his spiritual omnipresence. Life was simple. I did as Mom and Dad said: I prayed, "Lord, bless this food and drink, for Jesus' sake, amen." An ogre might live in your closet, or a monster under your bed, but as long as the nightlight was on and Mom was in the house, it would probably be okay. Meanwhile, from memory verses to Sunday school cards, stories read at bedtime to tagging along with Dad to the office, life was an intense and exciting learning experience.

When the world is whole and you are loved, you accept nearly all as a matter of course: three square meals, an old (English) Ford Counsel, grandparents who pampered you with tea and cookies, and the certainty that on top of all this God loved you, too. I am extremely nostalgic for those times and such faith. That nostalgia also informs my doubt today. I said earlier that I romance a woman I cannot have: I long for attachment to a community and God, for peace and quiet, confidence and happiness in believing — but it is gone.

I've already noted that we will return to conservatism, simplicity, agonism, and other features of enchanted faith to see how such features were transformed — or not — as faith developed down through to the present. The idea, remember, is to show how there is some underlying continuity, but also that there has been great change in the landscape of faith, as there has been over the millennia in Banaue. But the very fact that faith's features, its definition and content, changed over time raises the question of whether these changes are good — and right. Is one era's faith closer to the ideal than another's? Do we need to see the development of differing kinds of faith as progress? Regress? Or do we measure it all by some other standard, perhaps a church tradition? Or do we measure it by some communion's or theologian's view of what Scripture has to say of faith, if indeed Scripture has only one concept of faith? And how do the answers to such questions help or hinder me in my own struggles with faith and doubt? We'll return to these questions in the next and following chapters.

chapter 2

Literate Faith

⁓

Introduction

I started the first chapter by describing the rice terraces of Banaue. Located in Ifugao Province in the Philippines, the terraces are often described by Filipinos as the eighth wonder of the world. And the terraces, carved into steep mountainsides like steps, are remarkable: now, where once there was nothing but cliffs and steep inclines, there are thousands of square miles of cropland. But the terraces are disappearing in recent times. The dikes that hold the water in the rice terraces crumble and leak. As people stop farming the terraces, they fall into disrepair. If the trend continues, at some point — perhaps in a thousand years from now, perhaps longer — the rice terraces will be unrecognizable, having melted back into the mountains.

At what point did the Banaue mountains become the Banaue Rice Terraces? And when will they once again qualify as raw mountain, the terraces a dim memory for archaeologists to try to reconstruct? It is difficult to say, just as it is difficult to say when Europe's enchanted faith became something else, or when my childlike faith disappeared. Still, popular conceptions about faith changed sometime between the fourteenth and sixteenth centuries in Europe, while my conception of faith changed sometime between my eighth and twelfth birthdays. What is more, the changes in Europe's faith and my faith are in some ways analogous. In this chapter we'll explore the transition from enchanted faith to what I'll call literate faith.

Enchantment's Decline

Thousands of years ago, philosophers such as Socrates and Plato were already questioning the received wisdom about agons, the gods, and the way the world worked. Their doubts, combined with the emergent rationalism of Aristotle, were later nurtured in the philosophical schools of the Cynics, Stoics, Epicureans, and Skeptics.[1] The ideas these scholars argued about took fragile root and weathered several intellectual crises from the fall of Athens to the fall of Rome. After that Christian, Muslim, and Jewish scholars through the "Dark Ages" and up to the Renaissance discussed these now ancient ideas. The discussions they carried on in universities, seminaries, and monasteries were not the stuff of everyday life, nor did they carry much weight with everyday people. But this intellectual tradition was nevertheless hardy and inventive. Furthermore, many in this minority were influential churchmen who also helped shape the institutions within which most people lived their lives. Eventually, some of the richness of this critical tradition spilled over from academia into everyday society. Even if laypeople rarely understand the genesis of what came to be known as Enlightenment thinking, they were eventually caught up in its science, its new ideas about government, religion, and values. These intellectual currents slowly changed not only medieval scholarship, but society as a whole as well.

What happened to make the Western tradition of scholarship, which was rooted in ancient Greek philosophy, become incorporated into a worldview in which not just scholars, but also the masses of people, participated? And how did adoption of many of the attitudes, modes of thinking, and presuppositions of the Western intellectual

1. Jennifer Hecht, *Doubt: A History; The Great Doubters and Their Legacy of Innovation from Socrates to Jesus to Thomas Jefferson and Emily Dickinson* (San Francisco: HarperSanFrancisco, 2003), offers a readable and compelling account of doubt's critical role from Greece to the present. For the Greek story, see pp. 1-44.

tradition change faith, especially the faith practiced in the pews? The answer to the former question is complex, but one key factor is literacy. And the answer to the latter question, also complex, indicates the end of the enchanted worldview. These changes took place over hundreds of years, although, as we shall see, a few key events gave the coming change great cultural momentum.

1. Growth in Literacy

Increasing literacy, beginning as early as the twelfth century and in full bloom by the seventeenth century, was the most important reason enchanted faith slowly disappeared from Europe. Even before the invention of the printing press, literacy was making an impact on the everyday lives of more and more Europeans. For example, M. T. Clanchy traces how, in England, written documents such as property titles began to replace oral memory concerning property ownership soon after the Norman Conquest of 1066.[2] Such documents, read aloud, gave otherwise illiterate people opportunities to enjoy some of literacy's benefits — assuming, of course, that the land title confirmed their claims! And even before the printing press made books and pamphlets widely available at affordable prices, creeping literacy had made hand-copied personal prayer books, such as *The Book of Hours*, accessible to more and more people.[3]

Gregory Clark describes another reason for a gradual, inexorable growth in literacy over time. He notes that far more children of wealthy families survived to adulthood than did children of poor families, because the former had better food and health care. For example, during the early seventeenth century, twice as many (60 percent) children of rich Europeans survived to adulthood than did poor Europeans' offspring. However, the upper classes did not have the resources

2. M. T. Clanchy, *From Memory to Written Record: England 1066-1307* (Oxford: Blackwell Publishers, 1993), p. 52.

3. Clanchy, *From Memory to Written Record*, pp. 111-12; see also Diana Butler Bass, *A People's History of Christianity: The Other Side of the Story* (New York: HarperCollins, 2009), pp. 106-7.

to maintain all their children in the comfort that the parents were accustomed to. Younger children, in particular, were forced out of the upper classes and moved down the social ladder. While they could not take money or property down that ladder with them, they could take their education and literacy. As a result of this downward mobility, more and more people among the population at large, over time, could read and write.[4]

However, the single most important factor contributing to higher literacy rates was undoubtedly Johannes Gutenberg's invention of the movable-type printing press in about 1440. Francis Bacon would later famously argue that three inventions "changed the appearance and state of the whole world," namely, "printing, gunpowder, and the compass."[5] It was probably no accident that he listed printing first.

In any case, over the course of a few hundred years, first in the cities and then in the countryside, Europeans took to reading and writing like Canadian kids take to hockey. The shift ended oral culture and eventually created a culture in which the majority were literate, a shift that transformed Europe. According to Bernard Mehl, who puts it very succinctly, literacy was so valued that people eventually assumed that "to be schooled was to be holy."[6] Martin Luther would have agreed. He once

> urged the establishment of compulsory education arguing that a neglect of learning would result in "divine wrath, inflation, the plague and syphilis, bloodthirsty tyrants, wars and revolutions, the whole country laid to waste by Turks and Tartars, even the pope restored to power."[7]

Luther may have exaggerated the impact of literacy, but not by much. Catechisms, confessions, sermons in print and from the pulpit,

4. Gregory Clark, *A Farewell to Alms: A Brief Economic History of the World* (Princeton, NJ: Princeton University Press, 2007), pp. 128-32, 183.

5. Francis Bacon, *Novum Organum*, Aphorism 129.

6. Bernard Mehl, *Classic Educational Ideas* (Columbus, OH: Charles E. Merrill, 1972).

7. Quoted in G. Strauss, *Luther's House of Learning: Indoctrination of the Young in the German Reformation* (Baltimore: Johns Hopkins University Press, 1978), p. 8.

and tracts — not to mention the small matter of books — flooded Europe, spurring both more literacy and more awareness of new ideas. Europeans learned to argue Scripture amongst themselves, read confessions and catechisms aloud, and to sing out of personal Psalters. Elizabeth Eisenstein remarks on how this increase in literacy, and the flood of literature that went with it, changed European attitudes toward authority and theology.

> Bible printing subjected the authority of the medieval clergy to a two-pronged attack. It was threatened by lay erudition on the part of a scholarly elite and by lay Bible reading among the public at large. On the elite level, laymen became more erudite than churchmen; grammar and philology challenged the reign of theology; Greek and Hebrew studies forced their way into the schools. On the popular level, ordinary men and women began to know their Scripture as well as most parish priests; markets for vernacular catechisms and prayer books expanded; church Latin no longer served as a sacred language veiling sacred mysteries.[8]

Literate Europeans arguing about the latest tract out of Geneva or broadside from the Mennonites sometimes discovered that, though they disagreed with their village neighbors, they agreed with writers who lived on the other side of Europe. As a result, new kinds of communities, not restricted by geography, emerged around ideas, convictions, and dreams. These communities were most often religious movements — Lutheranism, Calvinism, Zwinglianism, Anabaptism, and so on. But movements around other ideas, such as humanism, or in commerce and the arts, also developed.

I grew up in this literate church. While I was bored waiting for church to start, I would read the church order — the rules for being a good church — in the back of the *Psalter Hymnal*, our hymnbook, to pass the time. The liturgy was achingly simple: words spoken and sung, without any drama or rites or color or processions, unless an

8. Elizabeth L. Eisenstein, *The Printing Revolution in Early Modern Europe* (Cambridge: Cambridge University Press, 1983), p. 161.

elder's handshake with the pastor before and after the sermon counted for something. The pastor wore a black suit or perhaps an unadorned Genevan gown. Books made the huge investment the church had traditionally made in the arts unnecessary, and the Reformers lost little time in finding biblical justification for doing away with such arts. In Protestant churches one found few decorations, few if any pictures of Jesus, and mostly abstract geometric designs in the stained glass windows. Church members delivered long lectures about evolution and unconditional election at men's and women's societies; but they certainly did not follow the stations of the cross or go on pilgrimages.

I loved that literate church. It was solid and safe, and the hymn-book addenda were endlessly fascinating. I loved that church partly because I grew up in a literate family. My grandfather, with his grade-three education, used to read Dutch theologians like Abraham Kuyper, and hundreds of similarly educated Dutch immigrants to Canada would beat a path to his backroom bookstore in the 1950s and '60s to buy systematic theologies and philosophies — published in both Dutch and English. My father, a high school graduate, spent his spare dollars on not one, but two complete sets of Bible commentaries. He displayed them with pride in a special bookcase he constructed under the bay window, in the center of the living room. Inductive Bible studies in which people "share" how they feel about Bible passages, instead of studying what biblical experts have written about them, would have absolutely befuddled my father and grandfather.

2. Writing out Conservativism

We have seen that literacy gave Europeans the resources and the habits of mind to question received wisdom. Literacy worked powerfully to make society, as a whole, much less conservative. How so? Well, for openers, written material works against the local consensus, whatever it may be. New information and ideas from the four corners of Europe, and from even further abroad, gave newly literate people a multitude of ideas and facts to think about. Over the course of a few generations, it was not just the local priest and neighbors who informed you about the shape of the cosmos, but Waldensians, Hussites, and maybe even humanists like Erasmus. People might discover that it wasn't their neighbor they agreed with so much as a pamphleteer from a city halfway across the continent. The increase in new and different ideas made the old conservatism harder to accept and live by.

I can trace how this happened even among my rural Dutch ancestors. I have a great-great-grandmother whose name was Jantje Rijkens. Her ancestors included a secretary to the bishop of Bern, Switzerland, in the twelfth century. Later ancestors of Jantje included a fourteenth-century mayor of the Swiss town of Solthurn. By the seventeenth century, however, the Rijkens were in trouble. The family had converted to an Anabaptist sect, while Switzerland was still solidly Reformed; in order to escape persecution, they joined other families who were traveling north in 1711 to the Netherlands in an "overland ship." The Netherlands was more accommodating to religious diversity, and the Rijkenses found relief from the religious persecution they had experienced in Switzerland. They founded Anabaptist churches in the province of Groningen. Ironically, after a few generations, few of the Rijkens were Baptists anymore: they had mostly converted to Calvinism, the religion of their onetime persecutors. People all over Europe were changing their minds, as my own family's journey from Catholic to Reformed to Anabaptist and back to Reformed would indicate.

In medieval Europe, both the society in general and particular individuals had been extremely conservative when it came to the adoption of new ideas. However, with the advent of literacy, "[i]nsofar as memory training and 'slavish copying' became less necessary, while inconsistencies and anomalies became more apparent after printed materials began to be produced, a distrust of received opinion and a fresh look at the evidence recommended itself to all manner of curious men."[9] In other words, literacy — and access to diverse opinions — made people, if not radical, at least receptive to new ideas.

9. Eisenstein, *Printing Revolution*, p. 194.

3. *From Mnemonic Devices to Spoken Literacy*

We saw in the last chapter that in the enchanted, oral culture of Europe, "faith" was inculcated in a number of ways: for example, in rituals, painting, plastic arts, and storytelling. However, the religion of the word abandoned all writing that was not contained within the alphabet or within the symbolism of just two, rather than seven, sacraments. But the enchanted world could not be contained in a book; so it slowly faded away.

Under the influence of literacy, both the form and content of preaching also changed. Preaching stopped using the bard's strategies of primary oral tradition to communicate; it had to adopt new rhetorical strategies suited to the new preaching situation — a church full of readers. Rather than commonplace stories and short lists of required moral actions, preachers adopted strategies such as *lectio continuo*, slowly preaching their way through the Bible, verse by verse, explaining at each stop along the way what the lexical, grammatical, and historical features of the text suggested about its doctrinal meaning. Meanwhile, many members of the congregation had their own Bibles open on their laps, or close by at home, to check up on the reasoning of the preacher. Usually they agreed — but not always.

Where oral, illiterate audiences relied on mnemonic strategies such as rhyme, repetition, and agonistic stories to help them remember the story and its significance, literate audiences came to value the printed text's complex linearity and the sustained doctrinal teaching that could come in preaching. And if they could not remember everything the preacher had covered, they could buy his sermons — or better perhaps, ones by the famous preacher in the next town — from their local bookseller. John Calvin's and Martin Luther's sermons became their Bible commentaries, and they are still appreciated today for their erudition as much as for their robustness. To get some idea of just how widespread and popular the religious writings of Calvin were, consider that between 1541 and 1565, Calvin's writings were responsible for 42 percent of all the sheets of print produced in Europe, while the Bible itself accounted for only 14 percent.[10] Calvin and other preachers

10. Pearce J. Carefoote, *Calvin By the Book: A Literary Commemoration of the 500th Anni-*

presented sermons orally in the image of written books, as if they were meant to be read with the ear. Audiences listened to sermons as readers. This is nowhere so obvious as in the conflicts of the old oral heroes, or agons.

4. The End of Agonism and the Advent of Linear Thinking

One specific feature of oral, enchanted European religion that I have discussed in the preceding chapter was the oral fascination with agons — those contests waged by heroes battling for good in the heavens — or in Jesus' case, those battling against evil in hell. Heroic stories were memorable, and faith consisted in knowing those *stories* rather than agreeing with certain theological *propositions*. But what happens when people don't need oral help remembering the story, because they have it — and all the other biblical stories — at their fingertips in the family Bible? Well, the story flattens out. Words on a page don't allow for the same sort of exaggeration. The rhyme, repetition, and meter of the storyteller are no longer needed.

But something else happens as well. Not only do people now have the literal story in the pages of the Bible, but they also have pamphlets, books, and sermons to interpret the stories on their shelves. Some of the European elite's scholarship and erudition begins to show up in the homes of regular folks. That scholarship is nonfiction. It explains the meaning of the Bible, compares different views of the nature of Jesus' presence at the sacraments, and lists the various steps of the *ordo salutis*, that is, the steps one takes on the way to salvation. This new literature divides the basics of the faith, now much more voluminous than what might be preached in a medieval sermon, into chapters, or Lord's Days, each explaining some doctrine.

The dramatic *story* of the atonement that we discussed in the preceding chapter — where Jesus defeats the devil in a cosmic battle in

---

versary of the Birth of John Calvin, Thomas Fisher Rare Book Library (Toronto: University of Toronto Press, 2009), p. 45. For this statistic, Carefoote quotes Jean-Francois Gilmont, *Le Livre réformé au xvie siècle* (Paris: Bibliotheque nationale de France, 2005), p. 48.

the depths of hell — is thus replaced by a rationalist *doctrine* of the atonement — "substitutionary atonement," to be exact. This doctrine has some biblical warrant; it was also sketched out by Augustine, and was fully developed by Anselm of Canterbury in the eleventh century. Substitutionary atonement uses a legal metaphor to explain how Jesus saved humans from their sins, and it is notable for its internal logic. Briefly, according to this theory, humans sinned, and so humans need to pay restitution for sin's damages. Unfortunately, no human can pay such restitution. Considering the damage sin has done to creation and to individual souls, not to mention to God's honor, no person has the resources to pay the fine that would justly cover such damage. Only someone with divine power and glory has the resources to pay such an enormous price. But humans are not divine. So God, in his grace, sent his divine son, Jesus Christ, to become human. As a human, Jesus, even though he did not personally sin, could justly pay the cost for human sins; as divine, Jesus had the capacity to pay for human sin. Jesus' resurrection proved that he had successfully done so.

Notice that the atonement story is now totally overshadowed by atonement theory. Theory consists of assumptions, premises, and logic that, one might hope, will lead to a reasonable conclusion. This kind of thinking, analogous to scientific analysis as well, has allowed literate people to make distinctions between the spiritual and the physical, to reason through the connections between superstitious acts and results, and to see inconsistencies between biblical orthodoxy and surviving pagan attitudes. And as this kind of thinking swept through Europe, becoming more and more commonplace in society at large, enchanted thinking made room and gave way. David Olson says this:

> Oral tradition depends upon rhyme and rhythm as well as dramatic deeds of gods and heroes if it is to be memorable and serve as the base of a culture. Writing relaxed these constraints on memorability. Equipped with an optimal writing system, that is, one capable of preserving in writing everything that could be said orally, the stage was set for the evolution of a new, now literate, form of discourse and hence of thought. The literate mode depended not on memorability but on stated principles, on explicit

definitions of terms, on logical analysis and detailed proofs. The result was *the end of enchantment* and the beginning of the modern conception of the world.[11]

This new "literate" form of discourse is often described as linear thinking: that is, one thing necessarily leads to another. Scholars such as Walter Ong and Marshall McLuhan long ago suggested that print — and the literacy that made use of this new technology — actually restructured human consciousness so that linear, rational thinking became much more accessible, and actually became second nature to literate people. Elizabeth Eisenstein puts it this way: "Increasing familiarity with regularly numbered pages, punctuation marks, section breaks, running heads, indexes, and so forth helped to reorder the thought of *all* readers, whatever their profession or craft."[12] She adds: "The thoughts of readers are guided by the way the contents of books are arranged and presented. Basic changes in book format might well lead to changes in thought patterns."[13] Olson concurs: "Writing and increasing literacy were undoubtedly instrumental in the development of a skeptical, scientific tradition."[14] Mitchell Stevens notes that "[p]rint enforces a certain kind of logic: one-thing-at-a-time, one-thing-leads-directly-to-another logic, if/then, cause/effect — the logic most of us have internalized."[15]

Only a few years ago, the suggestion by Walter Ong and Marshall McLuhan that literacy restructured human consciousness was very controversial.[16] But recent studies on brain plasticity, that is, the abil-

11. David R. Olson, *The World on Paper: The Conceptual and Cognitive Implications of Writing and Reading* (Cambridge: Cambridge University Press, 1994), pp. 36-37 (emphasis added).

12. Eisenstein, *Printing Revolution*, p. 73.

13. Eisenstein, *Printing Revolution*, p. 64.

14. Olson, *World on Paper*, p. 53.

15. Mitchell Stevens, *The Rise of the Image; The Fall of the Word* (New York: Oxford University Press, 1998), pp. 78-79.

16. Other important scholars who have argued that writing restructured consciousness include Eric A. Havelock, *The Muse Learns to Write: Reflections on Orality and Literacy from Antiquity to the Present* (New Haven: Yale University Press, 1986); and Jack Goody, *The Interface Between the Written and the Oral* (Cambridge: Cambridge University Press, 1987).

ity of the brain to physically rewire itself in response to new or different sensory inputs, have confirmed that the intuitions of Ong and
McLuhan were largely correct.[17] So, for example, after many chapters
on how brain scans illuminate how reading makes use of different
parts of the brain than watching TV does, for example, Maryanne Wolf
notes:

> The evolution of writing provided the cognitive platform for the
> emergence of tremendously important skills that make up the
> first chapters of our intellectual history: documentation, codifica-
> tion, classification, organization, interiorization of language, con-
> sciousness of self and others, and consciousness of consciousness
> itself.[18]

We shall see in chapter 4 below that choosing for other, electronic
media undermines an individual's ability to make use of these resources (i.e., they restructure consciousness again). For now, however, the key thing to remember is that literacy both changed human
habits of thinking, and that, in turn, the new habits made widely available the kinds of gifts Wolf describes. And then, with respect to faith,
literacy laid the groundwork for a very different kind of religious sensibility: one that focused on the linear rationality of doctrines argued

17. Many recent books examine this fascinating topic from a number of perspectives.
See, for example, Maryanne Wolf, *Proust and the Squid: The Story and Science of the Reading
Brain* (New York: HarperCollins, 2007); Norman Doidge, *The Brain that Changes Itself:
Stories of Personal Triumph from the Frontiers of Brain Science* (New York: Penguin Books,
2007); Steven Johnson, *Mind Wide Open: Your Brain and the Neuroscience of Everyday Life*
(New York: Scribner, 2007); Richard Restak, *The New Brain: How the Modern Age Is Re-
wiring Your Mind* (New York: Rodale Press, 2004); Gary Small and Gigi Vorgan, *iBrain:
Surviving the Technological Alteration of the Modern Brain* (New York: Collins Living, 2008);
and Stanislas Dehaene, *Reading in the Brain: The Science and Evolution of a Human Invention*
(New York: Viking, 2009). Two books argue whether or not modern media are changing
the brain for better or worse. Arguing for the worse is Mark Bauerlein, *The Dumbest Generation: How the Digital Age Stupefies Young Americans and Jeopardizes Our Future* (New York:
Tarcher/Penguin, 2008); arguing in favor of the ways contemporary media impact education and thinking for the better is Don Tapscott, *Grown Up Digital: How the Net Generation Is Changing Your World* (New York: McGraw Hill, 2009).
18. Wolf, *Proust and the Squid*, p. 221.

in texts rather than a faith memorable due to the incredible feats of its agonistic heroes. "Writing, they suggested, preserves statements and thereby opens them up to critical inquiry."[19] In fact, faith became not a matter of knowing the story and *caritas;* it became a matter of critical understanding and acceptance of propositions.

The importance of the transformation that literacy wrought for faith cannot be understated. The scientific method — or even merely the application of cause and effect to religious doctrine — must have worked powerfully against the whole notion of an enchanted world, where things like relics and spells had power. Jennifer Hecht elaborates on these changes:

> In the early Middle Ages, something curious happened to the ideas of faith and philosophy. For the first time, *belief itself became the central religious duty.* A new kind of doubt appears here, in response. This new doubt doubts the other side of the equation — us. This one is believer's doubt, and it hurts more. Whereas before there was not much reason to try to believe (it was more a question of what to say in public), now the religion is set up around the idea that belief is difficult and that we must work toward it.[20]

For now, instead of a story that everyone knew, faith had become a set of propositions that had to be proved and a set of presuppositions that might or might not hold. The reader had to decide.

5. Interiority

Other factors worked to change Europe's religious sensibility, sometimes hand in hand with literacy and sometimes independently. For example, over the course of the Middle Ages, Europeans became increasingly aware of their inner lives. Literacy was a factor here as well.

19. Olson, *World on Paper,* p. 36.
20. Hecht, *Doubt: A History,* p. 169 (emphasis added).

"Catechisms, religious tracts, and Bibles would fill some bookshelves to the exclusion of all other reading matter. The new wide-angled, unfocused scholarship went together with a new single-minded, narrowly focused piety."[21] And piety is a kind of interiority.

But literacy was not the only factor. Early in the Middle Ages, Christianity ran at several speeds. Rulers ruled. Peasants worked. And priests, monks, and religious scholars did the religious duties for society as a whole. This tripartite division of society was understood as being part of the structure of the cosmos. And what the priests and scholars did — worship, study, and pray — was seen as something that they did for all of society, freeing the peasants and rulers from focusing on those kinds of responsibilities. The most extreme among the religious renounced worldly goods, marriage, and sometimes even human company in order to transcend their worldly station and somehow get closer to the divine — on behalf of all people.

The trouble with this worldview is that it wasn't satisfying to many in the church, including many leaders. This was probably in no small measure because the clergy recognized that Scripture itself expected people to be personally engaged as Christians, rather than just prayed over by a religious caste. Therefore, throughout the Middle Ages there was pressure from the top to find a way for all Christians to run at the same spiritual speed, pressure that Charles Taylor says led to reform with a small *r*. So, for example, at the Lateran Council of 1215, Christians were encouraged to engage in confession in order to participate in communion. Confession involves self-examination, a personal evaluation of one's own moral and spiritual standing. Preaching orders such as the Dominicans called Christians to more intentional piety. Diana Butler Bass describes how the use of the rosary as an aid to devotion grew from the late twelfth century through the sixteenth century, making "the mystical path of the saints readily available to regular parishioners through a disciplined, meditative recitation of prayers [that] fostered an interiorized and individualized spirituality." Describing the popularity of the *Book of Hours* for laity that was slowly becoming more literate, Bass notes that "[t]hrough the Middle Ages the

21. Eisenstein, *Printing Revolution*, p. 48.

laity made what had become a clerical form of prayer their own once again, reclaiming for themselves an ancient practice of the church."[22]

Of course, this trend was encouraged by literacy as well. As people argued finer and more abstract points of theology or morality, their longing for more and more dramatic experiences of the divine increased. Puritans, for example, believed that all people needed a dramatic conversion experience in order to be sure that they were truly Christian (as we shall see in chapter 6 below).

Charles Taylor enumerates other, related factors. In the enchanted world, people tended to see death as another stage of life. A desire to die a good death — one marked by "grief and expectation, repentance and forgiveness — formed the practical spirituality of the medieval vision for dying well," and weighed much more heavily on people than the desire to escape judgment.[23] Perhaps because of surviving pagan attitudes, the whole Christian notion of judgment did not weigh heavily on people. They presumed the church was in the business of dispensing salvation. The presumption was that salvation was for all.[24] However, over time, as the church focused on the forensic account of atonement, people also tended to focus more on their own impending personal appearance before God the judge — then thought to be not at the end of history but immediately after death. Counting on salvation gave way to agonized self-examination as to whether or not the truth was in them. Taylor sums up by arguing the following: "In any case, there was something like an 'internal crusade' from the thirteenth cen-

---

22. Bass, *People's History,* pp. 179, 108.

23. Bass, *People's History,* pp. 117-19.

24. Zwingli — as well as some other early Reformers — was sure that the scope of God's grace was wider than we imagine today. He includes in the number of those saved: "Hercules, Theseus, Socrates, Aristides, Antigonus, Numa, Camillus, the Catos and Scipios; here Louis the Pious, and your predecessors, the Louis, Philips, Pepins, and all your ancestors who have gone hence in faith. In short there has not been a good man and will not be a holy heart or faithful soul from the beginning of the world to the end thereof that you will not see in heaven with God." Ulrich Zwingli. "A SHORT AND CLEAR EXPOSITION OF THE CHRISTIAN FAITH PREACHED BY HULDREICH ZWINGLI, WRITTEN BY ZWINGLI HIMSELF SHORTLY BEFORE HIS DEATH TO A CHRISTIAN KING; THUS FAR NOT PRINTED BY ANYONE AND NOW FOR THE FIRST TIME PUBLISHED TO THE WORLD." MATTH.11: "COME UNTO ME," ETC., 1536, ed. M. Bullinger (written July 1531).

tury on, mainly carried on by the preaching of the mendicant orders. A crusade against [several heresies and groups]; but also a standing campaign towards repentance, towards facing the facts of death and judgment, and acting accordingly." The more people focused on their own worthiness, the less they looked to "magical" rites for their salvation. It was now thought of as something having to do with getting one's soul right with God. People wielded their own magic.[25]

The impact of these changes was not restricted to the world of faith. The change in Europe's religious outlook was bound up in other intellectual trends. The Renaissance and Enlightenment, for example, were also influenced by the way writing made scholarly vocations more attainable through the multiplication of texts. Taylor, in particular, constantly calls attention to the variety and complexity of the many factors that led to today's secular society. So, for example, he connects the end of enchantment with a series of events that saw concepts such as "the law of God" evolve into concepts such as "natural order."[26] At first, natural order was thought of as providential; but eventually other, nontheistic ideas would also emerge.

Ultimately, with the advent of literacy, Europeans learned that there were other ways of thinking about the story. In fact, one could even theologize — theorize — about the meaning of the story. This, in turn, led to disagreements about theology as Christians relied more and more on rational arguments. The change in consciousness that this wrought made conceiving of the world as enchanted more and more difficult. Events needed rational causes. Salvation came to be linked with either works or faith; salvation by grace through faith even made people wonder how much faith they needed. Faith became an internal act of will, and it was faith not only in the larger story — something that Catholics and Protestants hung onto — but also acceptance of the right doctrines. Faith became assent to confessional summaries of "the truth." Doubt was the problem, and it became increasingly widespread.

25. Charles Taylor, *A Secular Age* (Cambridge, MA: Belknap Press, 2007), pp. 64-65, 68, 75.
26. Charles Taylor, *Varieties of Religion Today: William James Revisited* (Cambridge, MA: Harvard University Press, 2002), pp. 68-69.

Modernism

So what did literate faith become by the end of this era? The faith of my grandfather and the customers at his bookstore. It was faith constructed and imagined in the image of the book: the same linearity, rationality, and depth of information. At its best, faith was an intellectual commitment that had practical consequences for hope and loving. It no longer saw the world as charged with spiritual reality, but it saw the spiritual realm as one to inspire meaning and morality for worldly people. Literate faith was a stepchild of modernism.

First, this era is characterized by belief in progress. Even the language that was used to describe these times suggests as much. After the "dark" ages, Europe experienced a "renaissance," and then later, an "enlightenment." There was an explosion of knowledge about the cosmos, about physical processes as diverse as gravity and electricity. Each century celebrated a different kind of progress. The seventeenth may have seen it as better education for the masses. The eighteenth saw it as inalienable rights and nationalistic success. The nineteenth century saw progress in nations that stretched from sea to sea and could be crossed by trains. These days progress is mostly measured by the avalanche of information technology, electronic communication, and creature comforts and consumer baubles that people have access to — rather than by the achievement of any spiritual or philosophical ideals. But all through the modern era, whatever progress looked like, it was always believed in.

Second, the engine of progress was rationality, as well as its gifts, technology and science. Linear books with their assumptions, presuppositions, arguments, and conclusions became the infrastructure for faith, giving it an ordered and intellectual cast. It wasn't enough to know the Lord's Prayer or the Apostles' Creed by heart. Books, pamphlets, and sermons had transformed faith into the need to make a difficult choice between many competing creeds in a deeply fractured church. People thought of faith as a sustained argument, and they expected intense doctrinal conflict. Christians everywhere made peace with schism and separation from other Christians in the name of their idiosyncratic truths. The one holy catholic church of Europe became many creed-based and national churches.

Many scholars have remarked on how Christian theology adapted the intellectual infrastructure and modes of thinking of the Enlightenment. For example, Hendrik Hart writes: "To counteract the rational infallibility of scientific propositions, [conservative] Christians responded with the (equally rational) infallibility of revealed propositions. But a focus on [rationalistic] propositions was common to both sides."[27] This slavish mimicry of rationalist rhetoric is easy to illustrate. For example, the contemporary preacher Haddon Robinson argues that "expository preaching is the communication of a biblical concept, derived from and transmitted through a historical, grammatical, and literary study of a passage in its context, which the Holy Spirit first applies to the personality and experience of the preacher, then through him to his hearers."[28] One finds here the same emphasis on truth and the same emphasis on method, on rational propositions, and, interestingly enough, on experience or psychology that characterizes Enlightenment rationality. George Marsden notes that, "despite the conspicuous subjectivism throughout Evangelicalism and within Fundamentalism itself, one side of the Fundamentalist mentality is committed to inductive rationalism."[29]

Third, faith also became a matter of overcoming doubts. Such doubts were often engendered by the simple observation that most people in Europe had made different faith choices than you had — not to mention most people on the planet. Underscoring the problem of doubt was the sense that if one had Scripture, and one read it with care, one should be able to understand its central message in a commonsense way. But again, many people obviously did not. At the same time, not believing became an increasingly popular option, and this also made people realize that they would have to decide for themselves.

27. Hendrik Hart, *Setting Our Sights by the Morning Star: Reflections on the Role of the Bible in Postmodern Times* (Toronto: Patmos Press, 1989), p. 95.

28. Haddon Robinson, *Biblical Preaching: The Development and Delivery of Expository Sermons* (Grand Rapids: Baker, 1980), p. 21.

29. George Marsden, *Understanding Fundamentalism and Evangelicalism* (Grand Rapids: Eerdmans, 1994), pp. 117-18.

Fourth, for many Christians, the arguments for and the content of the faith were not enough to settle their doubts. These Christians often went looking for an experience that would confirm the truth as they understood it. While not usually becoming anti-intellectual, many religious movements — from the Brethren for Common Life to the Puritans to the conventicles of the pietists — sought out such religious experiences partly to confirm their faith in the face of doubt. Indeed, among charismatic Christians and Pentecostals today, such an experience is paramount. Such faith was also often intensely personal and interior, calling for individuals to have an inner life. David Wells observes:

> Reformation individualism produces people whose life choices and values have a seriousness and intensity about them that reflect their recognition of an ultimate, divine accountability. It is this sense of a moral universe presided over by God that drives this individualism to eschew all competing authorities, including those of the state, the Church, and most importantly, the self.[30]

Fifth, modernists of all stripes built institutions to further their convictions, their missions, and to teach a new generation. Whether it was a new denomination or a trading company or university or labor union or parochial newspaper, modernists understood the power of incorporation as a lever for their efforts to share the good news or profit from their ventures — or to control their flock. These institutions were organized on rational principles with a view toward accomplishing great ends. Such institutions accomplished much, but they would also, as we shall see in the following chapter, come under withering attack for their coercion and their obsession with control.

Sixth, the genius for building institutions and the drive to ever more interior and personal faith — along with constant battles about doctrinal propositions — led to more and more schisms. From conventicles to Congregationalists, dissenters to Baptists, Christians

---

30. David F. Wells, *No Place for Truth; or, Whatever Happened to Evangelical Theology?* (Grand Rapids: Eerdmans, 1993), p. 141.

seeking the right balance between experience and theology broke off into increasingly smaller communities from the time of the Reformation right through to the present.

Seventh, in line with the increasing emphasis on scientific method, faith presumed that as long as you apply the right grammatical and historical — that is, "scientific" or "rational" — instruments, ancient texts would reveal authorial intention. Ironically, the more the faithful insisted so, the more the church continued to fracture into different sects committed to different biblical interpretations. Ultimately, one result was that more and more people left the faith altogether, finding it too fantastic and too improbable, given the sad state of conflict and disagreement among "true believers."

What It Meant for Me

My childlike "enchanted" faith had a lot of momentum. In part this was because I grew up in a family and community that formed within me the habits of faith. My parents were quite intentional about this. As I noted in the last chapter, they walked the faith talk. Furthermore, I was blessed to be part of a family where this meant I would be surrounded by love, kindness, consistency, and encouragement. And thus did I, unconsciously at first, connect those kinds of virtues with faith.

But the momentum my faith developed was also due to the ways in which the institutions I was part of — church and school — shaped me. I went to Calvin Memorial Christian School in St. Catharines, Ontario. It was a parochial school with mostly very good — and also very Christian Reformed — teachers. This Christian education system extended all the way through college, and then through seminary, and stayed with me, but for a few courses at Toronto's York University, until I started my PhD studies. That meant that the ideas I encountered were mostly ideas that the leaders in my community thought safe; or, if they were non-Christian ideas, they were couched in rhetoric that made them seem untenable. Some people would call such an education brainwashing, but those who gave it to me called it nurture of children and obedience to God's desire that all of our lives be offered up to Jesus. For me, that education was rich, filled with teachers who loved me and my fellow students; but it was also one with a decided point of view, as indeed any education, including secular ones, must have.

At the same time, that education was a modern one in the sense that it was not rooted in an enchanted view of the cosmos. The fact that all of life was to be lived to God's glory did not mean that there were sprites and ogres and spirits under every rock and in every stream. The scientific method found a home in science classes. We learned about faith in Bible classes, in catechism classes, and in church. This still took a lot of time, but it was clear that faith was its own thing. On the other hand, in the church, family, and Christian schools I was raised in, nothing else gave faith a run for its money.

My own faith was unquestioning and eager. I was so taken with pleasing parents that approved of my interest in faith, and took so much pleasure in understanding the systematic structure of our faith, that I never really wrestled with its relevance. The interest I took in church and faith could, in a different family setting, have just as easily been an interest in rocket science or chartered accountancy. But it wasn't. And so, without ever having an existential struggle, I believed as the rest of my extended family did, and I came to believe in their systematic theologies and confessional catechisms. I knew the arguments for our point of view, compared to those of the Baptists, for example, and I understood that there was a way to describe a God who made decrees of election that led to the salvation of some and damnation of others as somehow just and loving. It was a puzzle, but I was curious. And the setting was safe, loving, and full of people who affirmed my interests. Doubt? Well, it never really showed up on my plate.

So, between the earliest days of my faith and the present, there has been both great change and great consistency. I realized that faith was not a given, the One Story that made sense of everything else for almost everyone else. That was a big change. But I also learned that the complexity and genius of the doctrines and institutions, as well as the love of the people "of faith," made faith an indispensable and enjoyable part of my life.

I loved reading, and I couldn't get enough of it. In fact, I think it is safe to say that I was so fascinated by so many different, often arcane, branches of knowledge that I was able to read about that I was usually far too distracted to do very well at school. When I was six years old, for example, I was sent to the hospital with stomach complaints. The doctors were unable to determine what the problem was: no ulcers, no invasive species, no problems at home that they could see. One nurse, making a late-night checkup, finally figured out the problem. At two or three in the morning she found me reading by the dim light from the hallway. I had a *Reader's Digest* open to an article entitled "I Am Joe's Liver." The doctor diagnosed a severe case of anxiety brought on by my reading way beyond my comprehension level, reading that had left me very worried that my liver or heart or stomach might go at any time.

I'm not sure how I learned to read so well so early — especially since I hardly knew a word of English when I started kindergarten. Once I picked it up, though, I couldn't stop. After the *Reader's Digest* experience, one of my parents brought home a grocery-store encyclopedia set. It was strictly bush-league compared to the *Encyclopedia Britannica,* but it had the virtue of being brief enough to be able to be read from cover to cover, all twenty or twenty-five volumes. Then came my first trips to the library. I carried home books on cars and planes and wars and jungles — sometimes, during the summer, two or three piles a week. I remember asking permission to go to the adult section of the library because I had read most of the books in the kids' department, or they were just too easy. I felt as if every librarian and patron wanted to throw me out of the science and transportation sections that I frequented because I was too little to be in the adult library. And then, at someone's suggestion, I picked up a book by Jules Verne. From there it was a short step to Edgar Rice Burroughs and Arthur C. Clarke and Isaac Asimov. I was hooked — and still am — on science fiction.

My interest in reading was rewarded by strong parental approval. As the oldest son, I loved that kind of approval. I can remember, when I was in grade three or four, receiving an assignment in school that involved writing a short paper — probably meant to be a paragraph — about the part of the catechism that discussed why Jesus needed to be divine to bear the burden of human sin, and needed to be human in order to be the right one to pay for sin. Something got hold of me, and I wrote — in a very neat longhand (which was very difficult for me, since I was fine-motor challenged) a ten-page summary of the genius of the catechism's answer. When I handed it in, my teacher thought it so good that he displayed it at the Christian School Teachers' convention. My parents basked in the reflected glow. My father, who at about that time was pursuing his own efforts to become an ordained pastor in spite of not having the prescribed education, encouraged me to do more. I learned early that my way to get approval and joy in life was not on the sports field or the party scene; I was too clumsy for the one and too shy and introverted for the other. But reading and writing, now that impressed the people who were most important to me!

In fact, it became a refuge that I probably overdid to the point of being antisocial. One of my most enduring memories of being a teenager has to do with reading too much. The family had decided to drive out to Pepi's Airport Drive-in to watch the planes fly in. All five of us kids and two adults were supposed to pile into our Chevrolet Biscayne, at a time when air-conditioning in cars was not routine, and drive on over. I demurred. I said that I wanted to stay home and read — in my basement bedroom. My father became angry. Turning on me, he complained loudly that I was a very selfish young man, given the way I ignored the family and all social events just so that I could read in my basement hideaway. It was time, he said, that I joined the human race. But mostly, I didn't. I stayed home, stewed for a while, and soon lost myself in whatever book it was I was reading.

It has been pretty much the same all my life. After seminary I kept a diary of all the books I read. I made sure it was at least one a week. By then my interests were expanding. Popular science, transportation, and good novels were still an important part of the mix, but books on anthropology, evolution, archaeology, and biography became part of the mix.

What does all this have to do with faith? you may ask. Well, my love of reading, especially social-science kinds of books, resonated with the role that books, articles, and writing sermons played in my ministry. Everything I read was useful for preaching. My sermons were informed not only by my wide reading, but also by the way I internalized narrative, both dramatic fictional narrative and good nonfiction narrative. I sensed that these all worked together, and it made the whole process of studying for, writing, and delivering sermons a real pleasure. The pleasure, in fact, was so real that, even as my reading brought me into contact with more and more difficult and challenging ideas, it completely overwhelmed any inclination I had to take such writing as a serious challenge to my faith. I think there was a part of me, deep inside, that argued that if intellectual heroes of mine like Richard Mouw, Nicholas Wolterstorff, Neal Plantinga, and John Stek could go on believing, if they could find a way to negotiate the many intellectual challenges to their faiths, then I must be able to as well.

In retrospect, it wasn't just that what I was reading was helpful for school or ministry. It was that reading somehow shaped the shelves and bins in my brain in such a way as to make it hunger for more of the same — more inferences, more deductive leaps, more facts, more organized ways of cataloguing all that I was learning. Marshal McLuhan, of course, has said that the medium is the message, and for me the medium was both reading (and its logic) and faith (with its logic). It wasn't that I didn't let the two of them come into conflict; together they shaped my sensorium.

Mention of some of the best professors I had brings to mind another important factor that helped keep me deeply engaged in the intellectual community I was raised in. I was the oldest son and there was no surer way to please my father than to boldly go where he wanted me to go. This started with his desire that I go to a Christian college. I was resisting, thinking that it would be nice to make a clean break of a merely okay high school social scene by going to a secular institution like the University of Toronto. But Dad let it be known that he wasn't too crazy about that choice. And, through a humorous turn of events, he got his way.

It happened that one day, near the end of my last year of high school, my father told me that my basement bedroom was beginning to look like the local landfill and that I needed to have it clean by the time he got home from work the next day. He said that if it wasn't he would impose strict sanctions. I said, "Sure," and immediately forgot the whole conversation. The next day I had a friend over after drama practice because he couldn't get a ride home. We were hanging out in my room when he pulled out some cigarette papers, a roller, and a pouch that contained not tobacco but marijuana. And he began rolling joints as we talked about this and that. When his paraphernalia was spread out all over my bed, I heard the upstairs door open and my father's heavy footsteps begin the descent downstairs. Dad, I realized, was going to check out my janitorial assignment.

It was time to think fast. I jumped off the bed, ran out of my room, slamming the door behind me, and bolted up the steps to meet my dad about halfway. "Dad, we need to talk!" I said. "Let's go to your office. I've decided to go to Dordt College." This so impressed my father that he turned on his heel and led me upstairs.

My friend and I were off the hook that afternoon, but I was on my way to a Christian college as a result of my quick thinking. And not just any Christian college. I was off to Dordt College in Sioux Center, Iowa. About an hour's worth of corn fields and feedlots from the nearest city of any size: Sioux Falls, South Dakota, to the north, or Sioux City, Iowa, to the south. I wouldn't be surprised if you never heard of either city.

What characterized Dordt was its single-minded commitment to the fact that its perspective on life and faith was just about the best thing in the world. The focus was on the intellectual tradition founded by an early twentieth-century Dutch (of course) prime minister and theologian, Abraham Kuyper. Courses at Dordt were taught from a Kuyperian perspective. The trademark notion was that every human endeavor, from education to politics, from medical care to law, could be done — indeed, had to be done — in a "Christ-centered" way, because every square inch of the universe belonged to Christ. In practice, this meant that liberal arts students had to master a set of standard texts by authors such as Herman Dooyeweerd and Hendrik Vollenhoven of the Free University of Amsterdam. If we were really focused students of this material, we might devote our lives to working for nonprofit institutions designed from the ground up to advance the complex Kuyperian perspective. If we were not really focused on getting to the depths of this worldview, we could stick with more basic texts by Abraham Kuyper and become Christian school teachers or Christian labor organizers.

A critical aspect of such studies was learning a system for categorizing all other thinkers by their main errors, which we did in order to more easily dismiss them. This went on a lot in my college apartment, all of my roommates being philosophy majors. Similarly, thinkers within the tradition had enough minor differences of opinion so that one could spend a lifetime arguing these, which was not necessarily a healthy diversion from asking more sensible and more basic questions.

What this kind of education did, more or less, was incubate those of us who engaged the education. We were so busy learning the good and true stuff that there was little opportunity to consider other stuff. We were heavily socialized to buy into the system by professors, friends, and parents, all of whom genuinely thought it was the best thing going. Somehow, what was missed in all of this was serious consideration of whether or not faith, in fact, was warranted or plausible. It was largely assumed, and I bought into it hook, line, and sinker. Partly it was fun trying to master the material. Partly it was that my friends turned out to be the students most engaged in this material, and so I went along to get along. And I internalized for myself the logic of this system — as well as its triumphalistic cast.

It was all incredibly exciting. We harbored the hope that, in spite of human sin, our tribe could create the institutions — everything from hospitals and nursing homes to universities and labor unions — that would bring a high degree of Christian coherence, justice, and whatever else is good about faith to every part of life. Better yet, this vision was not couched in fundamentalist legalism or moralism. We didn't dress funny. We listened to rock and roll. We drank alcohol. We smoked lots of cigarettes, and some pot in moderation. All of this, we believed, could be redeemed and transformed. So we paid attention to it and enjoyed it.

I was in love with the system and its language, concepts such as "sphere sovereignty" and *enkapsis*, creation ordinances and power organizations. I read copiously. I arranged the books on my shelf by the various theological loci. I honestly don't think it ever occurred to me that I might not want to believe, or that people who didn't believe what I did were seriously disadvantaged when it came to reality.

But the height of my love affair with literate, linear, bounded Christianity probably came during my years in seminary. In many ways, seminary was more of the same: Kuyper was still important, but my appreciation for other relatively conservative theologians was on the increase, and thus did seminary broaden my horizons. For the first time, I also became aware of the difficulty of interpretation, and so I decided that, though we always should try as hard as we can to get it right, if in the end we are wrong about some moral or doctrinal matter, it is more a function of a hard text than a hardened heart.

But I loved the linear. I even tried to model my theological method on the scientific method. In my last year at seminary I wrote a paper entitled "Theological Method and Incarnational Coherence." The first section was entitled "Four Presuppositions for Doing Theology as a Science," and the first presupposition was: "A Goal of Theology Is Theoretical Knowledge." Along the way I declared that, "rather than assess a theological theory's 'predictive accuracy,' doctrines should be assessed according to their teleological utility." I found such projects fascinating, totally relevant, and fun to engage in. I didn't notice that, while I was presenting my seminar paper, my fellow students' eyes were glazing over.

There was no need in my life for a conversion experience. I had texts. There was no need to keep me on the straight and narrow. I loved nothing so much as parsing the straight and narrow, including making some allowances for drifting onto the shoulders. I was so busy trying to understand my own tradition that reading Karl Barth was about as far off the beaten orthodox track as I had time for. And I didn't understand most of what he had to say very well anyway. And so I marched off to my first parish, sure of what I knew. I had enough emotional intelligence to easily get by with the pastoral work. And I loved words enough to write at least the odd riveting sermon without writing really bad ones too often.

My polite rage for order extended to most aspects of my work. I memorized Robert's Rules of Order so that council meetings would go smoothly. I read everything I could find about church administration.

I taught adult classes in my home on the structure (naturally) of the Gospel of Mark. And I loved going to meetings of our local group of Christian Reformed churches, where we discussed doctrine, schism, and the discipline of erring brothers (the erring ones were all brothers at that time).

In short, Calvinist Christianity had all the answers, and I never really doubted that I had the training to understand those answers and the wisdom not to press them too hard in case they didn't appeal to someone close to me.

chapter 3

Postmodern Faith: Loss and Doubt

Introduction

My metaphor for the changing nature of faith has been the Banaue Rice Terraces. The terraces are built on an underlying geological structure, the Philippine Cordilleras. And as much as the terraces change through the ages — from bottomland farms to thousands of square miles of carefully crafted terraces to the slowly eroding but beautiful scene of today — the underlying geological structure remains the same. Something about faith, even as we move through enchanted, literate, post-modern versions of faith, is similarly built on an underlying structure that seems timeless. And yet, the faith of humans is remarkably diverse around the world, and remarkably different from one era to another within the smaller scope of Western history and culture. This diversity, even within the Christian tradition, gives me pause, making me wonder what is essential about faith, and what is not.

I also see that in some respects I have recapitulated in my own life something like the historical phases that faith in the West has gone through. My childhood faith was enchanted. As I learned to read, I put childish things behind me and adopted a linear, rationalist, modernist framework for my faith. But lately I have come to question many aspects of that faith. Perhaps this questioning is analogous to the slow erosion of the rice terraces that has begun over the past fifty years as well. In this chapter I'll examine how postmodernism has begun to work against the modernist aspects of my faith. And in the next chapter, I'll look at how life lived in the embrace of electronic and virtual reality has also had a profound impact on society's — and my own — faith.

The Seeds of Personal Doubt

Doubt isn't like a switch that can be turned on and off. It works more like the slow erosion of a streambed by water, or of a mesa by the wind. So, even as I celebrated my faith and dedicated myself to proselytizing on its behalf, doubt slowly — sometimes irritatingly — worked to re-route and reshape my faith. I now remember my childhood days with an aching sadness, because what I freely received then I cannot now buy for all the money in the world. Faith is neither whole nor easy anymore. Life is not enchanted. I can't pinpoint the moment I first started doubting. I'm guessing that certain facts and events quietly built an infrastructure for doubt that it inhabited only when it was ready.

The first such events may have had to do with neighborhood kids who didn't go to my church. I played with them. We built a fort in the empty lot across the street. We collected chestnuts together, storing them in huge boxes that we moved from one backyard to another, one step ahead of the wrath of our parents. I liked them. But when I walked to my Christian school in the opposite direction of their public school, they sometimes yelled at me, "Dutchie, Dutchie, DP." DP stood for "displaced person," as in "war refugee," or "scum." A teacher told me to ignore the taunting because in the end God would make sure they got what they deserved. I remember wondering how it was that these otherwise good friends didn't have what it took to go to heaven.

I now live in Toronto, a very diverse city. Buddhists and Sikhs, atheists and Jews all live nearby in my suburban neighborhood. My wife, in her psychotherapy practice, often provides marital counseling for people in mixed-ethnic, mixed-race, or mixed-faith relationships. She tells me that these are mostly decent folks. The minute I stop to think about their hopes and dreams, I can't help but hope and dream with them. I realize that I've grown up in a cultural and religious "ghetto"

— in the best sense of that word, mind you — and so I have begun taking my own traditions, doctrines, and pretty soon my convictions with a grain of salt. I can hardly imagine that, in the midst of so much difference, my people were the ones who got it mostly right generations ago. It doesn't seem fair that my tribe of pale northern European Saxons got all the truth while others got so much less. Jennifer Hecht calls this "cosmopolitan relativism."[1]

So I started wondering idly: maybe there are more paths to God, even if only one is the shortest way. Or maybe God doesn't much care about what your particular revelation is, or what you think. After all, God never really made the effort to be as clear or comprehensive in Scripture as systematic theologians think they can be. Maybe what God really cares about, in the end, isn't the original sin of a mythic ancestor whose guilt somehow ends up on my books, but the real sins — or real good — that I or my tribe actually do. There is a pretty strong line of scriptural support for such a view. The parable of the sheep and goats, for example, describes a final judgment of the nations that is not about whether or not you are elect, or have the right conception of the divinity of Jesus, but about what you did for the "least of these my brothers" (Matt. 25:40). Even a brief review of history makes it very clear that so-called Christian nations have never had a great track record when it comes to ministering to the "least of these," whether they were colonial subjects in Indonesia or India, or the slaves they traded in the Atlantic triangle, or the poor farmers around the world that Western nations have doomed to poverty by their protectionist agricultural trade policies. As I write this, Western nations that have militarily occupied Haiti for generations, that have robbed Haiti of its wealth while protecting the interests of their Western corporations, that supported repressive dictators in the interest of stability while self-righteously and hypocritically declaring allegiance to human rights and democracy — these Western nations are delivering massive amounts of disaster relief to Haiti after the 2010 earthquake. Unfortu-

---

1. Jennifer Hecht, *Doubt: A History; The Great Doubters and Their Legacy of Innovation from Socrates and Jesus to Thomas Jefferson and Emily Dickinson* (San Francisco: HarperSanFrancisco, 2003), p. 286.

nately, it is a case of far too little, too late, to effect the lasting change that might one day help Haiti achieve even a modicum of prosperity and peace. When it comes to the least of these, Western nations seem to have a habit of beating them to within an inch of their lives, and then shaking their heads in disbelief and disgust while binding their wounds.

Cosmopolitan relativism is only part of why I began to doubt the black-and-white faith story I grew up with. Ironically, seminary — where no relativism was allowed — also helped create an infrastructure that doubt would later inhabit, mostly by expanding my intellectual horizon. Professors would say things that sent me to books other than those on the suggested reading lists. These alternative perspectives were fascinating and, as often as not, as plausible as the one I was learning to defend. I realized not only that each of the Gospels has its own unique voice but also that each Gospel contains historical elements that cannot be harmonized with the others, beginning with the Christmas story.

I learned that the creation story, and especially the flood story, had historical antecedents in Sumerian and Akkadian myths — the *Atrahasis Epic* and the related *Gilgamesh Epic* — that were much older than the biblical record. I read books that suggested very plausibly that Abraham was a dimly remembered legendary figure, and that biblical accounts of the Exodus from Egypt and entry into Canaan (Palestine) were exaggerated. I was appalled by the Bible's account of Israel's ethnic cleansing of Canaan, the slaughter of men, women, livestock, and even children to make way for God's people, and remain shocked that my professors tried to justify such genocide as God's will, which is still, after all, the most common justification of genocide. I realized that New Testament writers expected the immediate return of Jesus and were sorely disappointed when he didn't return in their lifetimes. The Nicene Creed turned out to be as much — or more — of a political document as it was a theological one.[2] The basis for

---

2. Any fair account of the early theological controversies in the Christian church will explain how this was so. A particularly riveting and well-told tale is Richard E. Rubenstein, *When Jesus Became God: The Epic Fight over Christ's Divinity in the Last Days of Rome* (New York: Harcourt, Brace, 1999).

the ecumenical creeds' explanation of the two natures of Christ, and of the Trinity, turns out to be a Greek philosophical concept that presumes upon some sort of shared universal substance that even God has. And so on. Although my seminary years deepened my love for Scripture and the history of doctrines, and certainly did not threaten my faith, those years made much that I had once simply taken for granted seem a lot more complicated — if not yet tenuous. At the very least, I would say that my education — and my investigations beyond the prescribed seminary reading — provided me with an agenda for doubt.

Serving as a pastor also impacted my faith. Interestingly enough, it wasn't the death, the wasting diseases, or the congregational bickering that challenged me. Though difficult, pastoral work in those contexts can also be inspiring: that is, they can be an opportunity to see how Christian attitudes of service and Christian hope really make a difference. However, the luxury of twenty or more hours a week with my Bible, while I was writing sermons on big issues such as evolution, homosexuality, apartheid, and women's liberation, did form me. I can remember struggling with the fact that what I was thinking was not always what I dared say in my sermons. And as I was thus struggling, I became less concerned with trying to figure out where God was drawing a line in the sand on these issues and more intrigued by why some people were so concerned with making sure that those lines were drawn as tautly as possible. Scripture did not speak to me with the same clarity that others, usually those more conservative than I, claimed it spoke to them.

As I studied issues like those mentioned above, as well as many others that were supposedly the reason for the divisions between my denomination and other conservative denominations, such as the Catholics or the Baptists, I also realized that many of the doctrines my tradition valued actually lacked warrant. Sometimes my tradition's attachment to such doctrines actually seemed to be in inverse proportion to the amount of attention they received in Scripture. Let me give you an example. Conservative scholars who have similar views about the authority of the Bible, and also similar beliefs about the hermeneutical principles that should be used to interpret Scripture, cannot agree on who should be baptized. Should babies born into Christian families be baptized, or should those baptized be adults who have had a conversion experience? One might think that if similarly conservative scholars, using the same conservative exegetical principles, cannot agree, they would at least admit that Scripture is not sufficiently straightforward about baptism to draw a line in the sand. However, we scholars seem incapable of this sort of humility, appealing instead to ancient decisions in our own traditions, which have been laid down for all time in confessions such as the Augsburg Confession or Canons of Dordt as the final word on such matters. Disagree with those confessions, and you are tossed from your faith community. Suggest a change to those confessions, and you fall under a cloud of suspicion and controversy.

But the question of adult or infant baptism just scratches the surface. Should women be allowed to preach? Can we say that God loves all people? Should we allow the use of musical instruments in the church? Can children participate in the Lord's Supper? Is the guilt of original sin passed on from one generation to another through birth, or representatively, or not at all? Scripture provides few clear or concise answers to any of these questions — though Lord knows, he (or she?) could have been a lot clearer about such issues in Scripture if it had really mattered. In fact, I sometimes imagine that Scripture's very lack of clarity on most matters is actually a mischievous invitation from God to concentrate on the parts about which there can be no misunderstanding. The greatest of these, of course, is love.

Again, the impact of my pondering of such things early on in my ministry was not to push me away from faith per se. But the questions did help build an infrastructure of observations, of habits of thinking, of curiosity and piety that doubt would later inhabit. I did come to the conclusion that the reasons people held onto one doctrine or perspective rather than another usually had more to do with their tribe, their church's ethnic or socioeconomic makeup, than with any original and deeply personal search of Scripture or wrestling with issues (for more on this, see chapter 5 below). It just seemed odd to me that the small band of mostly rural Dutch folks who just happened to be my ancestors had coalesced around a specific set of confessions, doctrinal traditions, and culture nearly two hundred years earlier — that they should ever be expected to have gotten so much right. Of course, in reality that doesn't seem plausible at all. So I decided that, as much as we insisted on Scripture as the basis for our theology, we really decided issues on the basis of what we were taught as kids, what we learned from our teachers, and how best we could maintain our social and career status quo. That is, family and friendship ties ultimately are more persuasive then syllogisms or proof texts. And thus I also looked at all the doctrines of my tradition, and at the coercive ways in which the church insisted we subscribe to them, in a new light. It seemed to me that, for all the talk about having a rational and sensible theology, we maintained our belief in that theology more through rationalization after the fact, and through using the church's means of enforcement, than actual conviction based on measuring those doctrines against other doctrines and against Scripture.

During my first years as a pastor, one event in particular had a very large impact on my earlier perception that my particular tradition of Christianity had gotten it all right. In Sarnia, Ontario, we ran an interdenominational Cursillo program. Begun in the Roman Catholic Church, Cursillo was a weekend event that invited people to reconsider their faith, their church membership, and the direction of their lives. After attending one such weekend, I signed up as a pastoral leader for another. The highlight of the weekend was supposed to be a communion service. Here people from many different church backgrounds — or maybe none at all — joined together to celebrate Jesus' death and resurrection, as well as our unity in the faith.

Each weekend event had two pastoral leaders. My partner on my weekend was a Roman Catholic priest. At the very moment of communion, he stood up and said that he could not participate. He wanted to, he said, but his bishop had forbade him to take communion with Protestants. So I would have to officiate by myself. Furthermore, said the priest, he would stand by the communion table and silently observe communion while not participating, as a mute reminder that the church we thought of as one and interdenominational was actually broken and fractured. He hoped his example would forever cure us of the notion that we were more orthodox, more right, and more holy than some other Christian sect. He hoped that his example would encourage us to work for church unity.

In some ways the priest was overly dramatic. At the same time, his silent witness got to me. As a pastor, I wondered which doctrines that separated me from my Baptist or United Church friends — never mind my Catholic friends — really justified having separate churches. Ironically, not only did we have separate churches, but once the Cursillo weekend was over, I knew that most of us would be engaging in proselytizing activities that would mostly add up to stealing other church's sheep. I thought we needed to unite around the far more important convictions we shared than the doctrinal distinctives that most people in the pews hardly understood. Therefore, even while I continued to love and admire my own tradition, I became less and less convinced that most of what defined that tradition should separate Christians.

Throughout this time I was the pastor of two churches. I prayed daily, regularly walked the labyrinth at a monastery, immersed myself in Scripture, went on spiritual retreats, and talked about my doubts with my closest friends and spiritual directors. I always believed, but it was, increasingly, with an edge of discomfort. Study, wide reading, and curiosity did not always confirm me in my childhood opinions. I struggled with dissonance, with more and more questions about things I used to take for granted. I had the public face of a true-blue evangelical pastor as always, but in my private life I was asking more and more questions and beginning to suspect that the answers I was entertaining were not all acceptable to the powers that be. The simple oneness of my childhood was forever fractured. I was no longer sure, and I knew it.

Traveling Doubts

Thus, slowly and subtly, over time, I found myself becoming less confident in what I believed, because study and experience were both changing my mind. The balance between my faith and my doubt began to shift. I realized, on my trip around North America in the "Bananer," that I doubted — with some faith left over.

But thinking back now, I see that two things were really happening. First, there was a certain amount of dissonance caused by my reading, which led me to change my mind about some theological issues. The reading I did led me to doubt positions that my denomination had taken and to look more favorably on positions that other denominations or theologians had taken. So, for example, I rejected my church's teaching on human evolution and homosexuality: I decided that we needed to accept evolution as a scientific theory and that we should welcome practicing gay persons fully into the life of the church. Ultimately, however, this dissonance never really challenged my faith in God, or in Jesus' resurrection, or in the big picture of Christianity, or even my comfort level with my church's confessions — even if I often wished we could be a bit less dogmatic about them.

The second thing that was going on was more fundamental, more basic to faith itself, not just about the doctrinal furniture. It was the beginning of my questioning of whether or not Christianity itself — and God as portrayed by Christianity — made sense. The year Irene and I spent on the road was full of that kind of basic doubt. As I write about it now, it seems to me that I can talk about this doubt's arrival and impact on me in a pretty rational and orderly way. The truth is, when I go back to my journal for that year, I see that I swayed back and forth between belief and disbelief, between certainty and uncertainty. There was no steady progression from one to the other. But it was as if different corners of my brain were holding onto contradictory ideas and maps all at the same time. My narrative, after the fact, is a lot more orderly than my journal shows that I felt at the time.

I think that the formative events that pushed me out beyond the comfortable cocoon of moving around the doctrinal furniture into a full-blown struggle with whether or not I believed can ultimately be traced back to a few overseas journeys I made as editor of *The Banner*. The first was to Japan, where I led a retreat on the meaning and experience of faith — an ironic theme, as it turns out. After the retreat I traveled to Hiroshima. The iconic atom bomb memorial, a partially destroyed, roofless building caught in a time warp, was disappointing. Nearby, however, there is a small park with a statue of a little girl, Sadako, who died of radiation-induced leukemia some years after the bombing. Her story is memorialized in a popular children's book my wife and I read to our boys several times, entitled *Sadako and the Thousand Paper Cranes,* by Eleanor Coerr. In the book, Sadako races against time to fold one thousand paper cranes in the hope that, as legend had it, she would be cured if she succeeded. Unfortunately, Sadako didn't get her miracle; she died just before she could fold the thousand paper birds.

The memorial was simple: a statue of Sadako with a paper crane on her shoulders. What moved me, though, were the hundreds of thousands — perhaps millions — of brightly colored tiny paper cranes children from all over the world sent to Hiroshima in memory of Sadako. As I watched, workers came with more boxes full of cranes, which they emptied on top of the others.

I remember thinking, *So many tiny busy hands from all over the world and so little healing to show for their efforts.* Somehow the connection between my boys' health, the tragedy of Sadako's death and her parents' helplessness to do anything about it, and the longing innocence all those paper cranes represented — altogether it had me in tears that night, alone in my hotel room. I remember thinking how odd it was for me to weep. I keep a tight rein on my emotions because I don't like to feel vulnerable. But there I was, for one of the few times in my adult life, with tears streaming down my face.

From the Sadako Memorial I walked over to the Atom Bomb Museum, which is not a place for people who prefer happy illusions. Dioramas showed people with melted flesh dripping from their bodies. I saw pictures of horribly mutilated victims of the bomb, as well as audio and video interviews with survivors. One display consisted of a few concrete steps marked by a black splotch. That bit of carbon was all that was left of a man who had been vaporized while waiting for his bank to open.

I cannot adequately describe how wrenching all this was. Add Nagasaki to Hiroshima, and also to what I knew about the fire bombings of Dresden and Tokyo, and what I'd read about places like Bergen-Belsen and Auschwitz and Stalin's ethnic cleansings. In any case, I was changed. Somehow Hiroshima lifted all that history out of the textbooks and laid it at the feet of my God. Not that I simply blamed God:

after all, this is what people had done to people. But God might have done something to save us from ourselves. He might have shortened history, and he might have listened to the cries of his people today the way the psalmists seemed to believe that God listened to them in their day — usually, at least. I say these things being fully aware of all the books written on the subject of theodicy, books that defend God's reputation in the face of evil. I understand that there are no easy answers and that the mysteries that surround the ongoing presence of evil are immense. Still, the emotional force of what I saw in Hiroshima made it difficult to turn to these halfway answers and their difficult rationalistic syllogisms with any confidence or relief.

Nevertheless, after Hiroshima I carried on. Like most people, I can compartmentalize my life when it's necessary. Hiroshima found a room at the end of a long dark corridor in my heart. But I didn't visit that room much; I had a job to do, a family to support, a life to live.

And that is how things remained for some time. A few years later, I visited East Africa to do another on-location story and analysis. In Kenya, I toured Nairobi's Kibera slum. Kids lucky enough to go to school were packed forty or fifty to each 225-square-foot dark, stuffy classroom. There were no pencils, pens, papers, or books to be seen anywhere. One in fifty homes had water or electricity. Inside the ghetto there were no sewers or roads, just open ditches full of human waste. Many of the children had distended bellies as a result of malnutrition. I had seen such things before — in Haiti, in Nigeria, and in Honduras. I wrote appropriate words, said the right things to my hosts, and filed those experiences away much as I had the one in Hiroshima. It helped that the Kibera story was mostly about the positive things our people and our money were doing in East Africa. As bad as things were, we were making a difference.

After Nairobi, I was invited to make a side trip to Rwanda, where our church was doing development work near Kibuye, on Lake Kivu, near the Congo border. In Rwanda, I was taken to a church in Ntarama, just outside the capital of Kigali. Five years earlier, members of the Hutu tribe slaughtered a thousand Tutsi tribe members and sympathizers seeking refuge in that church. When I visited there, the sanctuary was still strewn with the remains of hundreds of dead people. There wasn't any flesh left on the bones, but I could still make out the clothing draped over the skeletons. Personal effects littered the floor. Three skulls sat on the church's pulpit, including a child's; on tables running the length of the sanctuary were hundreds more skulls of the people killed there. I took photos. I said sad things to my hosts. As I remember it now, though, I didn't become too emotional.

From Ntarama I was driven to Bisesero. There, at what was meant to be a national monument to the horror of the genocide, was a mountain made of the bones of more than 15,000 victims of genocide. The mountain was several stories high. Again, I took pictures, made notes, and walked the path up the hill on which the Tutsis had made their stand. I did not weep, though I felt empty. And tired. After an hour I got in the car and went on to the guesthouse where I was staying in Kibuye. On that drive I can remember thinking that Rwanda is a country where no one looks you in the eye.

After supper I immediately fell into a deep sleep, only to be awakened, in the pitch dark, by the sounds of soldiers marching past my bedroom window, shouting at the top of their lungs. Normally, soldiers don't spook me, because I grew up seeing them as men and women standing at attention at Remembrance Day services or helping out during disasters, such as floods and earthquakes. In Africa, though, you see many more soldiers than you do here in North America, and they made me very nervous. Once, on my way to an airport in northern Nigeria, soldiers stopped our car more and more frequently as we neared the airport. They would throw boards with nails in them over the road. We would slam on the brakes. The soldiers, often looking like they were no more than seventeen or eighteen years old, would poke their machine guns into the windows and ask for a toll — a bribe — in order to let us continue. My missionary driver would (foolishly, I thought) refuse — on principle. This would make the soldiers mad. They would argue with the driver, raise their voices, and swing their AK-47s around.

So when I was awakened from a deep sleep by the sound of soldiers in Rwanda, it scared me silly, especially since I knew there were Hutu rebels in the hills who had attacked the town just a few weeks earlier. When all was finally quiet again, I got up. I was unable to sleep, and so I sat in the dark to reflect. But now something had pried open the door to that secret room in my heart. I was afraid. As in Hiroshima, I wept. Angry. I had seen more of death — not to mention the poverty, hunger, and corruption that attended it — in three days than I could handle. I shuddered and pounded my fist against the wall. I tried to cry myself to sleep, but I could not.

I've seen too much. Compartmentalization isn't nearly as effective as it used to be when you know that every day good people die horrible deaths. I have a friend in Zimbabwe who recently spent six months in a South African hospital after being beaten and left for dead by Mugabe's Zanu-PF goons. Despite the fact that I (and many others) have been praying for peace in the Middle East nearly every day for as long as I can remember, they are still killing each other over there. And when there is a lull in Iraq or Iran, the killing moves to Lebanon or Egypt or Sudan or Libya.

And so I wasn't sure someone was holding the whole world in his hands anymore. This is what Jennifer Hecht would call doubt based on the moral rejection of injustice and suffering.[3] I doubt because I wonder how God can allow this to go on when he claims to have already triumphed over evil in Jesus' resurrection. In light of these grievances against God, I've found myself lately getting angry when I hear people pray for old and sick aunts to get better, or for "traveling mercies." (Are there also "stay-at-home" mercies?) I wonder why, if God doesn't answer prayers to end genocides or famines, he would answer a prayer to heal a sick old lady. I am even angrier when I hear people say things like, "My aunt is better! What an answer to prayer!"

As if atheists don't get cures that seem miraculous sometimes, and as if the lifespan of Christians is notably longer than that of Muslims or Mormons. God didn't lift a finger to save the 200,000 who died in the 2005 tsunami. People from at least three faiths prayed to him that day for success and happiness and safety and peace. But they all died. And then, in a display of callous shallowness, some of the clergy of each of those three faiths pointed to the sins of the dead — especially the dead of other sects — as the reason God decided to punish them

3. Hecht, *Doubt,* p. xx.

with a tsunami. The ugliness of God as portrayed by such people makes the atheism of Ivan Karamazov appealing by comparison. With atheism the hard question is: "Where did the cosmos come from if there is no God?" With faith the question is: "Why does God allow things to go on this way?" Atheists and theists both have their theories, of course, but those theories (like most doctrines and theories) are all underwarranted. So now I am a doubter as well as a believer. I am an agnostic Christian.

Postmodernity's Argument

Besides the grinding poverty, genocide, and war crimes that I've witnessed, there are other reasons for worrying about whether God is helpfully engaged other than by making sure the sun rises and sets: modern war, with its atomic and hydrogen bombs, remote control missiles, and "shock and awe" attacks on civilian cities; lawless, murdering dictators in Africa, Europe, and Asia; modern finance from WorldCom to AIG; Christian rulers in the American empire who nevertheless insist that foreign policy should be conducted in the national interest rather than in the neighbor's interest. Politicians seem more interested in economic growth than climate change or the collapse in biodiversity.

Taken all together, the enumeration of such ills makes for a depressing reality. I understand that at one level most of this certainly cannot be blamed on God. People are responsible. On another level, however, Scripture asserts that God loves the world, and wants to save it, and was willing to lose his son to do so. So why the wait? Wasn't the resurrection enough to tip the scales already? If Jesus died as the compassionate God, the one who was willing to suffer in our place, why should so many people have to continue to suffer after his death?

Where I have often looked to God and wrung my hands in frustration at how slow he seems to respond to real need and suffering, other philosophers, who have less time for God, look at the long list of ills I've enumerated and blame modernity — the rational, progressive, literate civilization I described in the preceding chapter. These scholars are called postmodernists. Postmodernism is an intellectual critique of the modernist worldview that came out of the Enlightenment, which I described in chapter 1. Postmodernists often begin their critique by arguing that modernist elites have used science, rationality, and texts such as the Bible and advertising to maintain their positions of privilege, often at great cost to most other people and to the planet itself. Postmodernists look at the pollution that results from industrialization, the disregard for environment in the name of ideologies such as capitalism and communism, the mechanization of war that one sees as armies graduate from Gatling guns to gas attacks to guided missiles and worse — they look at such things and blame modernity.

I have a lot of sympathy for postmodern criticism. Hiroshima and Iraq and Chernobyl don't inspire confidence in the old regimes or their presuppositions. And they don't inspire confidence in the God of the old regime either, the God of whom Christians sing, "He's got the whole world in his hands." So what is postmodernity? What follows is a brief primer as a partial counterpoint to some of the key trends we have seen in modernity.

First, rather than place their faith in reason, postmoderns are suspicious of the way reason and her stepchildren, science and technology, have been used to oppress, to trick, and to rationalize on behalf of the powerful. From Agent Orange to atomic bombs — both of which have been used in combat only by the United States — from tailpipe pollution to oil-sands emissions, from dwindling jungles to growing aquatic dead zones, postmodernists see a pattern of moral failure, death, and destruction. While they acknowledge that here, in the First World, life can be very good, or at least very easy and full of entertaining diversions, our economic progress has meant marginalization, suffering, and death for many others in the world.

Second, rather than touting a faith in human progress, postmoderns mourn human loss, suffering, and inequity. "The Enlightenment faith in moral advancement through science, reason and rationality should have ended with the First World War."[4] They don't celebrate increased

---

4. Chris Hedges, *When Atheism Becomes Religion: America's New Fundamentalists* (New York: Free Press, 2008), pp. 113-14.

wealth, health, and leisure in the West so much as they are horrified by Treblinka and its many reiterations over the past fifty years, aghast at the collapse of fish stocks, and sad about poverty and disease that could be addressed except for a lack of will on the part of those who could afford it. They are concerned for the weak, the minorities, the hurting. They groan with all creation over what scientific progress has meant for the rest of the world, for qualities like love and understanding, and for the environment. It is not that postmoderns deny reason's power to discover new cures, or, for that matter, develop new weapons. It is just that postmoderns suspect that when science and reason are in play, they benefit the rich, powerful, and corporate to the detriment of the weak and marginalized.

Third, rather than submit to the powers, to the rational bureaucracies, to parties or corporations or denominations, all rationally and scientifically conceived to keep people in line while perpetuating their own existence, postmoderns tend to be very suspicious of human institutions and the power they wield. They think of the Vietnam War and fundamentalist Islam and the Catholic abuse scandal and Wall Street financial overreaching as instances of institutional violence.

This suspicion of institutions is rooted in experience and memory. Bob Sweetman argues that, after about 1850, Europe organized itself into many ideological communities: for example, secular communities from Marxist to monarchial, religious communities from Catholic to Reformed. Each of these communities was organized as a stand-alone "pillar" within which people could live their whole lives. The pillars proselytized to the extreme, because they saw themselves in a life-and-death struggle with other isolated pillars, always trying to win converts to their cause, whether religious or secular. The Dutch Calvinist pillar included churches, of course, where people could socialize and worship; but it also included Amsterdam's Free University, Reformed trade unions, the Anti-revolutionary Party on the political stage, several newspapers, radio stations, Christian day schools, and farmers' federations. The National Socialist pillar in Germany even had an army, the Brown-Shirts. At the national level, the people who were in power in those pillars cooperated, or didn't, to govern the nation as a whole and maintain the peace. While this pillarization found its most intense expression in the Netherlands, all European countries had similar social structures. But, Sweetman argues,

> throughout the second half of the nineteenth century, conflicts between competing ideological communities and their incompatible visions became ever more intense. Indeed, one could even say, albeit too simply, that their competition twice bubbled over into disastrous "world wars."

So, for example, National Socialism, Marxism, and Kuyperian Calvinism all proselytized with the view of convincing all of Europe, indeed all of the world at the time, that their vision of human flourishing was the right one. And, as we know, such proselytizing ended up, more than once, in armed conflict.

Sweetman argues that the race to American — and Canadian — frontiers made such pillarization a harder sell in North America; but capitalism, mixed with notions of manifest destiny, served as a similar organizing principle, except now for almost all segments in society. After World War II and the widespread and understandable European disillusionment with the ideologies of the various pillars, the conflict between the West's capitalism and the East's communism masked this disillusionment, until the fall of the Berlin Wall. Ultimately, however,

> [t]he cumulative effect of this ideologically induced violence led people of all ideological persuasions to slowly lose faith in the total visions that had played such an important role in the World War catastrophes.[5]

The resulting suspicion of institutions extends to traditional "religion" and churches. "Religion tends to authoritarianism as capitalism tends to monopoly," says Julian Barnes.[6] From the postmodern per-

---

5. Bob Sweetman, "Another Brick in the Wall: Why We Don't Join Institutions Anymore," lecture delivered at the Institute for Christian Studies Worldview Conference, September 27, 2008.

6. Julian Barnes, *Nothing to Be Frightened Of* (Toronto: Random House Canada, 2008), p. 82.

spective, the church is, like many institutions, just one more ideological franchise trying to increase market share and in that way increase its profit and power, often at the expense of its members as well as outsiders. The great scandals that saw churches condone, then cover up, and finally confess to the abuse of Native Canadians in residential schools doesn't surprise postmoderns. Neither does the parallel cover-up by archbishops and cardinals of their priests' abuse of young parishioners in the American Catholic Church. Nor does the Pew Forum on Religion and Public Life finding that "more than half of people who attend services at least once a week — 54 percent — said the use of torture against suspected terrorists is 'often' or 'sometimes' justified." This compares to only four of ten persons unaffiliated with any church.[7]

So when postmoderns criticize Christian faith, it isn't just systematic (read "pseudoscientific") theology or powerful male hierarchies that bother them. Christianity's commitment to its whole worldview and ideology is off-putting to them, including its know-it-all attitude and its insistence on one way to the exclusion of all others. I used to have in my home a missionary organ that had gone to Africa at the turn of the twentieth century. It could be packed into an 18-inch by 18-inch by 3-foot carrying case. The purpose of such a contraption, of course, was to teach Africans "real" Christian music. This sort of hubris is a microcosm of what postmoderns see writ large over all Christian enterprises and programs.

In Europe people simply left the church. Ironically, in North America, where the experience of pillarization wasn't so intense, conservative Christians since the time of Nixon and then Reagan have been trying to build on capitalism's success by making their family values and Christian conservatism the moral basis for a new round of pillarization. Many others, perhaps more cognizant of the ways in which the church has been used by ideology in recent history, are repelled by such efforts.

7. CNN, "Survey: Support for terror suspect torture differs among the faithful," April 20, 2009: http://www.cnn.com/2009/US/04/30/religion.torture/index.html (accessed May 1, 2009).

Fourth — and very importantly for someone like me, who is rooted in ancient texts and modern theologies — postmoderns do not believe in "methodologically secured objectivity." That is, postmoderns believe that our hopes, dreams, and prejudices have a profound influence on what we see when we look through a microscope or into a biblical text. There is no combination of following strict exegetical rules for grammatical and historical analysis that can give us back the exact original meaning of biblical texts or help us recover the original author's intent. Postmoderns argue that we usually see what we want to see, what our prejudices have taught us to notice, what our pocketbooks think will be profitable; we see whatever will keep the status quo on our side of the table.

Of course, these critics are not surprised when similarly conservative Christian exegetes use their historical/biblical/critical apparatus to arrive at very different conclusions about baptism, the nature and extent of God's love, or the relative importance of charismatic gifts. They point out that the conservative Baptists will use this "rational" apparatus to support the Baptist viewpoints they grew up with, while Reformed and Catholic scholars will do the same. So postmodern Christians want a new hermeneutic, one that focuses less on arguing these old, disputable matters and one that focuses instead on the margins, on the poor, the widow and the "least of these"; one that challenges the status quo, the rich, and the powerful, which the old hermeneutic usually figured out how to excuse; one that focuses on *caritas* instead of talk about love.

Fifth, postmodernism has a conflicted relationship with values. On the one hand, it has always taken the side of the marginalized, the poor, and the victim. This perspective is almost reflexive and suggests a very strong commitment to a certain set of values. On the other hand, in its often impolitic criticism of the status quo, of rules that limit human freedom, postmodernism seems very relativistic. This is especially true for people — like many Christians — who live according to that line in the sand.

Sixth, postmodernity, in rejecting science or rationality as the bedrock source of ultimate answers, and in being suspicious of institutional churches, is nevertheless very open to the contribution that *spirituality* can make to the quest for finding meaning and purpose. For example, postmodernist Stanley Fish, writing in *The New York Times,* quotes Terry Eagleton:

> "Why are the most unlikely people, including myself, suddenly talking about God?" His answer, elaborated in prose that is alternately witty, scabrous and angry, is that the other candidates for guidance — science, reason, liberalism, capitalism — just don't deliver what is ultimately needed. "What other symbolic form," he queries, "has managed to forge such direct links between the most universal and absolute of truths and the everyday practices of countless millions of men and women?"[8]

Graduate School

When I was in my first and second congregations, I was vaguely aware of the postmodernist critique. But it was my return to graduate school at Wayne State University in Detroit that really introduced me to postmodernism. This happened in two ways. It was first through texts and classes: I read Roland Barthes and Pierre Bourdieu with care, and I read other postmodern scholars more superficially. But I also became aware of postmodernism as a kind of academic spirit, and never more directly than when I took a course entitled "The Rhetoric of Oppression."

The professor began the course by inviting students to say something about where they were coming from and to explain why they were taking the class. The first student said that he was gay and thus interested in every aspect of homosexuality as a current cultural issue. He spoke briefly of the violence and discrimination against gays that he had experienced. He finished by saying that he hoped this class would help him understand how words were used to oppress gays.

---

8. Stanley Fish, "God Talk," *The New York Times,* May 3, 2009, "Think Again" column, a review of Terry Eagleton's *Reason, Faith and Revolution:* http://fish.blogs.nytimes.com/2009/05/03/god-talk/.

The next student said that she was a radical feminist and believed that women in our society were uniformly oppressed. She railed against the male bias in literature and institutions. She said that the differences between women and men were more important than the similarities, and that because of those differences only women would be able to give the world peace instead of violence, joyful consensus instead of cold rationality. She even professed faith in a pagan goddess. And she said she needed to understand how words could help. The professor nodded and smiled.

The next student was an African-American woman. She said that the only perspective that made any sense for her was Afrocentrism. She lamented how generations of prejudice, violence, and economic racism had ravaged her community. She said that if her community wanted to recover, it would need to turn inward to rediscover its roots and strengths. Only knowledge that affirmed her ethnicity could be of any value to her. The professor nodded and smiled — and so it went. Besides these classmates, the others included labor organizers, secular Jews, and a Marxist. And after each gave a short speech explaining why she or he needed to understand the "rhetoric of oppression," the professor nodded and smiled.

Finally it was my turn. I said I was happy that scholars could finally own up to their values and biases. Somewhat smugly, I told the class that a scholar I admired, Abraham Kuyper, had argued the need to do so a hundred years ago in his Stone Lectures at Princeton University. Kuyper argued, for example, that Christian scholarship would be different in some respects from secular scholarship. I said that I was an evangelical pastor who would try to do academic work from that perspective.

At that point the professor jumped up from his seat and insisted that working from a Christian perspective in his class would be absolutely inappropriate. "All through the millennia, Christians have been the oppressors," the professor said. "In the name of their God they've justified slavery and beating up gays and have kept women barefoot and pregnant. Well, that's over now. Christians have forfeited their right to speak. This is a class for and about the oppressed."

Now, I suppose there are many ways one could react to such a rejoinder: I could have stomped out of the class; I could have complained to the administration afterwards; I could have just kept going and kept my opinions to myself. In fact, what I did was sit down, totally deflated. I kept my mouth shut for the rest of the class. Fortunately, when my advisor heard my story, he took me to see the professor who had so effectively shut me down so that we could have a heart-to-heart talk. With the help of my advisor, we reached an accommodation. Over the years we even learned to appreciate each other's perspective.

But something else happened. When I heard this professor's story about how his relatives had survived Nazi death camps, and when I listened to his perspective on Jewish history and white racism, and Richard Butler's biblically inspired Aryan supremacism, it was difficult not to empathize with him and his people, who were finally — yet with some fear left over — peeking out from behind whatever shelter they could in the hope that the persecution that had lasted hundreds of years was perhaps, at long last, over. And I could not help but feel horror and shame that Christians at all levels of society had continually sponsored, sanctioned, and carried out that persecution. What was it, I wondered, about my faith that made things turn out so bad . . . so often?

But what I ran into, there in that class, was more than just one man's personal dislike for Christianity as a system. I ran into a newly emboldened, courageous, and subtle criticism of Christianity as a coconspirator in much of the world's problems. My professor had found in postmodernism a way to voice what he knew in his bones. Just because Christians espoused an enlightened, systematic, and rational faith, it did not mean that a deep and black magic in their collective soul was not really in charge. Postmoderns want to get at that black magic and its rationalist dress.

Postmodernism gave me the cover to look at my tradition much more critically than I had ever been used to. It suggested that perhaps I needed to think about trying to separate the essence of Christianity from what it had become over the past few hundred years as it became systemically complicit in so much of modern society's failures. And it undermined my belief in a single correct interpretation for any passage of Scripture.

Actually, a long time ago, before modernism, Augustine had already pointed out that any interpretation of Scripture that accords with Scripture's central message is appropriate: "Whoever finds a lesson [in Scripture] useful to the building of charity, even though he has not said what the author may be shown to have intended in that place, has not been deceived, nor is he lying in any way."[9] Modernity insists on restricting interpreters to a single, literal interpretation based on what the author meant, which limits our understanding of the endless depth of Scripture. Of such literalism Saint Augustine says: "There is a miserable servitude of the spirit in [the] habit of taking signs for things, so that one is not able to raise the eye of the mind above things that are corporal and created to drink in eternal light."[10] Postmodernism has given me license to agree with Augustine in this. I am not hung up on finding the one true interpretation of any one text; I decided to try on the multiplicity of meanings in Scripture that seemed consistent with the heart of Scripture. I guess you could say that I've learned from the premodern saints in our tradition to use some postmodern interpretive techniques like intertextuality and strong readings as heuristic means for multiplying the interpretations of Scripture — thus also increasing our depth of understanding of Scripture. In a similar way, the refusal to take "signs for things" allows me to focus on how the confessions underscore the love of God and neighbor rather than the multitude of doctrines the writers thought they understood best for all time.

At the same time, my new appreciation for the heart of Scripture and its multiple meanings has freed me from finding myself subservient to all those passages that don't easily fit into the larger picture of God's grace that is at the heart of Scripture. I don't worry about such passages very much. I don't strive to create false consistency that isn't really there, a consistency that only the modernist spirit insists must be there. I just trust that my inevitable interpretive mistakes made in love and hope are covered by God's love.

9. Augustine, *On Christian Doctrine*, 1:36, trans. D. W. Roberts, Jr., Macmillan Library of Liberal Arts (New York: Macmillan, 1958).
10. Augustine, *On Christian Doctrine*, III:9.

I was taking these graduate courses at about the same time that I was touring Japan and Africa and Haiti. The very experiential doubts I felt as an observer of some of the worst that humans can do to humans was, essentially, reinforced by what I was learning in graduate school about the history of interpretation and the nature of rationality. It is perhaps odd that, as a Calvinist, who should have had a good grip on human depravity, I had to really learn it by seeing it. And it is odd that, as a Calvinist, and thus one who believes in human depravity, I should be surprised that our tradition had not been able to objectively interpret Scripture or live out its fullest meaning in society's structures. In any case, the stage was being set for my year of crisis traveling across North America in an RV.

chapter 4

Oral Again: Digital Faith

⌒*ᴂ*⌒

Introduction

In his lively book *The Heart of Christianity,* Marcus Borg describes an encounter he had with a woman he met on a trip. She tells him, "I'm much more interested in Buddhism and Sufism than I am in Christianity." She makes this announcement "because they're about a way of life, and Christianity is all about believing. I don't think beliefs matter nearly as much as having a spiritual path and following a way."

Borg reflects on this woman's comments by noting the irony of it: Christianity, after all, was once known as "the Way." And he suggests that she is reacting against the "modern Western" notion (the Enlightenment notion I have described in chapter 2) that "faith means holding a certain set of 'beliefs,' 'believing' a set of statements to be true, whether cast as biblical teachings or doctrines, or dogma." Borg goes on to say that this perception of Christianity as "head knowledge" is widespread. He uses this observation as a springboard to describe his alternative paradigm for faith.[1]

Interestingly enough, however, I doubt that the woman would have been very sympathetic. Her objections to traditional Christianity notwithstanding, her description of following Sufism and Buddhism have

---

1. Marcus Borg, *The Heart of Christianity* (New York: HarperSanFrancisco, 2003), p. 25.

little in common with Borg's nuanced description of Christianity as "the Way" in his emergent paradigm for a postmodernist kind of faith. For example, this woman apparently did not understand — or wasn't troubled by the fact — that Sufism (actually a form of Islam) and Buddhism are religions full of mutually exclusive truth claims and divergent religious practices. Only someone who understands little about these religions, or one who isn't troubled by contradictions, would think otherwise. And while I can't draw too much by way of conclusion from this brief story, it seems likely that this woman has more in common with a fourth faith development than with postmodernism. That fourth trend is *secondary orality*.

"Secondary orality," or the second coming of the oral tradition, is rooted not in reflection or in a reaction to the intellectual heft of modernity, or in a reaction to modernity itself, but in important technological developments that, like the invention of the printing press hundreds of years ago, are having a profound impact on how and what people think. The technological developments at the center of this secondary phase of the oral tradition are all the electronic means of communication that have been developed in the last hundred years, but especially since television became widespread. Besides television, though, those electronic means have included the stereo and the computer, *Entertainment Today*, and Massively Multiplayer Online Role-playing Games (MMORPGs), cell-phone Tweeters, and Facebook fan clubs. Taken all together, I think of these developments as *secondary orality*, a phrase (invented by Walter Ong) that describes one of this trend's most striking features. These days many people choose not to read much. And if the oral tradition had a lot to do with enchantment, and literacy had a lot to do with modernist faith, then choosing not to read but to interact with others and the world primarily through electronic means is also going to have a major impact on the kinds of faith people hold to and experience. This chapter will discuss how the secondary oral tradition has impacted faith — including mine.

The Habits of Literacy

My wife and I have rarely, and then only briefly, owned a television. Our first used black-and-white set had a coat hanger antenna that drew in one channel — fairly poorly — from Rochester, New York, about twenty-five miles across Lake Ontario from where we lived, in Bowmanville, Ontario. We hid it in a closet because it was so ugly. A year and a half after we were married, we moved to Grand Rapids, Michigan, so that I could go to seminary, and we left the old TV behind.

After that, not owning a television was mostly accidental. We didn't have money to buy one; also, Irene and I were studying, so we didn't have time for TV either. It wasn't until we spent a summer in Barrie, Ontario, where I was a parish intern, that we realized that not owning a TV might be a good choice.

Irene and I were given the use of a furnished apartment, which included a television. I soon fell into the habit of watching it every night. The national news came on at 10 p.m. The sports, including the Blue Jays update, didn't come on till after the local news, at 11:30. So I started watching TV from 10:00 to 11:45 p.m. Except that, just to make sure I didn't miss the lead news story, I often quit reading whatever I had in front of me a bit earlier than 10 p.m., when I came to a chapter or section break. But then I decided I might as well watch all of *Cheers*, not just its last ten minutes, before the news. Within a few weeks, Irene pointed out to me, I was spending hours every night watching television. And I was spending it with my mouth hanging open, so focused that I was totally unavailable for conversation. I hardly touched the books I planned to read through that summer. I was fast becoming a television zombie.

Back in Grand Rapids, reflecting on our experience, we decided not to buy a television until our kids — we had one then — were old enough to both read on their own and enjoy it. We also decided that, instead of watching TV, we would take turns reading to our children at least an hour each evening. And so we did, until twelve or fourteen years later, by which time our youngest son, David, was reading independently. In the meantime, Irene and I had become a bit evangelical about not owning a TV, so we made the kids an offer in the hope we could keep television out of our house. What would they prefer? A new TV or a trip to Disneyland when the next space shuttle was supposed to blast off? They took the trip, saw the shuttle launch, and life went on without a TV. By now I was also in graduate school studying communication theory, reading Walter Ong and Marshall McLuhan and some early research on the effects of TV on reading, violence, and attention deficit disorder, all of which made it possible for Irene and me to add intellectual justifications to our no-television habit.

A few years later, when our youngest son flew off to the Czech Republic for his final year of high school, we became empty nesters. We bought the recreational vehicle that we dubbed the Bananer, and it came with a television as standard equipment. The TV hung out over the cab. We mostly watched movies and the news at ten o'clock. By the time we had driven from Grand Rapids to Charlottetown, Prince Edward Island, however, we began to feel bad that we had to stay up to watch the news, because we couldn't see the TV we had from our bedroom. So we went out and bought a TV for our bedroom. After nearly twenty-five years of marriage without TV, we now had two in our 240-square-foot mobile home.

During the ten years that I was editor of *The Banner*, I wrote only two editorials — of a total of more than 300 — about the benefits of not owning a television. On several occasions, however, people have characterized my time as editor by describing me as the guy who was against TV. I have also given a few public lectures about TV and how it shapes the expectations and skills of the audiences that come to worship and listen to sermons. Each time I spoke, audience members took sharp issue with my concerns about attention spans or the ways television actually rewires the human brain. These people would invariably point out that they had a TV — or better yet, several — watched a lot of it, and yet their kids were really smart. Others would compliment me for the talk and then rationalize their own television ownership by pointing out that they only rarely watched it — just their favorite shows, and news, and sports, and movies. I have rarely run into people willing to admit to watching TV for even a fraction of the average five to six hours a day that most North Americans watch it. People are very defensive about their television habits, rationalizing their consumption much like smokers do their cigarettes (or, in my case, cigars).

If truth be told, I guess not having a television (at least since we sold our RV) does even now give me a slight sense of moral superiority. On the other hand, I do own a computer. Last night, when I finished working on an earlier section of this chapter, at about 9:00 p.m., I thought I might pack it in and read a book for the rest of the night. But first, I thought, I should quickly check out how the Blue Jays were doing in spring training (on the Web), and what the fallout was for the Republican Party after Sarah Palin admitted to using the Canadian health-care system. By the time I had done so, and then followed a few related links, and then answered my email, including a peek at my Facebook page, and had my glass of wine — it was nearly eleven o'clock and time for bed. I did not touch my book. So now my wife and kids tease me by saying I'm addicted, not to television, but to the Web (or sometimes to Solitaire). I get very defensive when they say so, and I rationalize my Web surfing. But they are mostly right. I read less than I used to, and it now takes energy and focus to read. I'm more easily distracted than I used to be, and I dislike this in myself. I struggle against it. I do think I manage to keep my computer usage to reasonable limits. But the truth is, computer time cuts into my writing and reading time nearly every day. And I have to fight its allure. Like a cat in my lap, the computer is always on my desk, wanting to be stroked.

What I struggle with in my own life, society has, by and large, refused to struggle with at all. Somewhere between the premiere of *I Love Lucy* on CBS in 1951 and that of the vampire-themed *TrueBlood* on HBO last year, most North Americans put down their books, returning to them only as much as duty necessitated. We don't read much anymore. A recent study shows that, "[s]ince 1982, literary reading has declined by 28 percent in eighteen- to thirty-four-year-olds."[2] In

2. Gary Small and Gigi Voran, *iBrain: Surviving the Technological Alteration of the Modern Mind* (New York: HarperCollins, 2008), pp. 3, 4. Based on National Endowment for the Arts, *Reading at Risk: A Survey of Literary Reading in America*, June 2004, p. 6: http://www.nea.gov/pub/ReadingAtRisk.pdf.

that same age group, fewer than half read newspapers compared to older adults. Of course, by 1982, North Americans were already reading far less than their parents did in the 1950s.

Reading less, or not at all, has had a profound effect, not only on our society in general, but also on religion and spirituality. As a Christian agnostic, I've always been extremely curious to learn more, to find answers, and perhaps even to open the door to a level of certainty that would put my soul to rest. However, society is in the process of voluntarily giving up the means to nurture and answer such questions with the depth that modernity did. This chapter will examine why this is so. Along the way we'll discover that there are interesting parallels to be drawn between the oral, porous, enchanted era of human history and our present postliterate era. But there are differences, too.

Abandoning Literacy: Secondary Orality

What has happened over the past one hundred years or so is something like this. At first slowly, with the advent of electric communication such as the telegraph and telephone, then more quickly, with broadcast media such as radio and television and, more recently, the Internet, our ways of using literacy have changed dramatically. People today can still read, of course; but these days most people spend less time reading, and so they have much less practice reading with comprehension, or reading deeply. This is partly true because we tend to devote so much more time to nonreading activities, and especially to television and the Internet, than people used to. This is known as displacement. But not only do people spend less time with books now than they used to; evidence also suggests that watching even a small amount of television or other electronic media results in a lessened appetite for reading and less ability to make sense of the printed pages' potential for multiple levels of meaning, allusion, and complex rational linearity. Much of the research on brain plasticity, in particular, makes just this point. So, for example, summarizing several university studies, including brain scans of traditional readers compared to "digital natives," Gary Small writes: "While the brains of today's digital natives are wiring up for rapid-fire cyber searches, the neural circuits that control the more traditional learning methods are neglected and gradually diminish. The pathways for human interaction and communication weaken as customary one-on-one people skills atrophy."[3]

Similarly, after statistically cataloging how much less people today read than they used to, and how the younger you are the more jarring the difference is, Mark Bauerlein comments that "screen intelligence doesn't transfer well to non-screen experiences, especially the kinds that build knowledge and verbal skills." He goes on to note:

This explains why teenagers and 20-year-olds appear at the same time so mentally agile and culturally ignorant. Visual culture improves abstract spatialization and problem solving, but it doesn't complement other intelligence-building activities. Smartness there parallels dumbness elsewhere. The relationship between screens and books isn't benign. . . .

As "digital natives" dive daily into three visual media and two sound sources as a matter of disposition, of deep mental compatibility, not just taste, ordinary reading, slow and uniform, strikes them as incompatible, alien. It isn't just boring and obsolete. It's irritating.[4]

No wonder. According to research cited by Norman Doidge, brain scans show that different brain areas are involved in hearing speech and reading, which means that different kinds of comprehension are necessary when words come via TV or a book. Watching television — including computer screens filled with words — wires a brain differently than reading a book. Doidge goes on to observe:

3. Small and Voran, *iBrain*, p. 21. Stanislas Dehaene's *Reading in the Brain: The Science and Evolution of a Human Invention* (New York: Viking, 2009) is an extended treatment of how the brain circuitry probably originally dedicated to tracking animals and trails, inherited through evolutionary processes, has been co-opted by the brain for recognizing printed words. This book is especially helpful for understanding how extraordinary the ability to read is, and in a way, how easy it is for that ability to erode.

4. Mark Bauerlein, *The Dumbest Generation: How the Digital Age Stupefies Young Americans and Jeopardizes Our Future* (New York: Jeremy P. Tarcher/Penguin, 2008), p. 95.

Television watching . . . correlates with brain problems. A recent study of more than twenty-six hundred toddlers shows that early exposure to television between the ages of one and three correlates with problems paying attention and controlling impulses later in childhood. For every hour of TV toddlers watched each day, their chances of developing serious attentional difficulties at age seven increased by 10 percent.[5]

While the size and visibility of big-box bookstores and Amazon.com suggest otherwise, people now buy fewer books and finish reading fewer of the books they buy. While fads may steer kids — or at least a subset of them — to Harry Potter, the fad doesn't extend very far to other books. These days, in the United States, the average college graduate reads only two new books a year. As a society, we have traded in dime-store novels for TV serials and Scrabble for *World of Warcraft* — and Solitaire. At the same time, Christians have traded in catechism commentaries for short inspirational books full of bulleted lists and summary sidebars, both of which ease the reading and thinking load for the reader and relieve the author of having to construct a cohesive unifying narrative. Or, more probably, they read nothing at all. Instead of going to men and women's societies to read and learn and debate, we watch videos like *The Jesus Film* or *The Last Temptation*.

In a space of time even briefer than the two or three generations it took for northern Europe to trade the oral tradition for literacy, our society has abandoned high literacy for a cyber-culture alternative that is much less literate. In a few hundred years, some future historian may say of us, not that "to be schooled was to be holy," but that "to be plugged in was holy."

An interesting examination of the "less reading is better" phenomenon that characterizes contemporary society is found in Susan Jacoby's *The Age of American Unreason*. In a chapter entitled "Middlebrow Culture from Noon to Twilight," Jacoby describes how middleclass America in the mid-twentieth century presumed that reading

---

5. Norman Doidge, *The Brain that Changes Itself: Stories of Personal Triumph from the Frontiers of Brain Science* (New York: Penguin Books, 2007), p. 307.

was the path to success and happiness. Book-of-the-Month Club and encyclopedia sets sold by door-to-door salesmen are the enduring symbols of this era. The salient features of middlebrow America were: "an affinity for books; the desire to understand science; a strong dose of rationalism; above all, a regard for facts — [which] had been taken for granted by large numbers of Americans who wanted a better life for themselves and their children." In the end, however, the values of middlebrow culture died a slow death due to, among other things, the corrosive influence of television.[6]

These days most Canadians and Americans are poor readers. My current struggle to stay focused on books, something you could not have torn me away from when I was younger, is not unique. Even those who continue to read, read less and with less comprehension. Our culture has traded books for webpage views, words for icons, and study for entertainment. We have, in fact, become a society full of people who are merely functionally literate rather than deeply literate. We can read well enough to manage employee manuals, newspapers written for a sixth-grade reading level, spy novels written for an eighth-grade level, and so on. We can get by as readers, but the vast majority of us don't read with deep mastery. We read like little kids ride tricycles: for fun but not very well or for very far.

A host of scholars agree.[7] I will restrict myself, at this point, to noting just one more, an early critic of the new media, Sven Birkerts. A professor at the University of Michigan, Birkerts assigned his freshmen students to read a short story by the turn-of-the-century American writer Henry James. The students hated it. They couldn't get into it. They could make out the words, individually, but the syntax was odd. With effort, they could get through it; but altogether, they didn't get it. Birkerts writes that what emerged was

6. Susan Jacoby, *The Age of American Unreason* (New York: Random House, 2008), pp. 130, 126-27.

7. One evangelical scholar who has spoken out cogently about the new media and their potential effect on reading, faith, and church life is David Wells, *No Place for Truth; or, Whatever Happened to Evangelical Theology?* (Grand Rapids: Eerdmans, 1993). A good summary of his views, informed by Ong and McLuhan before brain plasticity was understood, can be found on pp. 198-203.

that they were not, with a few exceptions, readers — never had been; that they had always occupied themselves with music, TV, and videos; that they had difficulty slowing down enough to concentrate on prose of any density; that they had problems with what they thought of as archaic diction, with allusions, with vocabulary that seemed "pretentious"; that they were especially uncomfortable with indirect or interior passages, indeed with any deviations from straight plot; and that they were put off by ironic tone because it flaunted superiority and made them feel that they were missing something.[8]

Meanwhile, Back at Church

Christians and church leaders have been aware, at least vaguely, of these changes taking place around them for a long time.[9] They have tried to accommodate themselves and the church, but their success has been mixed. The basic issue is this: today's church and its members are left with the forms of literacy that were created for faith after the invention of the printing press, that is, systematic theologies, confessional statements, catechism training, sermons full of multiple truths, and important truth claims to ponder. Denominations are committed to very narrow confessional claims, but not many people in the pew are able to relate to those forms with much interest or understanding. You can't get people to meditate on the Belgic Confession anymore, to read John Calvin for pleasure, or to pick up books, such as Mark Bauerlein's, which might explain why this is so. As a result, the confessional, ideologically focused middlebrow church culture of thirty years ago just doesn't exist anymore, except among the church's oldest members and among that minority of highly literate and educated folks who often run the churches and seminaries. The doctrines that one presumably needs to believe to be Reformed rather

8. Sven Birkerts, *The Gutenberg Elegies: The Fate of Reading in an Electronic Age* (Boston: Faber and Faber, 1994), p. 18.

9. See, e.g., Pierre Babin, *The New Era in Religious Communication* (Minneapolis: Fortress, 1991).

than Methodist, or Catholic rather than Christian Scientist, are simply not understood by most churchgoers. Denominational elites in seminaries, church-affiliated colleges, and at denominational headquarters wring their hands because of the spreading ignorance; and they make heroic attempts to popularize denominational distinctives, not to mention just plain basic biblical and theological knowledge.

But they are failing — and failing spectacularly. People don't know what their church stands for compared to other churches, and they can't be bothered to read long enough to figure it out. As a result, the measure by which they judge churches isn't truth or tradition or perspective. Instead, more and more people hop from church to church looking for a great experience, for entertaining and engaging services, for connections with people and human services. It is no wonder that 41 percent of North Americans have switched churches at least once in their lives. The truth claims or distinctives of individual denominations just don't matter to — and don't even register with — most people.

One way that scholars have begun to think through the consequences of the changes I've been discussing here is to think of them as a return to something like the oral cultural context. Walter Ong, writing when the effects of the new media were just beginning to be felt, said "secondary orality" is that "in which a new orality is sustained by telephone, radio, television, and other electronic devices."[10] Ong was tentative about how secondary orality is similar to and dissimilar from the original oral tradition. He was writing about media before the widespread adoption of computers or the invention of the Internet. But what he says is highly suggestive. What follows are several characteristics of secondary oral faith and church life that, in part at least, mirror the characteristics of oral faith as I see it.

10. Walter Ong, *Orality and Literacy: The Technologizing of the Word* (London: Routledge, 1988), p. 10.

The Secondary Oral Tradition in Practice

1. Simplicity — or Ignorance?

In orality, simplicity in doctrine was a function of the limited resources people had with which to learn the complexities of the theology or philosophy of the churchmen. The gospel that lived for them, because they were unable to read or write, was the story itself rather than a framework of truths based on the story. Beyond the story, we saw that people might know the Apostles' Creed, the Ten Commandments, and some prayers. The church, at its best, encouraged its membership — practically everyone — to be obedient to their betters in both the secular and divine realms, to avail themselves of the sacraments and other observances, and to practice *caritas*.

This does not mean, of course, that academics in the oral era did not continue to develop theology in all of its myriad branches, or engage in sharp debate. But this happened apart from the daily life and church participation of most Christians. There were only a handful of universities and other centers for higher learning in Europe, and thus just a small group of elite scholars who understood the official dogma of the church. All this began to change as Europe became more and more literate. But the bottom line was that eventually a critical mass of Europeans made knowing as much as possible about their convictions an important life goal. As I have suggested above, to be schooled was to be holy.

However, these days, even though many people in the West possess expert knowledge in some field of human endeavor related to their work, they usually know little about the faith traditions that helped shape Western society. Literacy is often useful for getting by at work, but it has become optional in almost every other area of life. Few commentators have summed up the current status quo as colorfully as Bill McKibben, writing the following in *Harper's* magazine:

> Only 40 percent of Americans can name more than four of the Ten Commandments, and a scant half can cite any of the four authors of the Gospels. Twelve percent believe Joan of Arc was Noah's

wife. This failure to recall the specifics of our Christian heritage may be further evidence of our nation's educational decline, but it probably doesn't matter all that much in spiritual or political terms. Here is a statistic that does matter: Three quarters of Americans believe the Bible teaches that, "God helps those who help themselves." That is, three out of four Americans believe that this über-American idea, a notion at the core of our current individualist politics and culture, which was in fact uttered by Ben Franklin, actually appears in Holy Scripture. The thing is, not only is Franklin's wisdom not biblical; it's counterbiblical. Few ideas could be further from the gospel message, with its radical summons to love of neighbor. On this essential matter, most Americans — most American Christians — are simply wrong, as if 75 percent of American scientists believed that Newton proved gravity causes apples to fly up.[11]

In one of his famous "man on the street" interviews, Jay Leno asks a college student, "What is one of the Ten Commandments?"

"Freedom of speech," replies the college student. Leno asks a girl walking by, who identifies herself as an art history student, when Jesus lived. She thinks maybe about 30,000 years ago. Not a promising picture of her historical knowledge or her knowledge of one of the most important sources for Western artistic symbolism. Many more gaffes follow. And, in case some people think the Bible is the only thing Americans are ignorant about, Leno asks a man, "Who said 'Fourscore and seven years ago'?"

"George Washington."

Of course, making fun of the latest generation's ignorance has been the intellectual elite's favorite putdown for thousands of years. At the same time, one can't help but believe that there is something to the screeds written by people like Susan Jacoby, Thomas Friedman,[12] and

11. Bill McKibben, "The Christian Paradox: How a Faithful Nation Gets Jesus Wrong," *Harper's*, August 2005: http://www.harpers.org/archive/2005/08/0080695.

12. Thomas Friedman, *The World Is Flat: A Brief History of the Twenty-first Century* (New York: Farrar, Straus and Giroux, 2005). Friedman followed up his concerns about North American youths' sense of entitlement, compared to Indian and Chinese youths' sense

Max Bauerlein. Quite simply, when people no longer read much because they've taken up other activities, such as television or computer games; and if, when they do read, they often do so with less acuity and understanding than a generation earlier might have, because they have rewired their brain for other forms of sensory input — then discourse under the sacred tent and in the public square suffers. Like their ancestors in oral Europe, they know only what they can remember being told.

This puts both the church and other institutions under great stress. People no longer relate to the discourse that characterizes these institutions. And as the institutions struggle to deal with this new situation, the results are not always pretty. Perhaps this is most obvious in the political realm. While democratic discourse has always been rough and tumble, it has not always been vapid and idiotic. Scholars often point to the Lincoln-Douglas debates as an example of just how deep political discourse could be in another age. These days, however, after politicians publish the requisite biography or manifesto for their literate supporters, they resort to mass-media idiocy. From Joe the Plumber to Sarah Palin to Rush Limbaugh, political discourse (especially on the right) does not trade on depth of understanding. No matter how complex issues like global warming or nuclear proliferation or poverty are, people tend to focus on simplistic frames or personal attacks rather than understanding the issues in depth.

North American religion has always had a strong current of anti-intellectualism in it. Susan Jacoby notes that while an intellectual, freethinking type of faith developed in the United States after the Revolution, it was eventually overmatched by anti-intellectual fundamentalism. She thinks that it is "likely that poorly educated settlers on the frontier were drawn to religious creeds and preachers who provided emotional comfort without making the intellectual demands of older, more intellectually rigorous Protestant denominations — whether liberal Quakerism and Unitarianism or conservative Episcopalianism."[13]

---

that they must strive for an education, in *Hot, Flat and Crowded* (New York: Farrar, Straus and Giroux, 2008).

13. Jacoby, *Age of American Unreason*, p. 45.

Even evangelicals join in the dismissal of fundamentalism's intellectual aspirations. "Intellectual sterility" is one of its key features, says Mark Noll. "As a result of following a theology that did not provide Christian guidance for the wider intellectual life, there has been, properly speaking, no fundamentalist philosophy, no fundamentalist history of science, no fundamentalist aesthetics . . ." and so on.[14]

Fundamentalism, however, was slumbering in a quiet backwater of American culture until mass culture joined the fundamentalists in ignoring or dismissing large bodies of knowledge in the interest this time, not of frontier comfort, but of the warm glow of the television tube. As a result, Malcolm Muggeridge's oft-quoted observation seems right on the mark: "One of the peculiar sins of the twentieth century which we've developed to a very high level is the sin of credulity. It has been said that when human beings stop believing in God, they believe in nothing. The truth is much worse; they believe in anything."

2. Memorable — or Marketing?

At its best, the church coached oral Christians about the truths of the faith using a host of media and strategies that were all designed, in one way or another, to make the basic moral teachings, as well as the Christian narrative, memorable. The actual variety of methods used is stunning. Seven sacraments provided seven life opportunities to memorialize faithful living. Relics, icons, and symbols all provided opportunity to explain — and on occasion to excite — faith. Crusades and pilgrimages, in their own ways, channeled believers into high-commitment activities, or at least inspired believers to financially support them. And again, each was an opportunity, especially for preachers, to explain the faith. Simple, repetitive sermons that were, at their best, artfully designed with rhythm and imagery and commonplace stories made them memorable. Paintings, the stations of the cross (a

14. Mark A. Noll, *The Scandal of the Evangelical Mind* (Grand Rapids: Eerdmans, 1994), p. 137.

mini-pilgrimage, really, illustrating Jesus' march to death with each step along the way), feast days, morality and passion plays — these were all designed to help people learn and remember the basic content of the Christian faith.

In the highly literate era, some churches carried on with some of these practices, of course. In practice, the variety and intensity of many of these methods were toned down.[15] New practices that invited study and interiority — from catechism study to confession to responsive readings — often presumed a high level of literacy. In general, however, it can be said that Protestant worship was iconoclastic, word-centered, and much less concerned with being memorable outside of the spoken or printed word. Calvin did not so much as allow organ playing in Genevan churches, so plain was his approach to worship. The liturgy was simple: the singing was a cappella from the Psalms, and the sermon was long.

Today, unless pastors live in large urban areas where they don't need much market penetration to attract a demographically narrow crowd — readers, for example — the church and its preachers face an unenviable task. Their audiences are now made up of a mix of highly literate and secondary oral people. The skills that such people bring to worship, and the preaching moment, are very different. The readers are comfortable listening for extended periods of time, especially if the sermon is organized in a linear and rational manner, like a book. The readers are practiced at this discourse, and they appreciate depth and literary allusions. They know the larger narrative context of the biblical story, and they want to know how it is relevant to their contemporary hopes and dreams. We know less about secondary oral

15. Toned down, but not everywhere and all the time. In the West, Roman Catholics, in spite of Vatican II, are often still attached to muted versions of these rites. Travel to South America, or Africa, or the Philippines, however, and you are immediately struck by the fact that these kinds of rites still have a strong hold on the imagination of the faithful. When we lived in the Philippines, my wife and I were regularly awakened by religious parades, complete with icons and statues of the baby Jesus, outside our home. The ways in which societies that never went through the same kind of modernistic, highly literate phase of popular culture, but have adopted many of the forms of modern electronic media and have hung onto the rites of what we think of as another era, is an interesting study in itself.

worshipers, but we do know that they are impatient sitting through lectures. They have a highly developed eye for images, such as action and spectacle. They bring little knowledge of the story to worship, and little context. They might — or might not — be receptive to the kinds of memorable teaching methods the oral church used. Figuring it out is a trial-and-error process.

A few patterns for reaching secondary oral audiences are emerging. Liturgical traditions are refocusing on liturgy; and some rather spartan, nonliturgical traditions are rethinking their approach. So, for example, the United Church of Canada, after an abortive merger attempt with the Anglican Church of Canada, has nevertheless seen a very pronounced liturgical revival in the Anglican mold. Some evangelical churches have paid a great deal of attention to visual and dramatic ways of sharing the gospel. For example, I once attended a worship service in Ginghamsburg Methodist Church in Tipp City, Ohio, where the whole church was decorated like a racecar pit lane, with the pulpit area as a pit garage. The set included a real dirt-track racing car, tires, gas cans, and lots of trophies and racing paraphernalia. The music was by the Eagles and a few other secular groups, and for most of the service, scenes from *Days of Thunder,* the Tom Cruise and Nicole Kidman car-racing movie, played on a huge screen behind the stage. Not a second was wasted on silence for meditation or other purposes. The hour-long program was driven. The sermon — short, memorized, direct — walked the audience through the set while making the case that the church needed pit-stop-like teamwork if it was to achieve its mission. Little reference was made to scriptural narratives or doctrine, other than during a memorized Scripture recital. The music was so loud that I left with a headache. Books by the Ginghamsburg team call this "multi-sensory worship," and they come with CD-ROMs.[16]

The level of awareness that churches have of the underlying cultural dynamics that make the old-fashioned "sermon, prayer and a few hymns" style of worship less and less interesting to more and more

16. See, e.g., Michael Slaughter, *Out on the Edge: A Wake-up Call for Church Leaders on the Edge of the Media Reformation* (Nashville: Abingdon, 1998); see also Len Wilson, *The Wired Church: Making Media Ministry* (Nashville: Abingdon, 1999).

people varies a lot. Whether or not one enjoys church in the multi-media Ginghamsburg mode, it is clear from their books that they have given some serious thought to the effect of modern media on literacy and faith. Most famously, perhaps, in giving this serious thought is Leonard Sweet, with books such as *Postmodern Pilgrims: First Century Passion for the 21st Century World* (2000) and *SoulTsunami: Sink or Swim in the New Millennium Culture* (1999). In the latter book Sweet (and now others after him) insists that to be relevant — perhaps another word for memorable, at least in some contexts — modern worship must be "EPIC": experiential, participatory, image-driven, and connected.[17] Not much in such a description about faith, hope, or love.

In general, churches are using a mishmash of modern media methods to try and engage the audience. One such popular contemporary media method that I find particularly irritating is the "bulleted list sermon." Here the pastor picks a theme (say marriage or manliness) and says four or five or nine true things about this topic, each dutifully listed as a bullet point in a PowerPoint presentation. Each point is supported with a Scripture quotation to make it seem deeply grounded in Scripture, when in fact many of these biblical quotations are taken completely out of their narrative context. The whole process is extremely moralistic, and does nothing for helping the audience actually learn the biblical narrative as a whole. If the medium is the message, this medium shouts "pragmatism" rather than "discipleship," "success" rather than "service." Hymns, mostly from Contemporary Christian Music (CCM), are now played for the congregation rather than lustily sung by the congregation. Most of this music is a pale imitation of secular music (as many hymns have always been, I suppose); but the electronic amplification, the driving drumbeat, and bass guitar usually overwhelm audience participation, where Christian musicians in the past tended to borrow well-known secular music that could be easily sung. This is worship as a show, no matter how often the "worship leaders" playing such music insist that it isn't.

17. Leonard Sweet, *Postmodern Pilgrims: First Century Passion for the 21st Century World* (Nashville: Broadman and Holman, 2000); see also Sweet, *SoulTsunami: Sink or Swim in the New Millennium Culture* (Grand Rapids: Zondervan, 1999).

Beyond the church service, another method of choice for helping bulk up the knowledge and commitment of churchgoers takes the form of small-group ministry. Many of these small groups are mostly social, which serves an important community purpose, especially in large churches. But as far as knowledge goes, small groups usually don't travel far. Participants read Bible passages and are asked how they feel about them. The life of the mind, the insights of scholars, and the weight of the theological tradition and orthodoxy rarely make it to the coffee table.

Today's church is trying to find ways of reaching out to, educating, and embracing the new secondary oral audiences, as it must if it is to succeed. But it has not yet figured it out. Meanwhile, attempts to accommodate the new audiences have often led to conflict about worship styles and preaching. Large numbers of Christians, partly because of the individualism of our era and the cultural emphasis on authenticity (and for other reasons, as we shall see), simply drop out and practice their own private spirituality (or nothing at all).[18] Others doubt that the congregational setting is the right one, and so they leave the larger setting for the growing house-church movement.[19] Instead of a universal (European) church, or at least national and transnational denominations, we settle for communities that are smaller and unconnected to each other.

3. Syncretism

In the chapter on oral Europe, I noted that people had enchanted worldviews characterized by a porous thinking. In oral Europe there was no perceived division between the world of spirits and that of bread and butter. People presumed that the physical and spiritual

18. Charles Taylor, *The Malaise of Modernity* (Toronto: House of Anansi Press, 1991; 2003). This book contains a very good analysis of modern culture's obsession with authenticity.

19. For discussions of this trend, see Wolfgang Simson, *Houses that Changed the World: The Return of House Churches* (Waynesboro, GA: Authentic Lifestyle, 2003); see also Neil Cole, *Organic Church: Growing Faith Where Life Happens* (San Francisco: Jossey-Bass, 2005).

realms completely interpenetrated each other. People did not theorize
— or theologize — about religion, about God's existence; they simply
lived it, "as immediate reality, like stones, rivers and mountains."[20]
People presumed upon the enchanted world much as I, as a child, presumed upon the stories my parents told me about Jesus and God.

In chapter 2, I examined why this worldview broke down. The seeds
of doubt and alternative worldviews, which had long lain dormant in
the ideas of various philosophical and even religious groups, took
hold in the population in general with the advent of literacy. People
began to read, wonder, and argue for points of view that were dis-
tinctly different from the enchanted worldview. Other factors that
moved the common folk away from an enchanted worldview were
new modes of thinking, which were also influenced by literacy, that
ran to the more rational and scientific. The church encouraged a kind
of interiority that made people more reflective about their role in the
cosmos and how they thought.

The situation has changed again. Two factors are very important to
this current change. First, what seems to have happened is that the
postmodern suspicion of authority, hierarchy, and institutions has
become a society-wide intellectual fashion, probably because the purveyors of popular culture, who imbibed deeply of postmodern ideas
in university, have used contemporary media to share those perspectives. A list of examples stretches back almost fifty years by now, but
some notable markers along the way would include musicians such
as Pink Floyd ("The Dark Side of the Moon," "The Wall"), writers
such as Elie Wiesel *(Night)* and Kurt Vonnegut *(Slaughterhouse-Five)*,
television programs in the vein of *M*A*S*H* and *The Simpsons*, movies
from Stanley Kubrick's *Dr. Strangelove* to the *Matrix* trilogy. Overall,
popular culture has immersed audiences in a pervasive and thor-
oughgoing critique of traditional institutions. Given the ongoing
scandals involving clergy physical and sexual abuse, especially in the
Roman Catholic Church, the popular critique of religious institutions
is easy to believe.

Second, secondary orality also deprives people, much as the origi-

---

20. Charles Taylor, *A Secular Age* (Cambridge, MA: Belknap Press, 2007), p. 12.

nal oral tradition did, of the intellectual tools to thoughtfully analyze and evaluate intellectual alternatives or engage in sustained rational inquiry. Not only is the habit of critical thought lost, but the vast body of reflection that previous humans engaged in on matters related to faith and meaning, to life and death, is also largely lost to most people today. This is not because it is unavailable, but because it is unread. A further complicating factor might be that for those who do read, there is such a vast kaleidoscope of both thoughtful and quite ridiculous alternatives out there on the Web and in bookstores that people become lost.

The bottom line is that the intersection of these two factors, postmodern attitudes toward tradition and authority in popular culture and undisciplined and unformed intellectual habits, have opened society at large to a new kind of enchanted thinking. Many people do not now think that there is no dividing wall between the mundane and the sacred. They do, however, think that in both realms anything goes, and neither common sense nor hundreds of years of reflection on religion is a factor worth considering when they make up their own minds about spiritual matters.[21] Our culture is not enchanted as much as it is absolutely credulous. People do not see the divine folded in with the mundane, but are always porous to spiritual oddities and curiosities. As a result, when it comes to spiritual matters, our society is increasingly syncretistic. People will believe anything that appeals to them without any reference to rational, critical reflection or the teaching of institutions.

Other factors besides the two mentioned above also play a lesser role. Churches — and, for that matter, even service clubs like the Rotary and lodges like the Masons — are at a loss about how to motivate, recruit, nurture, and inspire a new generation of true believers. Catechesis in my own denomination has been largely abandoned. While some denominations in the Lutheran, Catholic, and Reformed tradi-

21. Some might argue that one person's common sense, say traditional Christian orthodoxy, makes about as much sense as one from another culture — Haitian voodoo, say. For a critique of the idea that the West's idea of rational religion is really not, see Pascal Boyer, *Religion Explained: The Evolutionary Origins of Religious Thought* (New York: Basic Books, 2001), esp. pp. 1-50.

tions support parochial education that helps form a new generation of believers, many don't. Instead, they may look to young Bible college graduates to be youth leaders, cross their fingers, and hope the kids catch it. In my experience, the basic idea seems to be that, if you can create a relationship with youth, they might take you up on your suggestion to stay in church. And, of course, you create relationships with youth by playing with youth — going to movies, outdoor attractions, and youth group evenings. Parents, in the meantime, who have stuck with church out of force of habit or in deference to their own upbringing, are just as confused as the churches are about how to turn their kids to faith. Statistics show that the younger you are, the less likely it is that you will go to church; and if you don't go to church, but are spiritual, you may as well make up your own faith, much as you choose your own alternative universe to play in online. As consumers, the young are used to getting what they want, not being told they can have any color they want as long as it is black.

So contemporary people, in the grip (though usually unaware) of postmodern mavens of modern culture and their own inability to thoughtfully consider alternatives, often believe in gods fashioned on a wish and a hunch. No image gets it quite as right as a cover of an *Utne Reader* a few years ago. Under the heading "Designer God," the magazine's cover is illustrated by a smiling boy with outstretched arms. He's wearing the yarmulke and locks of a Hasidic Jew, a Buddhist monk's robe, and a Christian cross; if you look a bit closer, you'll see two more necklaces, one a yin-and-yang symbol from Taoism, the other a star and crescent from Islam. On the boy's wrist there is a bracelet with little feathers, a nod in the direction of native spirituality. The article's subtitle asks, "In a mix-and-match world, why not create your own religion?"[22] The assumption behind mix-and-match religion is that what people choose when it comes to faith is at least as important as the internal consistency of the religion itself. This explains, for example, why Marcus Borg's seatmate wasn't concerned about the inherent contradictions in following the way of both Bud-

22. "Designer God: In a Mix-and-Match World, Why not Create Your Own Religion?" *Utne Reader,* August 1998.

dhism and Sufism. In fact, what really matters, as scholars such as Rodney Stark argue, is whether or not a religion — Christianity, something else, or something new — offers the believer benefits beyond what not belonging does. In his book *Habits of the Heart*, Robert Bellah describes Sheila, who mirrors just this sort of self-confidence. Sheila says: "I believe in God. I'm not a religious fanatic. My faith has carried me a long way. It's Sheilaism. Just my own little voice. . . . It's just try to love yourself and be gentle with yourself. You know, I guess, take care of each other. I think he would want us to take care of each other."[23]

In his book *After Heaven*, Princeton sociologist Robert Wuthnow includes a telling chapter entitled "Angel Awakenings." This chapter chronicles the stories people tell about their spiritual experiences. Some are Christian, some questionably Christian but within the ballpark, and others not Christian at all. One claims spiritual help of some sort saved her from falling into dangerous waters and drowning. Eight million Americans believe they have had a near-death experience where they glimpsed the other side. Eleven percent of Americans believe in channeling; 22 percent more are not sure, but they are open to the idea. Sara Kahn, one of the persons Wuthnow describes, is typical. She says that she has seen her spirit guide — an Englishman in a bowler hat — descend into her room. She says of her personal religious experience, "It's like having an orgasm. You can't describe it to someone else. You can say, 'It feels great.' But the description is inadequate. Spirituality is also something that each person has to experience for themselves."[24]

In fact, if you Google "personal relationship with God," you will discover that people from many religions use the same, or similar, self-centered language. Muslims, Baha'i, Hindus, and Mormons all claim personal relationships with their gods. Thus, for example, a recent *Newsweek* article quoted Megan Wyatt, a blonde Ohioan who converted to Islam, who says, "There are many ways to be spiritual. Peo-

23. Robert Bellah et al., *Habits of the Heart: Individualism and Commitment in American Life* (Berkeley: University of California Press, 1985), p. 221.
24. Robert Wuthnow, *After Heaven: Spirituality in America Since the 1950s* (Berkeley: University of California Press, 1998), pp. 114-41, 130.

ple find it in yoga. For me, becoming a Muslim gave me the ultimate connection to God."[25]

Modern faith is like that. People hear about it from friends, learn about it from their families of origin, read about movie stars who adopt it, and they want it, too. I'm reminded of the movie *When Harry Met Sally:* after Sally proves women can fake orgasms by having one in her seat in a café, another customer, who has been watching and listening, says to the waitress, "I'll have what she's having." Everyone is on his or her own spiritual quest. Such quests are part of our history. Whether it was sailors searching for the Northwest Passage or '49-ers looking for gold, North Americans have always hoped that by moving on they could find a better life. Now, in the absence of geographical frontiers, North Americans are transferring their rootlessness to spirituality.

You can't argue with people who say they've experienced a spirit guide from a past life, or who say they had a near-death experience of an angel leading them up, up, and away. You can't argue with people who go to an evangelical church and say that Jesus revealed to them that they should take a new job or pray for a friend. Religious people, regardless of their specific faith, always claim such things. And that's how it is in postmodern North America. Whatever our institutional religion, and whatever creeds and confessions we nominally hold to, what most of us want is an excellent spiritual experience. And we are so unfailingly polite with each other that we're not really up to questioning other people's experiences, or even sometimes insisting that the emperor has no clothes.

I personally became aware of this trend when I was in graduate school and realized that all of my fellow PhD students could define what Aristotle's concept of "epideictic oratory" was all about, and could explain the importance of social networks for corporate communication, because reason and theories mattered to these people. But the number and variety of faith choices that surrounded me was astonishing. There was a Wiccan, a Muslim or two, atheistic Marxists, and one or two New Age believers in Mother Earth and Gaea. After class

25. Http://www.msnbc.msn.com/id/9024914/site/newsweek/ (accessed January 2005).

was over and I would speak with them about their beliefs, they bristled when I suggested that ultimately only one of the many religions represented could ultimately be correct, or that their version of whatever faith they belonged to wasn't the orthodox version. The kind of rational thinking they brought to their rhetorical studies seemed to have no standing in their spiritual lives. When it came to faith, as far as these PhD candidates were concerned, rationality just didn't matter.

Discussing a 2002 Gallup survey, James Edwards concludes:

"Americans, little aware of their own religious traditions, are practicing a do-it-yourself, 'whatever works' kind of religion, picking and choosing among beliefs and practices of various faith traditions," says Gallup. People do not seem to know what they really believe, or why. The results are religious forms that are broad but not deep, emotionally intense but neither intellectually clear nor outwardly practiced. God is popular, the poll concludes, but not primary in people's lives. They believe in God but do not trust God.[26]

The trend towards syncretism is not just out there on the fringe of religious culture. Most people are not part of a new religion that mixes and matches odds and ends from different religions to make a new one like Cao Dai, a Vietnamese religion that mixes Confucianism, Taoism, and Buddhism with a little bit of Judaism; or Raelianism, a North American sect that combines Christian elements with belief in UFOs and cloning. Many nominal Christians mix and match but don't practice much — like Sheila and her "Sheilaism." And many more people who are otherwise members in good standing of their churches either don't know, or don't care much, about core teachings. Ask most Christians why they think they're going to heaven, and they'll answer "Well, I've tried to be good." In orthodox Protestantism this is called works righteousness, and it is at odds with the heart of Protestant theology's confession that people are saved by grace, not works. James Edwards calls this religious eclecticism.

26. James R. Edwards, *Is Jesus the Only Savior?* (Grand Rapids: Eerdmans, 2005), pp. 3-4.

Eclecticism — that is, picking and choosing — is a defining element of our individual religious autonomy. People (at least in the West) are not adhering to faith traditions with theological consistency, nor do they feel a need to. Nor are they opting for one set of beliefs over another. They are freely syncretizing — mixing and matching — beliefs that previously were thought incompatible and contradictory.[27]

4. Agonistic

I observed in chapter 1 that oral cultures told stories of battles that took place in the heavens, of outsized heroes and their incredible accomplishments. From Zeus to Thor, and Baal to Beowulf, oral cultures were agonistic. According to Walter Ong, this was primarily because agonistic stories were easy to remember. They were told over and over again, using rhyme and rhythm, becoming part of society's memorized cultural heritage. From the Iliad to the Atrahasis Epic, these stories embodied the values, the dreams, the gods, and the origin myths of oral people.

Agonistic stories fell out of memory after the invention of the printing press. People were more interested in facts and rationality than they were in fantastic stories. Books, with pages, chapter headings, tables of contents, and their ability to get inside the head and hearts of characters, made agonistic stories a footnote rather than the main event.

But now, anyone who has watched any movies or television lately knows that things have changed. The agons are back. From the Jedi of *Star Wars* to vampires, from wizards like Gandalf and Harry Potter to Transformers, agons fascinate people in today's culture. But the agons are not only alive and well in popular culture. Several years ago, the archdiocese of Chicago appointed — for the first time in its history — not a child-abuse-prevention staff person, but an exorcist. And just in case you think the Roman Catholic Church is going out on a limb on this one, consider this: even though exorcisms had all but died out in

---

27. Edwards, *Is Jesus the Only Savior?* p. 4.

Protestant churches as late as forty years ago, there are now, by some counts, at least three hundred evangelical parachurch exorcist ministries in North America. This is not a New Age fluke that takes in mostly flakes. For example, check out your local Christian bookstore. From the demon-under-every-bush fiction of Frank Peretti to the slightly subtler Nicolai, the antichrist in the *Left Behind* series of books and movies, to the more serious tomes on exorcism, such as Francis MacNutt's *Deliverance from Evil Spirits: A Practical Manual* and Joe Beam's *Seeing the Unseen: Preparing Yourself for Spiritual Warfare* — contemporary Christian fundamentalism is awash in fascination with outsized evil spirits below and battling angels above, with spiritual warfare and demon possession. All of this in spite of C. S. Lewis's injunction that giving the dark side too much time and attention is exactly the wrong thing to do if Christians want to keep it at bay.

Today's fascination with superheroes and their cosmic battles is, I believe, also symptomatic of a culture that is exchanging deep word literacy for the secondary oral tradition. These agonistic heroes work in today's culture, which is less than highly literate, because they're easy to watch on TV, easy to root for given the black-and-white morality that they embody, and easy to understand in that they have none of the interior life of someone like Hagar Shipley or Anna Karenina.

Related to today's fascination with a new breed of agons is the parallel fascination with celebrities. Whether in sports, on TV, or in the movies, or even in politics, contemporary society obsesses over the superstars. The world they live in is one the vast majority of fans will never know. Yet the magazines and websites such superstars inspire beat out pretty much every other genre. As John Lennon already knew long ago, these stars are more popular than Jesus, more powerful than speeding bullets, and more sexy and interesting than a virgin Madonna. Nor is this fascination with living and breathing agons foreign to Christians. In general, they are as happy to participate in the cult of the agon, buying *People* magazines and watching *Entertainment Tonight*, as are those who don't go to church. But Christians also have their own pantheon of worldly agons: from Mother Teresa to Rick Warren, to TV purveyors of miracles and wealth like Benny Hinn and Joel Osteen, Christians just love their superstars. They pack arenas and stadiums to hear "Promise Keeper" preachers pontificate on the health-and-wealth gospel or what it takes to be a real man and a successful man. And if they have healing in their wings (or at least self-esteem) or speak for the moral majority, but only require that you buy their books or send in a donation — the cost of worship is cheap.

The contemporary fascination with agons, though, might well be symptomatic of other religious values and qualities just below the surface.

Conservatism   In the oral tradition, we saw that conservatism was a function of not wanting to give up a structure or a thought or a skill that one had invested a great deal of time in learning. After all, there were no books. After teachers died, what you had was what was in your head. And that was precious! So change was looked on with suspicion. This suspicion extended itself to ruling classes, and provided them with uncommon political stability — at least with regard to the political order — even in the face of incredible instability when it came to food, disease, weather, and other "acts of God."

Secondary orality is similarly conservative, at least when it comes to power. For example, Roland Barthes says: "Statistically, myth [that is, agonistic storytelling to account for political reality, as in talk of evil empires and evil axes] . . . is on the right. There, [myth] is essential; well-fed, sleek, expansive, garrulous, it invents itself ceaselessly. It takes hold of everything, all aspects of the law, of morality, of aesthetics, of diplomacy, of household equipment, of literature, [and note this carefully] of entertainment."[28]

We live in an era of media convergence, where the channels of communication are about how the world really is owned by a few, and thus, necessarily, by the powerful. In our day, the masses, who rarely read or write, usually consume only those attitudes that fit with the hopes and dreams of the rich, who produce the media. At the same time, the secondary oral tradition's addiction to mass media and inability or lack of desire to dig for alternative worldviews that can still

---

28. Roland Barthes, *Mythologies,* trans. Annette Lavers (New York: The Noonday Press, 1991), pp. 148-49.

be found in books or offbeat magazines, if you look for them, cuts to-day's citizenry off from resources that would allow them to change their minds. Finally, as individuals, by and large they are conservative when it comes to maintaining today's structures and powers that be because they don't want to do the work — not the reading, or train-ing, or organizing, or the expenditure of time — to learn about new at-titudes and approaches. Interestingly, this situation is tailor-made for populist or charismatic leaders to win approval on the basis of their ability to stir and grab headlines.

On the whole, our Western secondary oral culture is also extremely well-to-do. Compared to the rest of the world, which is out of power and desperately poor, secondary oral cultures adopt an attitude that affirms their reality, and thus their place in it, an attitude that justifies our wealth and the rest of the world's poverty. Secondary oral think-ing, nurtured by media barons and comforted by Western entitle-ments, is conservative in that it is status quo thinking.

Agonistic Culture's Sense of Helplessness The secondary oral tradition — as evidenced, once more, in its fascination with agons — also fosters a sense of political and social helplessness that reflects a conservative attachment to the structures as they are, but that also in a way buttresses such structures. If the battles are between the superheroes and antiheroes fighting it out in the heavens or faraway battlefields or cave complexes, between what AOL once called a "mythic" Osama bin Laden and the stumbling, bumbling, tongue-tied Dubya Bush; or if the battles are between the free market and Third World dictators; or between Wall Street derivative bundlers and the department of the treasury — what sort of difference can everyday people make? Not much. We may have more money, more shows, and more gigabytes than any other generation has had; but along with many fewer books, we also have less to say and less we can do than ever before.

The agonistic worldview of the secondary oral tradition fosters a sense of being powerless and frustrated spectators. This frustration, in turn, undermines the democratic ideal, because citizens know and believe in their hearts that they cannot make a difference at the real power level. They don't vote. They try to get away with not paying taxes. And they disdain politicians, who, after all is said and done, seem to be spending as much time lining their own reelection war chests as taking on social and national Goliaths. This powerlessness makes itself known in two public reactions.

First, some of some of us are *simply co-opted by the system* and its structures. Realizing that we cannot change the system, and that politics of real change or different ideological paradigms are nonstarters, some of us, especially those of us who benefit materially from the status quo — which is to say, most of us — just go along for the ride. We read *The New York Times* or *The Toronto Globe and Mail,* we watch hours of television, we vote for the Liberals or the Conservatives in Canada, the Democrats or Republicans in the United States, we save like crazy for retirement, and we know virtually nothing about what it is like to be a Palestinian in Ramallah or a Zimbabwean in Kwekwe. Even Christians, who are supposed to be citizens of another kingdom in that we follow the path of loving God and neighbor, are hijacked into this nationalistic system. It reminds me of the so-called Stockholm syndrome, where kidnap victims fall in love with their kidnappers, the way Patricia Hearst did in the late 1970s, when she was in on a couple of bank robberies with the Symbionese Liberation Army, her captors. So, being powerless to make any real difference with the agonistic powers that be, some of us — I think most of us — are simply co-opted by the system. We don't ask questions for fear that the answers might require us to make some hard decisions.

One way that this attitude makes itself known particularly is how Christians, like everyone else, are focused on escaping and cocooning. Living for the weekend at the cottage, or creating ever more elaborate home theaters, or sticking to the well-worn path between church and home and school, where the politics and the battles are familiar and we feel we can make a difference (because the community is small) are common ways that today's Christians escape their feeling of powerlessness. Similarly, much of New Age spirituality is an elaborate search for significance and meaning away from the rational, dog-eat-dog world of our insignificance.

Second, feeling totally powerless in our agonistic world, some of us *adopt apocalyptic worldviews* that promise amazing escape from the way things are. The popularity of premillennial theology, like that of the *Left Behind* series, is a religious response to marginalization. When you can't go along with the evil secular-humanist government, you dream up scenarios where Jesus will save you, the ultimate deux ex machina via the rapture, while all the bad guys are left to deal with Armageddon and hell on earth. Of course, such scenarios merely reinforce the idea that there is nothing that can be done because, after all, the timing and ultimate solution is all in God's hands anyway.

More ominously, extremists who have strong ideological objections to the world powers, but feel marginalized, are likely to put their trust in charismatic leaders who can inspire them to sacrificial acts of courage, which will then help propel the world into a crisis, purify it, or force the gods to act on our behalf. The 9/11 plane bombings were such apocalyptic acts. And Aryan Nation racist terrorists, similar to Canada's Heritage Front, have for years been inspired by the apocalyptic novel *The Turner Diaries,* by the recently deceased racist William Pierce, which tells the story of how terrorist cells of racists use bank robberies, assassinations, and mass killing to precipitate a race war that exterminates all persons of color and gives North America back to white people.[29] In fact, as I write this paragraph, the newspapers are full of stories about white supremacist James von Brunn, who shot and killed a guard at Washington's Holocaust Museum. Von Brunn was a known associate of William Pierce and was very familiar with his book.

To sum up, we live in an agonistic culture; and that agonism is a product, at least in part, of our being a less than literate culture. We've turned back to the powers for an explanation of a world that we can't control. We have, by and large, responded to our powerlessness by becoming conservative with respect to the structures that we live within, by opting out or escaping into apocalyptic visions of the future, or by cocooning.

29. Andrew Macdonald [William Pierce], *The Turner Diaries* (New York: Barricade Books, 1978).

5. Community

In the old enchanted Europe nearly everyone shared the same enchanted worldview; so religion did not cut people off from each other. They were all part of one Holy Catholic Church that spanned Europe. Of course, there were fewer people in that world, and getting around wasn't that easy. People knew and communed with those who lived within walking distance, extended family members, fellow villagers and marketers, and those who went to Mass with them.

With the coming of literacy, what had been a single cloth was rent into many pieces. While the first divisions were large — between Catholics and Lutherans — they soon expanded to include Calvin's Reformed people and Menno Simons's Anabaptists, as well as national variations on all the main themes. By the eighteenth century, the pace of schism and division had only hastened. Divergent groups formed around many different theologies, personalities, and missions. But all the groups also functioned as tribes, too, so that the reasons for belonging, once the initial fervor that accompanied the new group's foundation wavered, eventually became pro forma, and people continued to belong because these congregations or denominations were *their* places — places of community, comfort, standing, and usually ethnic homogeneity.

The postmodern, postliterate church is even more fractured, especially in North America, where franchising has long been an alternative path to health and wealth for the entrepreneurial class. Not only do multiple denominations market to the religious consumer, but independent congregations, TV evangelists, and various self-help bookstore gurus do, too. People join churches less and less for doctrinal reasons, and more and more for the services churches can render. People are on the prowl for good preaching, youth groups, choir, certain kinds of music, a certain social cachet, great babysitting, and a host of other possible benefits of church membership. The most important reason, however, is relationship and friendship. Rodney Stark, of the University of Washington, has done a great deal of research on why people join the churches they do, and this is what he ultimately observes:

Knowing that he had written specifically on how and why religious movements succeed, I [the article's author, Toby Lester] called him and asked him to summarize his thoughts on the subject. "The main thing you've got to recognize," he told me, "is that success is really about relationships and *not* about faith. What happens is that people form relationships and only then come to embrace a religion. It doesn't happen the other way around. That's really critical, and it's something that you can only learn by going out and watching people convert to new movements. We would never, ever, have figured that out in the library. You can never find that sort of thing out after the fact — because after the fact people *do* think it's about faith. And they're not lying, by the way. They're just projecting backwards."[30]

In other words, people join churches — or continue to belong to churches they were born into — for social reasons. It is only as members that they rationalize to themselves why joining or staying makes sense theologically (I examine the social reasons further in chapter 8 below). They rationalize by adopting the beliefs of the church. Whether or not the beliefs make sense in some larger sense, or whether they are understood, is less important than whether or not adoption of the beliefs gives entry into the community.

The roots of this disregard for the beliefs of a church — and thus, of course, for much knowledge about the Bible — is the convergence of a postmodern suspicion of authority, in this case the authority of creeds and confessions and elders, and a suspicion of rationality, in this case the systematic in theology. And, from the other side, the secondary oral disinclination and inability to read creeds with pleasure or appreciation or a critical mind, along with the secondary oral displacement of time, leaves nothing over for church or spirituality that would actually take an investment of time.

30. Toby Lester, "Oh, Gods!" *The Atlantic,* February 2002: http://www.theatlantic.com/doc/200202/lester (accessed March 29, 2009).

Curricular Features

Postmoderns lean toward bulleted lists rather than books or lectures. Bulleted lists can be projected on walls, and hence they offer a sort of outline for sermons or lectures. Bulleted lists also provide a way around the need to keep a sermon or lecture on a linear narrative. Each item in the list offers a new opportunity to head off in a new direction, while offering the appearance of organization and direction; the bullets do not actually need to follow from each other or build on each other. Often, as in the "Seven Promises" of a Promise Keeper, they are loosely organized around a larger topic and allow the speaker to avoid using any unifying narrative at all. Meanwhile, the use of electronic equipment resonates with the newly wired, nonreading sensorium. If preaching is to succeed, preachers must return to the insights and methods of oral preachers to relearn how to attract and hold the interest of nonreaders.

Summary

The last two chapters have examined what became of literate Christianity, the Christianity I was raised in. Two movements, one primarily intellectual and the other decidedly not, postmodernism and the secondary oral tradition, influenced not only society at large, but me in particular. In a word, the critique of modernism that is at the heart of postmodernism resonated in me. Yet, even as I struggle against the symptoms of secondary orality in my own life, I'm appalled by where its indifference to rationality and reading is taking us as a society, and as a church.

The interplay of postmodern and secondary oral currents leaves me with very mixed feelings. I realize that over the past number of years I have definitely lost my appetite for working in the institutional — and especially national — church. Perhaps quite a bit of this has to do with the church's stubbornness when it comes to changing its moral position on issues such as homosexuality, and its stubbornness about not allowing more variety of opinion when it comes to confessional standards, even as many people in the pews have long ago stopped thinking about the confessions at all. In my denomination there have been recent attempts to change the form of subscription that ministers must sign in order to signal their agreement with the church's confessions. The attempts have met with failure, even as people in the pews — and pastors, I'm sure — understand less and less about the doctrines they are supposedly subscribing to. I think that I'm frustrated by this intransigence in part because I've changed my mind. But I'm also frustrated because I can no longer accept the hubris that comes with being so sure "we're right" about so much. This is especially true because it seems clear to me that most people and pastors don't join churches for theological reasons in the first place. The continued insistence on a sixteenth-century formulation of doctrinal purity represents an unwillingness to wrestle with the disappointing historical legacy of churches — and the reasons why people really belong to churches.

But I've also lost my appetite for the institutional church because I have seen, as the editor of a denominational magazine, that as an institution the church is a rough-and-tumble place dedicated to its own survival, growth, and pragmatic success. Not ruffling feathers, when such ruffling might result in fewer members, takes precedence over being honest, straightforward, and talking about change. I realize that my lack of trust in institutions also has deep roots in postmodern perspectives on the totalizing, proselytizing, hierarchical, and coercive ways they work.

I also find the secondary oral acceptance of the status quo when it comes to powers and principalities very disheartening. I often find myself wanting to make a stand against that acceptance. But then I come face to face with my own introverted nature and the energy that being "public" takes. I worry about losing my pension and my standing in the community. I find that, in many ways, I have submitted to the status quo along with everyone else. One of the spiritual issues I deal with daily is the disappointment I feel about my own addiction to the world the way it is.

The secondary oral interest in the heroic and apocalyptic is, for similar reasons, disheartening. It is rooted in abandoning more reasoned approaches to our tradition with the help of words and philosophical legacy, and leads to the acceptance of the status quo, as noted above. At the same time, the secondary oral rediscovery of the aesthetic and the image has great potential for offering churches new direction and energy, though so far this rediscovery appears to have little resonance with high art and aesthetic excellence.

One aspect of secondary orality that is especially tragic is the loss of narrative. I see it everywhere. People don't read narratives, and they don't understand stories that have multiple levels of meaning. And many seminary graduates who preach can't preach narrative, in spite of all the current homiletical emphasis on it. Spending a year on the road, my wife and I heard many more sermons that went nowhere and focused on abstract ideas that were poorly articulated than we heard those that retold the scriptural story. And we encountered a lot more PowerPoint presentations that were a jumble of barely related points around a broad theme than we ran into compelling, tightly knit sermons about a single memorable theme. When was the last time a person meaningfully memorized the six points, each with two or three subpoints, that she heard and saw in a PowerPoint presentation? This is where the secondary oral tradition really comes up short when compared to the primary oral tradition. Orality always had a strong emphasis on teaching the story, and participants knew how to listen to the spoken word. These days, audiences who are used to television and computers don't know how to listen, and have no practice in following metanarratives.

In summary, postmodernism has left me very unhappy with a modernist, rationalist, literate kind of faith. But in the current consumer-oriented, always new, liturgically bereft, self-help, nonnarrative congregations, I am also lost and unhappy. I am left with a faith that is nothing like what is expected of someone who is still a member of a conservative confessional church. It is a faith that I don't know where to park, nor for its nurture can I find like-minded people. I'm left uninterested and languorous with respect to the institution of that church; yet I have a cultural-tribal love for its people and the history I share with them. That makes for loneliness and a difficulty in finding a new community and learning new rules. After ten or fifteen years of having to hide rather than nourish my introversion, it has just overwhelmed me. At the same time, I'm not depressed. I am more positively and authentically engaged in hard faith questions than ever before.

Where all this leaves me is sort of shell-shocked. Not happy with how the church has uncritically adapted itself to the secondary oral tradition and yet troubled by the postmodern, I'm feeling out of sorts, not sure where I belong. I am attracted to starting over personally on religion but not to re-creating an institution.

Not a Hypocrite

So I have not always doubted. All my life, people who loved me — my mother and father, my wife and teachers — have lived as if faith is the thing in our bloodstreams that makes life worthwhile. Yahweh is the one, the only God. Sing. Pray. Worship. So I did . . . and I do.

You could even say that the God of Christians and Jesus, his divine son, have always been the center of my being. As an adult I fashioned a life out of preaching their names. The problem is that I've never seen the face of God and have never heard a still, small, quiet voice. I've never had the epiphany that so many other Christians claim to have had. Having seen what I have seen, I am wracked by doubt. Is this Jesus really a stream of living water? He seems too small, too insignificant, too far away. Will I live forever on a new earth? Is the New Testament — poorly written in Greek and all of it awash with inconsistency and ambiguity — really a word from God? Not a day goes by that I do not wonder whether the answers I proclaim are the right ones. Over time, I've come to doubt whether or not it is fair that I preach with clarity and conviction when I rarely have those for myself.

In the introduction I spoke of a walk along Rustico Beach on Prince Edward Island. When I reached the lighthouse at the far end, I turned around, and now with the wind at my back, I sang, "Jesus, remember me when you come into your kingdom." Just that line, over and over, at the top of my lungs, for about twenty minutes or so. Reflecting on what I'd seen in my travels and what I was reading about every day in the papers, I was tied up in knots. I meant my sung prayer with all my heart and soul. I suppose it must seem odd to most people that faith — or the lack of it — can rile me up so much. Why not get exercised, instead, over how the Blue Jays or my mutual funds are doing?

I don't know. Sometimes I wish baseball were my passion. In my religious life, I wish I could get up on Sunday mornings, pull the tie tight around my neck, march off to church, and sing at the top of my lungs while never giving anything but God's grace a second thought. But I can't. And sometimes, given the culture I grew up in and the certainty of so many professional religious people around me, I have even wondered whether my doubt disqualifies my faith and brings my leadership roles in my Christian community into doubt.

Sometimes I wonder whether or not I'm a hypocrite.

But now, in midlife, I don't want to leave the ministry: I would lose my place in the community. The denomination I grew up in is home. Sometimes, by God's grace, you just find yourself there and you rest in the fact that no one will make you leave. I can't leave. And, to be perfectly honest, if I were to leave the ministry or my denomination, I'd also lose the opportunity to preach, one of the things I'm best at. I actually want to believe so badly that when I get behind that pulpit, I do.

And yet, I also don't know. I certainly don't know the way some of the pastors do whom I have heard at councils and synods, men who get up and proclaim with complete certainty — as far as I can tell — their awful judgments: gay couples are damned, women should keep their mouths shut, and if you don't believe we're all descended from Adam and Eve, you don't believe the Bible. Well, I guess I'm in trouble.

I've come to understand my doubt and uncertainty only by degrees. Neal Plantinga, one of my seminary professors, once suggested that, for some people, faith just doesn't get their feet to dancing or their hands to clapping. That's me. I feel constitutionally incapable of believing with all my heart, soul, and mind. Instead, faith churns in my heart and as often as not seems preposterous to my mind. When it comes to faith, I have two left feet: I'm made for stumbling. It seems to me that faith is as abrasive and difficult as the waves that pile up on the shore, eroding the shingled bluff, so that what was once firm eventually comes crashing down.

chapter 5

So, What Is Faith, Really?

cw

Oral Faith

So far, we've seen that the nature and content of faith, like the Banaue Terraces, have changed and evolved over time. In the oral era, people had an enchanted worldview that perceived all of life and all things as cut from a single cloth that had spiritual and physical dimensions, not that they themselves would ever have put it so theoretically. Speaking of the early Christian era before the church became handmaiden to the secular powers and principalities of the state, Diana Butler Bass observes:

> Throughout the first five centuries people understood Christianity primarily as a way of life in the present, not as a doctrinal system, esoteric belief, or promise of eternal salvation. By followers enacting Jesus's teachings Christianity changed and improvised the lives of its adherents and served as a practical spiritual pathway.[1]

1. Diana Butler Bass, *A People's History of Christianity: The Other Side of the Story* (New York: HarperOne, 2009), p. 27.

Literate Faith

As Europe became more and more literate, this faith was dramatically transformed. Rather than rely on the church and its clergy to tell the story and explain the obligations of faith, people picked up the Bible for themselves and came to their own conclusions. The opportunity to focus on Scripture's printed word, as well as the flood of commentary that attended the widespread adoption of printing changed the human sensorium, making a more linear and rationalist approach more accessible to more people. Faith, like the world itself, took on the nature of an object to be explored and theorized about. Developing a personal piety and choosing between the several available doctrinal systems became important religious duties.

This linear faith was the one I grew up with. I remember that, as a teenager, when I made my profession of faith in order to become an adult member of the church, the elders, who had to give their permission, asked me to appear before them to answer their questions. Not one of the elders asked me about my relationship with God, or whether I would be good, or what I felt about the Christian life. Instead, they wanted to know how I defined the Trinity, and what was meant by "covenant" and "gratitude." They wanted to make sure that I understood the substitutionary theory of the atonement, rather than whether or not I knew the story of the atonement.

Postmodernism

Postmodernism was fundamentally unhappy with the Enlightenment status quo, and especially with its unwavering belief in scientific and technological progress. While not denying the power of reason, linear thinking, and the sciences, postmodernism isn't as optimistic that humans will use these technologies for good ends. While not always averse to spirituality, postmoderns doubt that texts such as the Bible can really be understood apart from the motivations of those who read and use them, and so they worry that such texts will be used — as they have often been used in the past — to exploit the weak, the poor, other races, and those marginalized in other ways.

Like Christians at their best, postmoderns are also deeply concerned with those on the margins, the weak, and the oppressed. But true to its critical way of thinking, postmodernism also has little energy or patience for Christianity's institutions and doctrines. For all of its questioning of Enlightenment values and presuppositions, postmodernism is at its heart an intellectual critique of Western civilization, and as such it is highly literate. While some postmodern values are mediated to society at large through the influence of postmodernists in the arts and media, its influence as an intellectual movement is limited in the population as a whole.

For Christians, the postmodern critique is a serious one. Christianity and secular power have often been allied as oppressors of people, their ideas, and their freedoms. From religious wars to inquisitions, persecution of minorities to cover-ups of sexual and physical abuse by its clergy, Christianity has usually fallen far short of the just moral vision of Old Testament prophets and Jesus' Sermon on the Mount. To the degree that faith has been identified with doctrines, or institutions, or progress, or power, or growth, or healing, or success, it becomes more and more difficult for postmoderns to credit.

The Secondary Oral Tradition

The secondary oral tradition is characterized by another change in the "human sensorium," so that linear, rational thinking just doesn't resonate with people anymore. In large measure, this is due to the new fascination with electronic media, which makes use of different kinds of brainpower. Less linear, secondary orality inculcates a kind of disregard for consistency so that people feel free to — and often do unconsciously — design their own religious practices, mixing and matching attitudes and practices from several sources. The lack of reading or any deeply informed critical reflection makes secondary oral people prone to following the latest trend while sticking with the status quo overall. Now, instead of worrying about whether the atonement is an agonistic drama about Jesus saving us from hell, or a complicated legal theory, most people just figure salvation is God's business, especially for nice people like them. Religion, to the degree that it interests them, ought to support their well-being, health, and wealth — while being entertaining as well.

I also personally struggle with the constrictions of the contemporary secondary oral tradition. I find that modern media and marketing impact me, too. My attention span is reduced while my wants have increased. But I abhor designer Christianity, the loss of cultural and religious memory, and fear that my own fall from modernist certainty in some way suggests my own grasping after a designer religion.

My Faith

My own sense of all this is that I'm intrigued by the aesthetic variety of the oral tradition, and especially the aesthetic palette of orality's storytelling, though I cannot even begin to fathom the enchanted worldview. The lack of literacy also restricts oral people's access to information and different ideas, making them easy prey for those in power, much as secondary orality restricts information and perspectives, making today's cultural innocents easy pickings for big business and the latest media-generated fad or consumer-savvy church.

I am also a product of modernist Christianity, and as such I've always courted a lover I could not have — certainty. But this is, in large measure, because ultimate religious truth lies outside the investigative competence of modernity. However, knowing that does not make believing easier. And the older I became, the less certain I was. At the same time, I love the game of doctrinal, rational religion — with the familiar constructions, order, and politics that I have mastered. Fitting it all together reminds me of when I was a child discovering the joys of my Meccano construction sets. But lately I find that I'm a tourist, I'm on the outside looking in at modernity, standing in front of the Empire State Building, say, or the Eiffel Tower. I roughly know how people did it. I know a lot about the general principles: materials, stress, digging foundations, rivets, concrete, and so on. I love to explore these things (and I have books on how things work). But I can no longer even dream of doing this stuff myself. I feel a lot like I did when I stood on the lip of the Banaue Rice Terraces: on the one hand, I'm deeply impressed at the breadth of vision and the magnitude of the engineering; on the other hand, I also see that the whole thing is crumbling, and that it no longer works very well for the people of today's world. It doesn't feed me. It is passing. And what will follow it is hard to say.

So now what? I feel the weight of the erosion of the terraces. I'm unhappy. I doubt. And I try to reconstruct my faith. Reviewing my history, above, I'm most intrigued by the story and *caritas*, the rationality and depth and new ideas possible with modernity, the critique of power inherent in postmodernity, and the desire to speak to the secondary oral tradition. And all this in the context of doubt that I cannot, in the end, dismiss.

Given all these choices and flavors, what really is faith? As much as I would love to offer an easy, one-size-fits-all answer, this turns out to be the most difficult question, one that I have studiously avoided so far. One obvious way to answer this question is to ask, What does Scripture say faith is? But the answer from Scripture itself is complicated by the fact that the intended audiences of Scripture were people, by and large, who could not have conceived of contemporary doubt as an issue that needed to be addressed. Even the fool who said in his or her heart that there is no God was not understood to be an atheist; rather, he or she was someone who simply refused to take God or his revelation into account.

The real faith issue that runs through the Old and New Testaments is that of trust. The story is about a God who made promises to the Israelites — made a covenant with them — and expected, in return, that they keep some promises about justice, mercy, and faithfulness in return. In this covenantal sense, biblical faith is as far as possible from modernist notions of a *propositional* faith: rather, it is about sticking with one lover rather than running off with another. It is about being a true bride for Christ, about troth rather than truth.

Given the other, adulterous options — Egyptian and Canaanite gods, and later the Greek and Roman pantheon and philosophies —

why should anyone choose to keep covenant with Yahweh, to trust in him? Yahweh, after all, let his people suffer in Egypt and demanded a solitary kind of devotion that was odd in the ancient Near East context and still odd in our relativistic, syncretistic culture. He seemed, to the outside observer, to often abandon his people to military incursions, to exile, and finally to long-term occupation and eventually near-annihilation. In what sense could the Israelites trust this God rather than those of the powerful Assyrians or Romans?

With respect to Jesus, the trust asked for is even more complicated. There were other narratives about gods who died and were resurrected. The Christian approach to the gods' interactions with humans wasn't unique or absolutely improbable, from an ancient point of view. The real problem with Jesus was that, as a historical person, he was not that impressive compared to the gods of several other pantheons. He did miracles, but so did other miracle workers. He taught well, but so did the Pharisees and Sadducees, the Epicureans and the Stoics.

Especially galling was Jesus' death as a criminal on the cross. This was not a heroic or impressive death. Nor were the subsequent accounts of his resurrection that convincing. Certainly, Thomas and the travelers to Emmaus and the Pharisee Saul, for example, had heard the stories during Jesus' lifetime, but they were not impressed enough by them to turn to faith. It took personal appearances by a resurrected Jesus to convince them. But then, just when his personal appearances might have brought him to the attention of the crowds, Jesus again went away, leaving quite a bit of confusion as to what had really happened. And, once departed, he also did not leave his followers with a consensus understanding about what his resurrection really meant. They continued to go to the temple sacrifices, for example; they continued to exclude Gentiles from their midst; and they continued to keep the Old Testament purity laws. In Jesus' absence, the world didn't seem much changed, which called his victory into question. He had taught that all Jews should follow his way, but they never were more than lukewarm about his teaching or the resurrection, preferring to stick with the ancient religion of Yahweh or the surrounding pagan religions. His first followers — at least until Paul's conversion

— were people of little account. When Paul, in turn, wrote that Jesus' story of crucifixion and resurrection was a stumbling block to Jews and foolishness to Greeks, he knew what he was talking about. Those first believers — even as late as the writing of the book of Revelation — expected Jesus to return any minute. From their perspective, he had promised! Up to my writing this last sentence, he has not yet done so. So, in what sense could this Jesus, rather than Yahweh or Zeus, be trusted?

To sum up, the Bible story was told by its authors with a very different audience in mind than the one that is reading it now. They wrote to inculcate trust, while we wonder about divinity and existence. Paul Achtemeier gets at some of this dynamic while nicely summarizing the trust aspect of both Old and New Testament faith.

> One enters that new [covenant] relationship with God by accepting what God has done for sinners in Christ. Such acceptance is what Paul calls "faith." Again, a better choice of word would be "trust." In modern English, "faith" often means assent to the validity of some intellectual content. But Paul uses that word not to get his readers to assent to the existence of God and Christ, but to place their trust in God and Christ to fulfill what they have promised. In that way, human beings leave their rebellious ways, which have separated them from God (that is, their sin) and now enter a positive relationship through Christ in which they seek to act in accordance with the divine will for humans that Christ displays. For that reason we use the phrase "righteousness through trust" rather than "justification by faith."[2]

So, Scripture's stories and teachings are designed to convince an audience that it is wiser to trust in God or in Jesus — and act as if they trust — than it is to trust in any other god. And, given that they had few options and could take it on considerable authority, medieval oral people did trust in God and Jesus. But the question that people

---

2. Paul J. Achtemeier et al., *Introducing the New Testament: Its Literature and Theology* (Grand Rapids: Eerdmans, 2001), p. 308.

through the highly literate era wanted answered was not whether they should trust the God of Scripture rather than some other god. No, now people had two other questions: What exactly must I believe about God? And, increasingly, does belief in a supernatural God make any sense at all?

With respect to that first question, Scripture actually says less than most people might suppose. We need to lighten up and relax when it comes to making oversized claims about what Scripture really means to say. God has not provided enough guidance to prevent the church from disagreeing on a good deal when it comes to baptism or election or evolution or the exact nature of Scripture's authority, to name just a few topics. So Christians should focus more on those things that most people are pretty sure are central in Scripture. In a brilliant and compelling turn of phrase, Brian McLaren calls this "a generous orthodoxy."[3] Paul mentions faith, hope, and love, for example, as deserving special mention. "Faith" here is faith as trust. Truth doesn't even rate as one of the big three. And Jesus says about love, especially love of neighbor and God, "Do this and you will live" (Luke 10:28). He doesn't say, "Accept this or that proposition, and love, and you will be saved."

The way one expressed trust in God during the Old Testament era was through fidelity, the worship of Yahweh alone. While eventually — perhaps late in the monarchy — such worship involved all kinds of laws (rarely kept or enforced in Israel's long history), it fundamentally consisted of "engaging in a life that embraces the large intentions of YHWH, which are marked by compassion, mercy, and forgiveness."[4] Or, as the prophet Micah sums it up in a passage that brings trust and obedience together into a single statement, we are called "to do justice, to love kindness, and to walk humbly with [our] God" (Micah 6:8).

Saying that the church needs to lighten up and relax about doctrine, demanding less in the way of affirmation than it historically has,

3. Brian D. McLaren, *A Generous Orthodoxy* (Grand Rapids: Zondervan, 2004).
4. Walter Brueggemann, *Reverberations of Faith: A Theological Handbook of Old Testament Themes* (Louisville: Westminster John Knox Press, 2002), p. 77.

is not to say that theology should be ignored. I'd love to see more people take an interest in theology and imaginatively plumb the depths of Scripture for insight about God, humans, and the world. However, Scripture isn't focused on doctrine to the degree that our traditions or our institutions are. It is focused on God's large intentions. Jesus himself is preoccupied with love of God and neighbor. Ironically, it isn't failure to love or do justice that church synods prosecute, but failure to accept their particular propositions.

Which leaves open the question of whether belief in — or trust in — God makes any sense at all. In the beginning of this book, I suggested that it would not be an apologia for faith — an argument to believe. So, rather than make a long and decidedly modernist argument for faith, I'll merely quote someone who makes sense to me on this issue. Leslie Weatherhead says:

> Those who have never had the numinous experience? They must pursue the way of argument as far as it can take them, and then make a leap of faith in the direction of the trend of the evidence, acting *as though* it were sound. Reason will take us so far on firm ground. But then there must be the leap *in the same direction,* if the truth of those facts in religion which are only reached by faith are to be enjoyed. Faith is not a leap in the dark, or, as the schoolboy said, "believing what you know to be untrue," or treading a road that is contrary to reason and superstitiously running in another direction. It is taking the road of evidence as far as it will go and then, with the energy provided meditating on the character of God as Christ revealed him, making a leap of faith, only to land finally in a conviction as strong as proof can supply.[5]

This is an old approach: it is rooted in modernism while acknowledging that modernism's most impressive tool, rationality, can ultimately take us only so far. At the same time, it is the best I can do, even while I see that this definition is more an explanation of faith as proposition than as trust. Also, I say this fully aware that many of the

---

5. Leslie Weatherhead, *The Christian Agnostic* (Nashville: Abingdon, 1965), p. 79.

reasons why I can't personally give up faith are rooted in motivations beyond rationality. I want to trust Jesus for no other reason than that I want to. Why? My upbringing was good, and both its moral and religious teachings are deeply rooted in my psyche. The overwhelming influence of Christianity in Western tradition carries me along with many others. The call to live a godly life marked by a love that mirrors Jesus' sacrificial life is intellectually compelling — even urgent. Humans have evolved to believe. The unity of Scripture, despite its diversity, speaks of a mysterious guiding hand that I can't easily dismiss. And in moments of greatest despair, or loneliness, or even joy, I find that the hope of redemption and the promise of God's providence are things that I cannot help but hope for, something that I ultimately explain by the mysterious work of God the Spirit in my soul.

So, haltingly — and with much leftover doubt — I continue to believe, to trust. And I often think of what Lewis Smedes wrote about this problem, when arguments were at an end. "Without Jesus we are stuck with two options: utopian illusion or deadly despair. I scorn illusion. I dread despair. So I put my money on Jesus."[6] I trust Jesus. But for what?

The Hope of One Who Does Not Know

Every Sunday morning I get up and go to church. For the past twenty years, I've mostly gone as someone who sits in the pew and listens. I have often been disappointed. Sometimes it has to do with the artlessness of the preacher, which is inexcusable in a secondary oral setting, where the aesthetic dimension of preaching now is more important than it has been in four hundred years. Sometimes I'm disappointed because the preacher nags. If I hear another sermon about the three things we have to change in our church if we want to grow, or the five things I need to do to have a happy marriage, or the seven promises I have to keep to be a good father, I will be sorely tempted to punch the preacher

6. Lewis B. Smedes, *My God and I: A Spiritual Memoir* (Grand Rapids: Eerdmans, 2003), p. 177.

in one of his soft spots. Such preaching, besides trading on the idea that Christianity is a pragmatic matter of applying the right methods appropriately baptized to solve any problem, simply doesn't square with Scripture. And it misses the boat entirely when it comes to telling the old, old story — a story that fewer and fewer people know well (for reasons that we've discussed). But mostly, when my faith flags, and when I'm not sure, and when I'm tied up in knots because of my doubt and the fact that I don't know anything for sure, I go to church to hear about the consolations of the gospel. Especially the kinds of consolations that speak to my lack of knowledge and my continual doubt.

And sometimes I hear a word from Scripture that stops me cold and sends me home — if not dancing, at least full of joy and hope. One such passage is Luke 23:34, where Jesus is dying on the cross. He looks out over the perjurers who lied to convict him and the torturers who nailed him down while he screamed and the crooked politicians who laughed to make it so. Jesus looks them all over, and rather than curse them and die, he prays: "Father, forgive them, for they know not what they do." I go to church to hear such things.

I recently saw a movie about forgiving someone who doesn't know any better. It was the Oscar-nominated *Away From Her,* based on a short story by renowned Canadian fiction writer Alice Munro, which tells the story of Grant and Fiona. She has Alzheimer's and has to move to a nursing home. When, after a thirty-day settling-in period, Grant is finally allowed to visit Fiona, she no longer knows who he is. Worse, in the meantime she has taken a shine to fellow resident Aubrey. Fiona helps Aubrey play cards; she helps him in and out of his wheelchair; and she even holds Aubrey's hand — all in the presence of her astonished and heartbroken husband. Fiona does not know what she is doing.

Grant reintroduces himself to his wife, to spark her memory. It doesn't work. He sits for hours in the lounge, watching Fiona, but she just complains, "My, you are persistent." Fiona doesn't know what she is doing anymore. This is very tough on Grant. One can see the anguish etched in his face, especially when he drives Fiona by her favorite places and she doesn't remember. But Grant keeps on visiting, and perhaps even more remarkably, he obviously forgives his wife. In fact, Grant's forgiveness is so complete that, when his wife falls into a deep depression when Aubrey goes home, Grant tries to convince Aubrey's wife to send Aubrey back to the nursing home so that Fiona will be happy again. Grant understands that, at bottom, Fiona just doesn't know. And so he forgives her.

I'm sure you can see where this is going. Just as Grant forgives his unknowing wife, so Jesus forgives the unknowing Pharisees and Romans for what they are doing. Amazing! Of course, if you think about it, what Grant forgives is actually just a tiny hint of what Jesus forgives on the cross. While Fiona can't help not knowing, the Pharisees and the Romans should have known better. The Pharisees, for example, knew that the charges that put Jesus on the cross were trumped up; Pilate understood that the trial was a miscarriage of justice; the Sadducees knew that Jesus had healed the people of all their diseases; the soldiers understood that crucifixion was torture and quite enjoyed raping little Jewish girls and pillaging Jewish wealth. So where Fiona didn't know anything and Grant forgave her, those who crucified Jesus actually knew quite a lot. In fact, perhaps the only thing they didn't really know — though Jesus had certainly told them often enough — was that he was the Son of God.

And yet, while his arms were bound to the cross by rough cords, and nailed to the cross with iron; while his face was matted with blood and his nakedness was visible for all to see; while he was suffering pain that we can barely imagine — that is when Jesus prayed to God to please forgive those who were doing this to him, because they didn't really know who he was, though even the sign on the top of the cross, "King of the Jews," referred to the fact that Jesus had tried to address their ignorance.

"Father, forgive them, for they know not what they do." This is one of the most amazing glimpses of grace in the entire Bible. And I live in hope because, if Jesus could be so gracious to those who crucified him, then he will be gracious to me, too. I live in hope because in those words I can see more clearly than in almost any other place in Scripture what God's true attitude toward humans is.[7] How could I

---

7. Ironically, the passage is not well attested, though there are other passages in Scripture that similarly speak of God's amazing grace for all, even those who do not fol-

ever fear how such a God would treat me when I finally come face to face with him? Even when I am not sure about some doctrines or truths that are hard to know for sure.

"Father, forgive them, for they know not what they do." Amazing to hear such words from the cross, but in a way completely consistent, too, with what Jesus himself had taught:

> But I say to you who hear, love your enemies, do good to those who hate you, bless those who curse you, pray for those who mistreat you. Whoever hits you on the cheek, offer him the other also; and whoever takes away your coat, do not withhold your shirt from him either. (Luke 6:27-29)

Jesus asks us not only that we do to others as we would have them do to us; he also asks us to do as he does.

There are other passages that similarly illuminate God's character. "Come unto me, all ye who are weary and heavy laden, and I will give you rest." "Love keeps no record of wrongs." "All things shall be made new." "And, as in Adam all sinned, so in Christ shall all be saved." This is a God I want to trust, with all my heart.

Yet, as a culture, we've grown used to it. We expect grace, more or less figuring that dispensing grace is God's business. Or we don't think we really need it. We've stopped worrying about hell, not because we don't think it exists, but because even the moral midgets among us think we deserve better. The promise of grace doesn't make our heads spin or our eyes lose focus. I remember, for example, the Sunday I preached my best sermon ever. It was my first summer assignment while I was a student at seminary.

I thought I had outdone myself. My theme was "Saved by Grace." Writing the sermon had been a struggle. I had tried, over and over again, to find the right words to describe the wonder of grace. In the

---

low him. In his textual commentary on the New Testament, Bruce Metzger rates this passage "C," which suggests considerable doubt about whether it comes from the hand of Luke. For a good book on other passages about the surprising extent of God's grace, see Philip Gulley and James Mulholland, *If Grace Is True: Why God Will Save Every Person* (New York: HarperCollins, 2003).

end, I spoke of how grace was more stunning than a 21-gun salute catching a child by surprise. I said grace offered a bigger bang than all of Canada Day's fireworks could, even if they were all shot off at once from one spot. And so on, with several more such illustrations, until I was sure that everyone understood just how amazing grace was.

In the foyer afterwards, an older lady approached me and asked if I was open to some gentle criticism. I saw that I didn't have any choice. "Well," she said, "that sermon was okay, as far as it went. But you fell short when you spoke of grace. You didn't help us really see just how incredible grace really is. You didn't cause my head to spin and my eyes to lose focus like they should when I hear about grace."

Well, my head was spinning and my eyes were losing focus! I took her criticism of my sermon as a personal defeat, at least for a little while. Reflecting on it now, though, I see that she was right. My sermon had fallen short. But I also see now that it really wasn't my fault. The problem is with Jesus' forgiving grace itself. "Father, forgive them, for they do not know." No one can fathom such love. As Paul once said: "May you have power with all God's people to understand Christ's love. May you know how wide and long and high and deep it is. And may you know his love, even though it can't be known completely" (Eph. 3:18-19).

The Past as Future: Living in Hope

Still, how can we live in confidence that such love, such grace, is for us? I think the place to turn to for an answer is the Psalms. When things were at their worst, the psalmists still had hope for the future because of a certain kind of relationship they had with the past.

Psalmists often struggle with a profound sense of God's absence — of hopelessness. Take Psalm 77, for example. "I cry aloud to God," says the psalmist, "that he may hear me" (Ps. 77:1). But far from hearing, God is silent: "Will the Lord spurn forever and never again be favorable? Has his steadfast love ceased forever? Are his promises at an end for all time? Has God forgotten to be gracious?" (vv. 7-9) Is it not a common problem? None of us has ever seen God, and that is a big issue for faith. Doubt and uncertainty are threads woven into every literate Christian's faith.

So when the psalmist cannot connect with God, and when the psalmist is wracked with doubt about God's gracious presence in his life, what then? The Bible contains beautiful promises: "Blessed are the pure in heart, for they shall see God." Or "God will wipe every tear from our eyes, and there will be no more death or mourning or crying or pain." But the psalmist doesn't turn to God's promises. It strikes me that if God seems invisible on account of pain and doubt, then God's promises will seem iffy, too. Doubt makes believing promises and trusting difficult. That's exactly how it was for the psalmist: "Are his promises at an end for all time?" (v. 8).

What happens next, however, is fascinating. When doubt and uncertainty about whether God was still there for Israel ran thick, when promises seem implausible, then the psalmist looks backwards into the unchangeable past. "I will call to mind the deeds of the Lord; I will remember your wonders of old" (v. 11).

"I will remember your wonders of old." The character of a person — his ability to love or her ability to keep a promise or their trustworthiness — is most visible in how he or she has acted in the past. Consider the story of Peter and Joan, married for twenty years. One day they found themselves in the kitchen hurling words at each other like stones, missiles with which both had fully intended to hurt the other. When it was over, Joan and Peter felt like twenty years of marriage had been destroyed in twenty minutes of verbal terrorism. What now? Looking to the future didn't help them — at least for the moment. The fog of war had obscured the future. All they had left was the past, and that is what they turned to. At one point, Joan said something about how Peter was being as dumb now as he had been the first time they had a fight. Peter said that he remembered it differently: Joan had been the obstinate one. In the stony silence that followed, Joan pulled out some old love letters to prove her point. Instead, she laughed at how they had written each other. Peter — still not feeling very happy — asked what was so funny.

She showed him and in spite of his dark mood, Peter couldn't help but smile when Joan read him his old words — about a perfect honeymoon cottage and a more perfect bride. They remembered going to Muskoka and how it had rained all week and how they had loved every minute of their cabin fever. They pulled out a photo album, full of pictures of children growing, houses lived in, and old friends. And slowly, as Joan and Peter talked about the past, they remembered their very own lovely, personal miracles of long ago.

What the psalmist, like every Israelite, remembered with special fondness was how God had safely led Israel out of Egypt through the Red Sea. The psalmist remembered how Pharaoh and all his blood-thirsty hosts had come after the Israelites with murder on their minds, and he remembered how God had saved his people then by showing them a dry way through the Red Sea. "The waters saw you, O God, the waters saw you and writhed. . . . Your thunder was heard in the whirlwind, your lightning lit up the world; the earth trembled and quaked. Your path led through the sea, your way through the mighty waters, though your footprints were not seen" (vv. 16-19).

It is interesting that God's footprints were not seen. No one has ever seen God. But on that day of their salvation the Israelites attributed it to God. And remembering how God dealt with his people in the past gave the psalmist trust for today and hope for tomorrow. The Lord's answer to the psalmist's sense of abandonment was the remembrance of miracles of long ago. All our todays are rooted in our yesterdays. And yesterday, says Scripture, God did great things for us. In Jesus, he died, forgiving even those who did not know what they were doing, though they should have.

What It Means

If the apostle Paul had painted a picture of what the psalmist remembered so vividly, even though it was far in his past, Paul would have entitled it the "baptism into Moses." Paul writes: "I do not want you to be unaware, brothers and sisters, that our ancestors were all under the cloud and all passed through the sea, and all were baptized into Moses in the cloud and in the sea" (1 Cor. 10:1-2).

The phrase "baptism into Moses" is an odd one. It is odd because one does not think of being baptized into people, but into water. And the whole point of the Red Sea story is that the Israelites didn't even get wet. But the meaning of the phrase, given the story of the Exodus that so encouraged the psalmist, is really quite clear: those Israelites "baptized into Moses" were the ones who escaped the terror of the sea on the east and the armies of Pharaoh on the west. Those baptized into Moses were the old men and women, the children and servants, and all the fathers and mothers who watched the sea walls cave in on Pharaoh's army once they themselves had safely passed through. Those baptized into Moses were the Israelites whom God saved by splitting the Red Sea when Moses raised his staff.

The apostle Paul mentions baptism into Moses only once. But he mentions baptism into another person, Jesus, several times. In Romans 6, Paul says, "Don't you know that all of us who were baptized into Jesus Christ were baptized into his death?" And in Galatians 3, Paul says, "All of you who were baptized into Christ have clothed yourselves with Christ. There is neither Jew nor Greek, slave nor free, male nor female, for you are all one in Christ Jesus." Baptism into Jesus means about the same as baptism into Moses does. Those baptized into Moses were the Israelites God redeemed when Moses was God's special ambassador. Those baptized into Jesus are all the people that God redeems through the one greater than Moses, namely Jesus.

Paul actually mentions our being "in" Christ 164 times in the New Testament, out of 384 times that he uses the word "Christ." The church and its people are said to be *in* Christ. So what does that mean? "To be 'in Christ' is to be in the new historical order created by Jesus Christ and kept alive by his Spirit." Again, "being in Christ, then, is to be within the rule of Christ, and within the liberating domination of the Spirit."[8] To be "in Christ" is to be alive today in the world that has been forever changed by the love of one who even forgave those who did not know.

A new situation? A new history? What can this mean? Well, the Bi-

---

8. Lewis B. Smedes, *Union with Christ: A Biblical View of the New Life in Jesus Christ* (Grand Rapids: Eerdmans, 1970), pp. 65-66.

ble speaks of life outside of Christ as life in the flesh, life under the law, and life in sin. Life under the law is unnecessary now that Christ has destroyed the law (Col. 2:14). Paul means that at a certain time and in a certain place, history was changed, or happened, on account of something Jesus did. He nailed the law to the cross. Or again, Paul pictures evil as a cosmic despot who seeks mastery over humans. But at the cross, in demonstrating his love, and at the grave, by rising from the dead, Jesus dethrones the despot and his rule enters a new and vital and vigorous stage. To accept this new rule of Jesus, and to bow before him is to be "in Christ." "Therefore, if anyone is in Christ, he is a new creation; the old has passed away, behold, the new has come" (2 Cor. 5:17).

But a further consequence of being in Christ, Lewis Smedes argues, is that it makes us "part of a program as broad as the universe." This is where faith comes in. As much as our society has made the private and the personal and wealth the key to the meaning and purpose of life, scriptural faith teaches us that, in imitation of Jesus, we should make our neighbors and God central — concerns that put me, myself, and I into proper biblical perspective and into a positive relationship with all those others who do not know. Smedes says:

> The design of Christ's new creation is far too grand, too inclusive to be restricted to what happens inside my soul. No nook or cranny of history is too small for its purpose, no cultural potential too large for its embrace. Being in Christ, we are part of a new movement by his grace, a movement rolling on toward the new heaven and the new earth where all things are made right and where he is all in all.[9]

Ultimately, then, my doubt — and no doubt the ignorance of those who do not know Jesus as even I do — is covered by the love of Jesus, who forgives those who do not know — and those who doubt. And looking back, I see that the new situation Jesus lived and died for has become the ultimate reality of the whole universe. And in imitation of

---

9. Smedes, *Union with Christ,* p. 92.

him, I see my Christian life's purpose as being an ambassador of that new law of love. Even though there is much else I remain unsure of.

Conclusion

There are three matters that still require some reflection, matters related to the powerful influence of the modernist growing fascination with — and the secondary oral tradition's capitulation to — the inner life and experience. The faith nurtured by this experiential focus is often described as having a personal relationship with Jesus. I don't think we can have one. Second, we'll examine the notion that faith is a way of getting out of life what we really want, that faith has cash value, as it were. This, in its own way, is a variation of the notion that faith is all about *my* hopes, dreams, and well-being. Finally, I want to examine how the intersection of legalism, doctrine, and tribalism undermine faith. Then, in the final chapter, I'll sum it all up.

chapter 6

Faith Is Not a Personal Relationship with Jesus

╭╮

What Christians Say

While Irene and I were on our yearlong journey through North America in our RV, we attended many different churches. One of them was a Methodist church in rural Louisiana. Early in the worship service the pastor insisted — not once, but several times — that "the meaning and purpose of life is to have a personal relationship with Jesus."

The claim irked me. As a child I was taught, in keeping with the Reformed bent of my tradition, that the purpose of human life was found in the cultural mandate: it encourages us to rule the garden and love each other to the glory of God (Gen. 1:26). This take on the meaning and purpose of life suggested that creation was somehow incomplete and culturally raw, and both needed to make progress to become all that God wanted them to be. In a sense, the cultural mandate made humans co-regents, even co-creators with God.

At the same time, I was also taught that Christians were supposed to seek justice and defend the cause of the poor, the widows, and the fatherless (Isa. 1:17). Jesus himself taught that the purpose of life is to love God above all and our neighbors as we love ourselves (Matt. 22:36-40). These notions, as honest as they were about human failure, also spurred great bouts of institution-building as we sought through political action groups and church relief agencies to do just these things, in as thoughtful and effective a manner as we could imagine and plan. Jesus also taught — and most of the New Testament illustrates — how Christians are supposed to make disciples and teach them how to obey Jesus: in other words, we were taught that we were supposed to grow the church as an institution. But I never heard while I was growing up, though it may have been whispered, that Christians were supposed to have a personal relationship with Jesus Christ. Such talk would have struck us as soft — probably Pentecostal.

And yet, this sort of language is now very common, even among Christians in the Reformed tradition. I think they take their cue, in part, from the tenor of evangelical Christianity. Rick Warren writes that, "This is what God wants most from you: a relationship!"[1] Henry Blackaby, of "Experiencing God" fame, writes: "Knowing God . . . is a relationship with a Person. It is an intimate love relationship with God."[2] A recent Newsweek/Beliefnet poll suggests that 75 percent of Americans say that a "very important" reason for their faith is to "forge a personal relationship with God."[3]

At the outset, I should say that there is a way of interpreting these words that makes some grammatical sense, though this isn't the sense in which most evangelicals use it. That is, according to orthodox Christian doctrine, Jesus is a person, both human and divine. Thus, when we relate to Jesus the person — through prayer perhaps, or through obedience to his command to love God and neighbor, or even by accepting the proposition that he died so that we could live — it might be said that we have a personal relationship with him. But I don't think that's what most people mean when they say that they have a personal relationship with Jesus. Most often, I think, people use the phrase "personal relationship" in a much plainer sense: they mean that they relate to Jesus very much like they relate to other people they know.

Philip Yancey's discussion of a personal relationship with God is a

1. Rick Warren, *The Purpose Driven Life* (Grand Rapids: Zondervan, 2004), p. 70.

2. Henry Blackaby and Claude V. King, *Experiencing God: Knowing and Doing the Will of God* (Mukati, the Philippines: Church Strengthening Ministry, n.d.).

3. Newseek/Beliefnet Poll Results: http://www.beliefnet.com/News/2005/08/Newsweekbeliefnet-Poll-Results.aspx (accessed Jan. 22, 2009).

good example of this common usage, but also of its problems. In his book *Reaching for the Invisible God*, Yancey echoes a long list of evangelical leaders since the Great Awakening by describing a personal relationship with Jesus as if it really were a "two people physically in the same room experience." Yancey writes that "getting to know God" is a lot like getting to know a person: "You spend time together, whether happy or sad. You laugh together. You weep together. You fight and argue, then reconcile." But a little later he notes that this is not as easy as it sounds. Jesus is not, after all, physically present. So Yancey adds that with God we shouldn't expect a relationship between equals. The problem, he says, is that we want God to be like us — tangible, material, perceptible, audible — while God "shows little interest in corresponding on our level."[4] But if God shows little interest in corresponding on our level, then how do we spend time together, laugh together, weep together, fight and argue and reconcile together? Why would you call such a relationship a personal relationship?

To give Yancey full credit, he does feel the weight of these awkward questions. He tries to resolve the problem through indirection. A relationship with God, he says, is like a relationship with a spouse you love but are not with. You miss your spouse; your heart grows fonder, so much so that you feel the absence of the spouse as a sort of presence. Well, perhaps. But again, this absence of someone you love as a mysterious presence sounds more like postmodern rhetorical criticism, like a search for what is lost in the traces, than the sort of "personal relationship" Yancey began by describing.

Telescoping his exasperation with such objections, Yancey also offers a brief summary of philosopher Alvin Plantinga's notion that belief in God is properly basic.[5] Plantinga's work is erudite and persuasive. Even so, a dense, closely argued, philosophical justification for the appropriateness of belief in God, which is what Yancey is referring to here, isn't the same as an actual personal relationship with God the way Yancey first describes it, even if it does fit well with the more

---

4. Philip Yancey, *Reaching for the Invisible God: What Can We Expect to Find?* (Grand Rapids: Zondervan, 2000), pp. 108, 110.

5. Yancey, *Reaching*, p. 103.

scholarly approach to faith that I'm used to in my bookish, modernist tradition. The mention of Plantinga, famous for his philosophical argument for the existence of God, reminds me that others have covered this ground before Yancey. In his *Proslogion,* eleventh-century theologian Saint Anselm of Canterbury complains, in the fashion of the psalmists, that God doesn't seem very personal. In fact, God seems far, far away.

> I have never seen thee, O Lord my God; I do not know thy form. . . . What shall thy servant do, anxious in his love of thee, and cast out afar from thy face? He pants to see thee, and thy face is too far from him. He longs to come to thee, and thy dwelling place is inaccessible. . . . Heavy loss, heavy grief, heavy all our fate!

God responds to this prayer by revealing to Anselm a famous philosophical proof for the existence of God known as the ontological argument. One commentator notes: "Even if it is a sound proof, however, it is a far cry from the explicit personal love from God for which he longs."[6]

Academics, aware of the problems that go with having a personal, vital, immediate relationship with Jesus do not always resort to philosophy. Sometimes they water down their definition for what would count as a personal relationship. Clark Pinnock tells the story of how a note reading, "From about half past ten in the evening to about half an hour after midnight, Fire," was found pinned to the inside of Blaise Pascal's coat when he died. The note seems to speak of a dramatic experience Pascal had and wanted to remind himself of. Pinnock goes on to say that not everyone has this intense and numinous kind of encounter with God.

> At the other end of a spectrum is the quiet ordinary perception of the goodness and mystery of existence. In essence religious experience is rooted in a sense of wonder at the awesomeness of being

---

6. Quoted in Daniel Howard-Snyder and Paul K. Moser, *Introduction: Divine Hiddenness:* http://www.ac.wwu.edu/howardd/hiddennessintro.html.

which leaves us feeling dependent upon something unconditioned, something which is the source of all reality. Though by no
means easy to define, and more intensely felt at some times than
at others, it is a human experience widely attested and lying at the
background of our lives most the time.[7]

Experiences like Pascal's are not what most evangelicals are talking
about when they insist on the necessity of a personal relationship
with Jesus. But Pinnock's alternative, a feeling of being "dependent
upon something unconditioned," certainly isn't what Yancey is talking
about either. And since Pinnock gives quite a bit of weight to "a
widely attested human experience," he also raises the question of
what we are to think of followers of traditional African religions, Hindus, or Muslims who have this experience as well. So we're left with
trying to account for the plain sense of what evangelicals seem to be
saying when they speak of a personal relationship that is pretty much
the same kind of relationship they have with other people. Jesus
speaks, they listen. They hurt, Jesus comforts. Jesus walks, they follow. They are not sure, Jesus reveals. He's with them all the time. He's
as close as the rest of the family. What can evangelicals mean by this?

Not a Shared Experience

At least some committed, believing evangelical Christians do not
claim to have this sort of personal relationship with Jesus. Some,
given the insistence that such a relationship is essential, are actually
concerned and confused by such claims. Consider, for example, the
contemporary Christian artist Chris Rice, who in a song about faith
admits that when it comes to finding God, he's never seen the signs
that other people claim to have seen. And in the chorus he sings of
faith that "finding You is like trying to smell the color nine."[8]

---

7. Clark Pinnock, *Reason Enough: A Case for the Christian Faith* (Downers Grove, IL:
InterVarsity, 1980), p. 41.
    8. Chris Rice, "Smell the Color 9," *Short Term Memories*. Rocketown Records, 2004.

Rice is saying that while he "simply believes," he feels somewhat estranged from other Christians because he isn't having the sort of experiences they claim to have, and that seem consistent with having a personal relationship — signs, revelations, or even a simple word. This, by the way, is a problem that I suspect many young people, in particular, wrestle with when they are told they have to have a personal relationship. In the absence of some personal sense that Jesus is speaking to me or walking by my side, some teens just don't know what to make of peers or teachers who say, with my Methodist preacher friend, that some such sort of experience is the most important thing.

As pervasive as the language of "personal relationship" has become, it confuses many Christians. As a pastor, I met quite a few people who experienced doubt, or perhaps anger, because they didn't experience Jesus the way their Christian friends seemed to. They can't say they've felt his presence, listened to his voice, or argued with him. After a while they begin to feel left out, like the only person at a Pentecostal worship service who isn't speaking in tongues. I've had people in my office who are caught between worship that wasn't connecting for them and a spouse for whom exactly that kind of worship was the sine qua non of life. They feel deficient, as if they're missing something essential to their well-being. And they feel like frauds, because the very frequency and offhand familiarity of "personal-relationship-with-God" talk creates rhetorical pressure to conform, to nod, to say "yes, I know what you mean," when they don't, and to act as if such a relationship is the universal reality of all Christians.

Furthermore, if such language confuses Christians, imagine what non-Christians must think of it. They know Jesus hasn't walked on the earth for nearly 2,000 years. Even if they were to grant the possibility of what conservative Christians confess, namely that Jesus is now sitting in his human flesh at the right hand of God the Father, unbelievers also know that there isn't any mail or phone service between God's throne and our homes. For most such people, talk of a personal relationship with Jesus must seem as unlikely and strange as New Age talk of channeling spirits from other planets or dimensions.

A little historical perspective might be helpful here. This is actually a very old problem that has surfaced over and over again for literate Christians, such as Anselm, who cannot, on the one hand, live in an enchanted world anymore, but who have tried, on the other hand, to rationalize Christianity, but now miss the experiential aspect of faith. For example, one of the things that Puritans are remembered for is that they believed that real Christians should have powerful, unmistakable conversion experiences that would set their hearts at ease about the presence of God in their lives and transform them with the desire to live a holy life. As it turned out, however, many of them just never had this required conversion experience. And it wasn't for lack of trying. They were baptized as infants, believed as children, went to church for a lifetime, and prayed for the experience daily; but having never received it, they never made the "profession of faith" that was required to take up full responsibilities and privileges of their church membership.

One such privilege that only confessing members enjoyed was permission to baptize their children. Now, if my church were to say to me, "You can't baptize your children here because you have not had the requisite religious experience, in spite of hoping for it all your life," I'd leave that church for one that would be a bit more understanding of my own faith journey. It is a mark of the religious stubbornness of these Puritans that enough of them hung in there with churches that wouldn't allow them to be full members that some of them started practicing what has become known as the "halfway covenant." For the sake of the church's institutional survival, nonconfessing church members were finally allowed to baptize their children, in the hope, I suppose, that the children would have the conversion experience that the parents might have longed for but never had themselves. In the end, however, the failure of so many good Puritans to have the proper conversion experience contributed more to that church's demise than the halfway covenant did to bolster it.[9]

---

9. A good summary of the controversy can be found in Sidney E. Ahlstrom, *A Religious History of the American People* (New Haven: Yale University Press, 1972), pp. 158-65.

Secular Language Transforms
Christian Hopes and Expectations

The language of personal relationship with Jesus has at least as much to do with secular culture's influence on Christianity as it has to do with the Bible. Charles Taylor notes that "a striking feature of the Western march toward secularity is that it has been interwoven from the start with this drive toward personal religion, as has frequently been remarked."[10] Robert Bellah argues that the language of "personal relationship" especially flourished when, in the nineteenth century, "science seemed to have dominated the explanatory schemas of the external world, [and in response] morality and religion took refuge in human subjectivity, in feeling and sentiment."[11] By this account, the triumph of science meant that faith had to make a strategic retreat to private experience.

Indeed, today's secondary oral society is one where experience and feeling reign, for reasons I have examined in chapter 4. It is worth repeating, however, that religion freed from some of the rational and linear constraints of modernity becomes extremely uncritical in its choice of sources, authority, or even good sense. Syncretism leading to "designer religions" is common. As religion retreats from the world of linear rationality, it seeks a home in experience, as does much of contemporary secondary oral life. Some even call it the "experience" economy. Marketing mogul Marilyn Carlson Nelson puts it this way:

> Anyone who views a sale as a transaction is going to be toast down the line. Selling is not about peddling a product. It's about wrapping that product in a service — and about selling both the product and the service as an experience. That approach to selling helps create a vital element of the process: a relationship. In a world where things move at hyper speed, what was relevant yes-

10. Charles Taylor, *Varieties of Religion Today: William James Revisited* (Cambridge, MA: Harvard University Press, 2002), p. 13.

11. Robert Bellah et al., *Habits of the Heart: Individualism and Commitment in American Life* (Berkeley: University of California Press, 1985), p. 46.

terday may not be relevant tomorrow. But one thing that endures is a dynamic relationship that is grounded in an experience that you've provided.[12]

Our society is individualistic and competitive at home, at work, and in the public square. People can easily feel beat up. Our society is also a materialistic one, full of cars and furniture and boats and clothes and toys. Yet none of these things satisfies our longing to get in touch with that genuine trace of God's divine image that still exists somewhere deep inside each of us. Our society is full of people who don't live where they grew up, whose families and friends are on the other end of the continent, and who now feel disconnected. The inability to trust, which is a result of repeated dislocations, is becoming a common experience. These days everyone longs for a divine connection that will ease the pain of their human dislocation in the midst of so much material plenty. We are waifs when it comes to meaning, unable to engage the accumulated wisdom that can be found in any library or tradition. Instead, we look for it in endless miles of shopping-mall corridors or computer game avatars. Since we have eternity set in our hearts, we want an epiphany: we want to experience God. And I suspect that that longing is enough for a lot of people to mistake just about any intuition or good thought or warm fuzziness for being Jesus. Jonathan Sachs says that in this situation people will go far to get that personal relationship:

Vast swaths of personal relationship have been commodified and offered for sale in a seemingly endless proliferation of new services: counselors, spiritual guides, personal trainers, style advisers, shopping consultants, massage therapists, aromatherapists, aerobics instructors, exercise class leaders — the whole spectrum of what Robert Reich calls "paying for attention."[13]

12. Marilyn Carlson Nelson, quoted in Leonard Sweet, *Postmodern Pilgrims: First Century Passion for the 21st Century World* (Nashville: Broadman and Holman, 2000), p. 32.
13. Jonathan Sachs, *The Dignity of Difference: How to Avoid the Clash of Civilizations* (New York: Continuum, 2002), p. 77.

Leonard Sweet writes: "Moderns want to figure out what life's about; postmoderns want to experience what life is"[14] Therefore, tourism — not automobile manufacturing — is the U.S.'s largest export industry and its second-largest employer (after health). Why? Because tourism is an experience industry. And as far as the automotive sector is concerned, don't forget how an ad for BMW cars puts it: "Engineering. Science. Technology. All worthless . . . unless they make you feel something."

Marsha Witten probably says it best:

Secularity is affecting the internal contents of religion — its ideology, speech, and practice — forcing it to undergo serious changes. In this view, modern culture exacts a toll from traditional religious beliefs, articulations, and behavior, elbowing religious tenets and pronouncements into increasing conformity with the norms of the secular world. Topics of elemental religious concern — the nature of God and his relationship to humankind . . . [are] subject to adaptation as religion strives to make its place within modern secular culture.[15]

Witten is not alone in understanding that modern secularity transforms the language, and thus the inner workings of today's religions. Charles Taylor, reviewing the import of William James for today, observes:

All experiences require some vocabulary, and these are inevitably in large part handed to us in the first place by our society, whatever transformations we may ring on them later. The ideas, the understanding with which we live our lives, shape directly what

14. Sweet, *Postmodern Pilgrims*, p. 33. Sweet can be faulted, perhaps, for his division of history into modern and postmodern phases without distinguishing between postmodernism as an academic movement and the secondary oral tradition as a contemporary Zeitgeist subject to some postmodern influences. Postmoderns tend to be academics; secondary oral people, though heavily influenced by some postmodern cultural trends, are not necessarily postmodern themselves.

15. Marsha Witten, *All Is Forgiven: The Secular Message in American Protestantism* (Princeton, NJ: Princeton University Press, 1993), p. 6.

we could call religious experience; and these languages, these vo-
cabularies, are never those simply of an individual.[16]

Ultimately, Witten points out that contemporary North American
Christianity, including evangelicalism, has traded the theological and
linear language of religious conversion, sin, and repentance for the language of personal relationship. The language of personal relationship
fits the experience economy; the traditional language of conversion, of
trading faiths via a dying to oneself, does not. The language of personal
relationship also fits with the contemporary suspicion of institutions
and authority. Finally, it also allows people to believe whatever they
want to believe apart from the constraints of tradition or rationality. A
personal relationship, after all, is *my* relationship; therefore, *I* define it.

The bottom line is that the huge emphasis contemporary evangelicals put on a great personal experience of and with Jesus as the be all
and end all of Christian faith has little or nothing to do with Scripture
and everything to do with taking from our culture what it thinks human happiness is all about. Commenting on the need for an inner experience, David Wells notes:

> There is an irony in all of this that appears to be entirely lost on
> those at the heart of it. They labor under the illusion that the God
> they make in the image of the self becomes more real as he more
> nearly comes to resemble the self, to accommodate its needs and
> desires. The truth is quite the opposite. It is ridiculous to assert
> that God could become more real by abandoning his own charac-
> ter in an effort to identify more completely with ours. And yet the
> illusion has proved compelling to a whole generation.[17]

Thus the language of personal relationship is also highly idiosyncratic. Since there is no theological consensus on what a personal relationship is, and since different religious denominations — institutions that might once have offered reflection and direction rooted in

16. Charles Taylor, *Varieties*, pp. 27, 28.
17. David Wells, *God in the Wasteland: The Reality of Truth in a World of Fading Dreams*
(Grand Rapids: Eerdmans, 1994), pp. 100-101.

their traditions — don't have an official teaching on what such a relationship would be, we've drifted into a position that a personal relationship means whatever the individual wants it to mean. People who claim to have a personal relationship with Jesus are, like many secondary oral people, creating their own designer religion away from the constraints of traditional learning and authority.

The Bible on Personal Relationships

So what does Scripture say about personal relationships with God? On the one hand, Scripture speaks powerfully about the providential nearness of God. God is David's shepherd and restores his soul (Ps. 23). God promises Israel that when she passes through waters or fire, he will be with her (Isa. 43:1-5). Similarly, Jesus promises that where two or three come together in his name, he will also be there (Matt. 18:20). While Paul is in Corinth, Jesus appears to him in a vision and promises him safety, saying "for I am with you" (Acts 18:10), much as he promises to be with the apostles to the end of the age as they teach and baptize (Matt. 28:20).

In a different vein, however, Jesus suggests that he is most present to us when we receive others in a Christ-like manner. "He who receives you receives me, and he who receives me receives the one who sent me. . . . And if anyone gives even a cup of cold water to one of these little ones because he is my disciple, I tell you the truth, he will certainly not lose his reward" (Matt. 10:40-42). Such teaching is important. But a relationship between persons is not always a personal relationship in the way that the phrase is usually used — perhaps always used — in our cultural settings. Providential nearness is usually not what people using the phrase are talking about.

Ironically, the Bible also speaks often about God's distance. Notwithstanding Psalm 23, God's presence to David was not so personal that God was able to advise him about Bathsheba or counting soldiers or how to raise Absalom. And the prophets insist on God's providential presence in Israel because the Israelites themselves cannot sense it, as they stumble from one disaster to another. God's presence to the apostles, after the ascension of Jesus, is only via visions like Paul's, or Peter's in Joppa, or John's on Patmos. In one such vision, while Paul is in Corinth (Acts 18), Jesus assures Paul that he is watching over him. One assumes that Jesus needed to say that, because otherwise Paul might not sense Jesus' presence.

The Gospel of John actually wrestles with what the personal absence of Jesus will mean for his followers. "I am with you for only a short time," says Jesus, "and then I go to the one who sent me. You will look for me, but you will not find me; and where I am, you cannot come" (John 7:33, 34; 8:21). It sounds like Jesus is saying that we cannot have a personal relationship with him in anything like the way we assume we will have personal relationships with anyone else. This should, at the very least, make us very cautious about describing a personal relationship, as Yancey does, using the language of personal presence. Jesus shows himself personally to Thomas; but you can almost hear the ache in Jesus' voice when he speaks of those who are alive today, who have not had the kind of personal encounter Thomas did. "You [Thomas] believe because you have seen. But blessed are those who have not seen, and yet believe" (John 20:29).

God's presence, even when, according to the Exodus story, it is experienced directly, also happens to be ambiguous and hard to trust. When the pillar of fire by night, and cloud by day, accompanied Israel to the Promised Land, speaking loudly of God's presence, Israel did not trust in God or make a choice for obedience because of that. In the New Testament, God came to humans in the flesh — in the form of Jesus — but it was so ambiguous a presence that, while Jesus walked on earth, few recognized him. Even the disciples, who had the closest of personal relationships with Jesus, barely understood him until after the resurrection.

In the absence of Jesus, who has ascended into heaven, we do have something else, of course: the presence of the Holy Spirit, which was made known to us at Pentecost. Jesus says, "I will not leave you as orphans; I will come to you" (John 14:18). A chapter later, Jesus explains: "When the Counselor comes, whom I will send to you from the Father, the Spirit of truth who goes out from the Father, he will testify about me" (John 15:26). "Unless I go away, the Counselor will not come" (John 16:7). Most doctrine of the Holy Spirit turns on such texts, insisting that God is most present to us through the illuminating work of the Spirit as we search God's word, Scripture. Furthermore, the testimony of many Christians through the ages is that the Spirit's presence can be mysteriously and wonderfully known.

But as a spirit, the Holy Spirit's interaction with us is also ephemeral. Jesus makes a point of telling us that, though the Spirit is real and powerful, it does not make itself known to us 24/7. "The wind blows where it chooses, and you hear the sound of it, but you do not know where it comes from or where it goes. So it is with everyone who is born of the Spirit" (John 3:8). All of which is both wonderful but also achingly not quite enough. As a follower of Jesus, I want more. The sum of the matter, as far as the Bible goes, is this. We have a kind of relationship with God: he is the creator, we are the creatures; Jesus the savior, we the saved; the Spirit reveals the truth, but only if we read Scripture. While Scripture claims that God longs to embrace us, and has set in motion Christ events that will allow him to do just that, we live before the consummation. We try to interpret Scripture correctly, but our differing interpretations have split the church into thousands of splinters. We want to love perfectly, but anger, misunderstanding, and fear drive us apart. We pray every day for peace in the Middle East and elsewhere, but for two thousand years those prayers have gone mostly unanswered. We want the same kind of personal relationship with Jesus that we have with a beloved spouse or child. But we cannot have one.

Antidotes

In the face of all this longing, I want to resist the temptation to impose on God my own imperfect definition of what an epiphany must be like. Just seeing the back of God was just about more than Moses could stand. Even when God showed Abraham all the stars of heaven and walked with him through the sacrificed cows, Abraham laughed at the promise of a son. Elijah's encounter was through a sound that came to him out of sheer silence. An angel touched Mary, Joseph, and the Bethlehem shepherds, and it put the *fear* of God into them. Not one of these encounters was sentimental or romantic; not one of them offered guidance concerning career choices, purchasing priorities, or college plans — those kinds of things I've often heard Christians claim Jesus has revealed to them. In fact, I think that by insisting on a personal relationship, as if God were just another pal, we are making God small, sizing him to fit our social construction of what a God should be like if we could have any God we wanted.

We should beware of falling into the trap of thinking we need to have a certain kind of (hyped) experience to know that we're Christians (or that there is a God). The hoped-for experience isn't necessarily going to be available to everyone. Ruth Tucker describes the "thaw" in the midwinter of faith:

> Those who are troubled by a sense of abandonment and silence need not strive for a summery spirituality — nor need they contemplate the option of walking away from the faith. There is a place for them on the barren wintry landscape, where the January thaw may provide a welcome respite. But "the spiritual January thaw will not last," writes [Martin] Marty. "Enjoy the warmth and sound it brings, the heart tells itself, but know that this is not a dispelling of winter, only an interruption."[18]

We must come to grips with the fact that "personal relationship" means many different things to nearly everybody by acknowledging this variety in our homes, churches, and denominations. I am not a great fan of Fowler's six-stage approach to faith, but it seems to me that his work is, at the very least, a reminder that not everyone is at the same place when it comes to faith, and we need to work with that by avoiding generalizations about what a personal relationship with God has to be.[19] We especially need to avoid the trap of making some fellow believers feel less than Christian, or uncool, or overly holy, or

18. Ruth Tucker, *Walking Away from Faith: Unraveling the Mystery of Belief and Unbelief* (Downers Grove, IL: InterVarsity, 2002), p. 164.

19. James W. Fowler, *Stages of Faith: The Psychology of Human Development* (New York: HarperCollins, 1981).

whatever, because they have or have not arrived by experiencing the right kind of personal relationship. As Christians, we also need to come to terms with God's absence. Jesus is not present in the flesh. God has not rearranged the stars to say, "I exist." One presumes it would be easy for him to do so.

And, as far as we can see, Jesus is also not present to prevent human suffering. I've tried to be a pastor to parents who have just had a Down syndrome child. After a car accident, I had to officiate at the funeral of a man's wife and only child. I've seen hundreds of rotting bodies — victims of genocide — in a little church in Nterama, Rwanda. And readers will all have their own stories to add. For such situations we need to recover the psalmist's language of lament: "You have taken my companions and loved ones from me; the darkness is my closest friend" (Ps. 88:18). And here ends the psalm, the psalmist's fist raised to heaven, because God certainly is not present. In a world full of suffering, injustice, and inequity, we need more of the psalmists who cry out to God with raised fist because he seems absent than we need people glibly speaking about their personal relationship with God.

We need to recover the psalmist's language of lament because it fairly represents how we should feel about Jesus' absence till he comes again to make all things new. This is especially true, I think, for our young people. We all know the dual phenomena of young people desiring both reassuring and intense experiences, including intense and reassuring worship experiences. Leonard Sweet describes "postmodern pilgrims" as people who not only want "all is well with my soul" worship, but also worship that cries out to God to come again and make all things new, because they are not all right now. I'm not against experience; I just want to make sure that it is connected to our tradition's deepest wells rather than individual and subjective interpretations of feelings that are characteristic, not of faith, but of secondary orality's inability to delve deep or long. Interestingly enough, it isn't just older folks who question contemporary worship's inability to occur in anything other than praise mode. Seventeen-year-old Marjorie Corbman recently wrote a surprise evangelical bestseller entitled *A Tiny Step Away from Deepest Faith*. She comments on her use of an old Christian liturgy for morning prayers: "I gush over the liturgy, over a thousand years old, to whoever will listen . . . [including] Christians of various denominations sick of contemporary Christian music that can sound more like love ballads than hymns of worship."[20]

But finally, what about the language of faith? In an odd way, saying you have a personal relationship with Jesus makes faith unnecessary, doesn't it? And given Scripture's overwhelming interest in faith, to the complete exclusion of insisting one have a "personal relationship" with God, what I'd really like to see is a revival in the language of faith. I would like to suggest that, rather than saying, "I have a personal relationship with Jesus," we say instead, "I believe in Jesus." Or, at least, "I try to believe in Jesus." The bottom line is that faith is what we need precisely when there isn't the black-and-white certainty that goes with a personal relationship, as most people understand such things. Unlike Thomas, we who believe today are blessed when we have not ever seen Jesus or heard his voice or touched his wounds (John 20:29). We are blessed, in the end, because we don't have a personal relationship, but believe anyway. This is the language of the Beatitudes; in fact, I sometimes think of the blessing Jesus gave Thomas as the tenth Beatitude. People who have not seen and yet believe — people of faith — are like the poor, those who hunger, those who weep, and those who are persecuted. They are in a very tough spot. They are experiencing the fallout of sin in a broken world. But somehow they are getting along anyway. They are blessed because the kingdom of God will, one day, be all in all. But not now. And they cannot miraculously evade the experience of Jesus' absence and the conviction his absence requires by claiming a personal relationship. Therefore,

> [faith] contains the notion of distance between the deity and man. . . . It suggests a reaching beyond experience, even a holding on against experience; it speaks of a trust which can at times become totally blind; and it has the undertone of the "not yet," of living by a promise.[21]

20. Marjorie Corbman, *A Tiny Step Away from Deepest Faith: A Teenager's Search for Meaning* (Brewster, MA: Paraclete Press, 2005), p. 52.

21. Hendrikus Berkhof, *Christian Faith: An Introduction to the Study of Faith* (Grand Rapids: Eerdmans, 1979), p. 16.

So where the language of personal relationship has a very questionable pedigree rooted in secular pressures to demythologize God, as well as a therapeutic culture that wants to turn God into a warm fuzzy, the language of faith is deeply rooted in Scripture. Whereas the language of personal relationship is always ambiguous and inexact, meaning whatever the speaker happens to privately mean, the language of faith is deeply examined, as two thousand years of reflection and shelf after shelf of books in any theological library will attest. Whereas the language of personal relationship sounds, on the face of it, implausible or perhaps even impossible, at least as far as the plain sense of such language goes, the language of faith serves as an invitation to ponder mystery and overcome unbelief. The apostle John put it this way: "This is [God's] command: to believe in the name of his Son, Jesus Christ, and to love one another as he commanded us" (1 John 3:23). Faith — whether as intellectual assent or trust or a concrete love for whoever is your neighbor of the hour — is Christ's own invitation to get into a proper relationship with him.

chapter 7

Faith Has No Cash Value

~*~

The Dreamers

Some years ago I wrote a little story to illustrate a sermon on keeping the faith. At the time I liked the story quite a bit. Now I'm not so sure. It goes like this:

Once upon a time, in a faraway land, there lived some dreamers who dreamed of a Promised Land where the sun shone warm, the rains came in their season, and a refreshing breeze always blew. In the dreamers' Promised Land green forests kept tune to choirs of singing birds and valleys wore the colors of a hundred different kinds of wildflowers.

When the dreamers awoke, they decided to sail to the Promised Land of their dreams. So they built themselves a ship and cast off. As they left the harbor, all the diamonds in this world that meant anything to the dreamers were conjured up merely by the sunlight sparkling on the sea.

Soon, however, the sailing turned out to be a disappointment. Many dreamers became seasick, and those who didn't were too busy sailing the ship to do much nursing. Many of the dreamers were so miserable, then, that they hardly had the energy to dream their dream.

A few days later, just when most of the crew was feeling better, the ship fell into the grip of a wild storm. The dreamers feared for their lives then, and were so busy fighting to survive that they hardly had time, anymore, to sleep or dream. The Promised Land faded from view.

Finally, though, the storm also passed. For a few hours, most of the dreamers even dared believe in the Promised Land again. Unfortunately, when the stars came out, they realized that the gale had blown them far off course. So they had a meeting. Some of the dreamers still spoke passionately of their dream and of the Promised Land. But others pointed to the torn sails and tangled lines and battered masts. They worried about dwindling supplies and spoke of scurvy.

In the end the crew chose to give up their quest and sail for the nearest port. The dream would just have to wait; they had lost faith.

Just then, when it seemed that things couldn't be any worse, the dreamers' ship was becalmed. After the seasickness and the howling storms and the decision to give up, the wind stopped blowing. And as day followed day and the relentless sun beat down on them, the water ran low and the food disappeared and the dreamers stopped dreaming altogether and sank into despair.

Then some of the crew raised their fists to heaven, and shouted, "How long, O spinner of dreams? Will you forget us forever? How long will you hide your face from us?"

Some others, feeling sorry, wept and whispered, "How long must I wrestle with my thoughts and every day have sorrow in my heart?"

Still others blamed the captain, or the mate, or the chaplain. They muttered, "How long will my enemies triumph over me?" As they pondered their painful lot, the dreamers were reduced to bitter remorse.

Only a very few of the dreamers still managed to dream — briefly, in snatches, and during troubled sleep. They would come on deck afterwards and search the horizon. One day, one of them noticed a bit of flotsam drift by the ship. And it made her think.

She looked up into the sky then, and watched a gull lazily floating by. And she realized that these things — the flotsam and the bird — were rumors of glory.

And so it was that the dreamers — and even those who no longer could — learned that, even when the wind doesn't blow, the sea currents flow. Even as the crew raised their fists to heaven, the ship kept on drifting along the Gulf Stream to the Promised Land. Out of the depths of their despair, the dreamers learned to have faith in the unfailing love of the spinner of dreams.

I first published this story as a sermon on the nature and quality of faith and hope in *Pulpit Digest*.[1] A few months later I ran into an old friend, who had read the sermon in a library and had been so moved by it that he wept over it right there in the stacks. He told me that the sermon's conclusion gave him hope during a very troubled time in his life. What could I say? I was glad that my sermon had made a difference.

The story is sweet, even if a bit melodramatic. Unfortunately, I cannot preach it in this form anymore. The last time I did, I realized that I felt as if I was duping the congregation. Is it true that even when the wind stops blowing the sea currents will nevertheless always continue to flow for people of faith? Do all believers — say, those in Zimbabwe — really get the miracles they dream about? I'm not sure you could convince a friend of mine of that, a Zimbabwean refugee who spent months in the hospital as a result of two murder attempts by Zanu-PF goons. Or what about the Christians who died in what they thought would be the safety of church grounds in Rwanda, mowed down in a racist genocide in which their pastor was complicit? Did they get their miracles? "The Dreamers" is a heartwarming story, but lately I find it difficult to assume that all journeys begun in faith and hope end well enough. My faith in happy endings is not as confident as it used to be.

---

1. John Suk, "The Dreamers," *Pulpit Digest* (January/February 1993): 49-52.

Pragmatic Faith

"The Dreamers" embodies a kind of spiritualized version of modernity's faith in progress. The progress here, however, is not the progress that society as a whole will make with the aid of science, but the progress individuals can make if only they make use of the right religious methodology. So, if we pray frequently enough, and with enough vigor, and with enough prayer partners, and with enough certainty — we will get what we want. If we have enough faith he will heal us (as well as our aunts, in-laws, and coworkers) of all diseases. And if we behave in this life while believing in God, we will also earn our final just reward — eternal life. Altogether, when viewed this way, faith is actually very useful. It has, as William James would say, cash value.[2] I call it pragmatic faith.

Pragmatism, according to Baldwin's old dictionary of philosophy, is the prescription "of the means necessary to the attainment of happiness." When it comes to religion, pragmatism often credits faith for its wonderful, practical, desirable results, such as unity, healing, emotional health, or even racial reconciliation. What the pragmatic believer — often unconsciously — values isn't so much the truth or doctrines; no, what matters is the church's usefulness. Putting it a bit more theoretically, William James says: "If theological ideas prove to have a value for concrete life, they will be true, for pragmatism, in the sense of being good for so much."[3] He thinks of pragmatism like a hallway that gets us to where we want to go. Or perhaps like a ship that gets us to the far shore.

The expectation that faith, whether understood as a way of life, as it was in the oral enchanted era, or understood as acceptance of certain propositions about God, as was more common in modernism, should result in some kind of special favor has actually been part of nearly every religion for a long time. John Bright, who wrote the classic book *The Kingdom of God*, points out that this pragmatic attitude to-

2. William James, *Pragmatism*, Great Books in Philosophy (Buffalo: Prometheus Books, 1991; first published in 1907), p. 26.

3. James, *Pragmatism*, pp. 35, 32.

ward faith was already present in ancient pagan religions. In the following passage he reflects on the fact that the Jews have been exiled from their homeland in Israel to Babylon.

> The pagan, be he ancient or modern, will understand it as the function of religion *to repay him in tangible terms for his worship.* He will desire this cozy understanding with his god: that his prayers will return him protection, his dollars more dollars. Nor will he be likely to stick with a religion that does not do this. It was a great temptation, therefore, for a Jew — in whose paganized mind Yahweh had failed him — simply to sink into the background and cease to be a Jew. No doubt many did.[4]

Jesus himself said, in a very enigmatic passage, that if we but had faith as large as that of a mustard seed we could tell mountains to throw themselves into the sea. As far as I can tell, no one has ever had faith that large, though there have been occasions when moving mountains before they erupted or before landslides buried the people who lived below them would have been a great blessing. In a Christian novel from the 1950s, Grace Irwin describes what happens to the faithful — in this case, Andrew Connington, a businessman and grandfather of the novel's hero — when they live their faith as they should and God desires.

> His conversion meant more to Connington than he could ever put into words, though, in time, he became a lay preacher and exhorted class-meetings and larger gatherings with quiet fervor. His business, too, prospered unpredictably. As it enlarged, he hired assistants from among his new friends at the City Road Chapel; and their industry and thrift rewarded him with increased financial returns. His success, the more remarkable because an awakened conscience forbade him to profit by the unprotected child labour then customary, was attributed by him to

---

4. John Bright, *The Kingdom of God* (Nashville: Abingdon, 1953), p. 131 (emphasis added).

Divine Providence and accepted as responsibility for which he must render strict account.[5]

Extreme forms of pragmatic faith are found in what is sometimes called the health-and-wealth gospel. Megachurch pastor Joel Osteen preaches: "Your praise is sending out your faith. That's allowing God to arrange things in your favor." He continues: "God is not moved by our tears . . . but God is moved by our faith. . . . When you get your faith out there that is what moves God."[6] Osteen means, of course, that such faith moves God to move things in the believer's favor. Kenneth Copeland, another television evangelist, thinks of faith as some kind of spiritual force. As "the force of gravity . . . makes the law of gravity work . . . this force of faith . . . makes the laws of the spirit world function."[7] In a recent Internet posting he explains how this faith-force fixed ruptured discs in his back: "That's the kind of thing that happens when we make the faith connection. We open the door to THE BLESSING of God and His goodness pours into our lives. Sickness becomes health. Poverty becomes wealth. We start living like the overcomers God made us to be."[8] Copeland preaches a gospel that equates the depth of believers' faith with the worldly success they are likely to experience. And he suggests that one excellent measure of the depth of one's faith is the size of one's gifts to Copeland's ministry.

Osteen and Copeland are two of the more dramatic examples of health-and-wealth approaches to Christian faith. In general, however, most North American Christians think of faith at least in partly pragmatic terms, much as I have for most of my life. Many Christians seem to think that God has some special kindness in store for them if only they'll believe it or in him; he will nudge them toward success if only they'll look to him for it. So, for example, Alan Wolfe rather humor-

5. Grace Irwin, *Least of All Saints* (Grand Rapids: Eerdmans, 1957), p. 12.
6. http://www.dailymotion.com/video/x7lazu_joel-osteen-says-if-you-believe-all_webcam.
7. Kenneth Copeland, *The Laws of Prosperity* (Fort Worth, TX: Kenneth Copeland Publications, 1974), pp. 18-19.
8. "Living in the Reality of God's Blessing": http://www.kcm.org/index.php?p=real_help_content&id=1279 (accessed Mar. 12, 2009).

ously describes a women's prayer meeting at an evangelical church in a New York suburb. These women actually pray using Robert's Rules of Order. They start the meeting by making sure that old business has been covered. They do this by going through the previous week's prayer requests and determining which prayers have been answered and which ones are still open. Having cleared last week's agenda, the women move to new business. Here they share their current concerns. Wolfe notes that these mostly involve illness and healing, personal finances, and real estate — personal health and wealth.[9] The underlying idea seems to be that in order to receive what they want and need, all they need to do is ask with a believing heart. The rules of order presume on that faith and God's response by regularizing the whole process, moving it out of the realm of hope and longing, mystery and doubt, into the realm of regular business. Given their presumption of a pipeline, one wishes they had prayed for peace in Palestine or liberation for Tibet!

Focusing on the procedures of faith in order to enhance faith's pragmatic effectiveness is also evident, these days, in the ways numbered lists are often used to enumerate the rules or steps one needs to follow to be a really successful Christian. I first became aware of this trend when I studied the Promise Keepers movement. Their best-selling book, of course, is entitled *The Seven Promises of a Promise Keeper*. Their sermons and literature are full of lists. At a stadium event for pastors in Atlanta, for example, those in attendance heard from:

- John Maxwell, who offered seven steps toward finishing well, one of which included "ten commandments" for avoiding sexual temptation.
- Bill McCartney, who listed nine marks of a disciple and seven considerations of the blood covenant (although he only got through four of them).
- Randy Phillips, who shared five things you need to do to become part of God's family.

9. Alan Wolfe, *The Transformation of American Religion: How We Actually Live Our Faith* (New York: Free Press, 2003), p. 23.

- Wellington Boone, who explained the five principles for timeless worship and the four stages of entering into a prayer relationship, not to mention the four steps of revival.

Notice that each of these lists was offered in service of a better life.

Pragmatic focus on procedure has also been evident in another evangelical phenomenon of late, the "concert of prayer." In these concerts, those praying are led through a series of highly choreographed steps that somehow enhance the prayer. So, for example, at the same Promise Keepers conference mentioned above, David Bryant instructed the audience on how to properly come before God. He told the audience to 1) lean forward where your are; 2) bow your head; 3) breathe deeply; 4) pray a prayer to be cleansed just as bodies are cleansed, by breathing; 5) whisper a song; 6) raise head, look up, and lift voice; 7) pray what comes to your heart, aloud; 8) remember how seminary training only gets us approximately close to God; 9) stand; 10) open your hands in front of you; 11) raise your hands; 12) repeat after me. Bryant had the audience follow these steps alone, and then, holding on to the people beside and behind you, in groups of three and five. And so on, with more instructions about what to pray and whom to pray with. One of the key premises of such "concerts" seems to be that the more people who pray for the same thing, the same way, the more likely God is to answer that prayer. Procedural correctness and high capacity give prayer power, using language that describes prayer as a technological device that humans use at their convenience to achieve ends that suit them.

Kenneth Burke defines all such appeals to order and numbered lists and instructions as appeals to "agency." He says that the appeal to agency derives its prestige from "the grammatical fact that it covers the area of applied science, the area of new power."[10] What Burke means, in short, is that when someone's language is full of references to procedure and numbers, to rules and directions, he or she is unconsciously doing two things. First, he or she is borrowing the language of mod-

10. Kenneth Burke, *A Grammar of Motives* (Berkeley: University of California Press, 1969; originally published in 1949), p. 286.

ernism, the language of science. And second, he or she is presuming, perhaps unconsciously, a worldview commitment to pragmatism.[11]

Of course, religion doesn't have to be pragmatically oriented. In fact, most scholars — including Marsha Witten and Robert Wuthnow — see pragmatic faith as evidence of the secularization of North American religion, that is, the slow process by which American faith accommodates itself more to the secular trends of society at large than to the traditional teachings of Christianity. Or, as Bright might put it, the slow paganization of North American religion. These days sin is soft-pedaled as "mistakes," or something that we need to be healed of, or the absence of positive vibes. God's immanence is emphasized over his transcendence. And faith is seen as a repertoire of techniques that bend God to human hopes and dreams.

Although pragmatic faith's interest in method, numbers, lists, and rules bespeaks its debt to modernistic linearity and concern with scientific procedure, it adds up to a faux intellectualism at best, one that shows little appreciation for historical accounts of faith or for the kind of methodological checks and balances that are a part of real science. In fact, the focus on bulleted lists, television, and other technological means that are most commonly used to spread the good news inherent in pragmatic faith; the uncritical acceptance of pragmatic worldviews at odds with key biblical themes; the use of participatory rites; and the belief in deux-ex-machina solutions to life's everyday problems — all these together make this a very secondary oral manifestation of a faith that still has some modernist elements.

Thus, says Robert Wuthnow, once upon a time faith was a matter of spiritual production: people produced children to populate pews, sent out missionaries to make converts, and spent their time and money building churches and religious institutions. Faith, in other words, suggested obligation and commitment. Now, however, instead of faith being a matter of spiritual production, it has become a process of spiritual consumption. Christians now "let professional experts — writ-

11. For more on the Promise Keepers' pragmatic worldview, see John Suk, "Onward, Christian Soldiers," in *The Promise Keepers: Essays on Masculinity and Christianity,* ed. Dane S. Clausen (Jefferson, NC: McFarland, 2000).

ers, artists, therapists, spiritual guides — be the producers while they consume what they need in order to enrich themselves spiritually."[12] That is, people believe and go to church in order to receive the institutional benefits of church: good choirs to sing in; great youth programs that keep kids out of trouble and in league with other good kids; fine preaching that inspires and informs; and networking possibilities. Even if this isn't a prosperity gospel that suggests God has special gifts in mind for the faithful, it is a very pragmatic and self-centered gospel. People believe because faith has added benefits: cash, salvation, success, or membership. Faith is not a commitment or conviction so much as it is the price of admission.

I can think of little positive to say about such faith. Although I long for the consolations of faith — hope for the future, the notion that life has meaning and direction, the good news that Jesus' suffering and death speak of God's love for humanity — I cannot credit faith in the divine pursued for a secular advantage. No one puts it as succinctly as Leslie Weatherhead, who says that "one would rather promote the most crude belief in luck, both good and bad, than encourage the attitude of special protection." He then goes on to quote the late E. Griffith Jones:

> "The piety that sees a sign of divine favor in escape from a sudden danger which destroys other lives, is a spurious and egotistic travesty of the faith that knows that 'God spared not His own Son, but freely gave Him up for us all.' The true Christian will ask for no immunity from the common lot, for no freedom from the hardships of experience, for no miraculous deliverance from impending calamity, but he will ask for the power to overcome the world in a spirit that is courageous as well as meek, militant against all forms of evil while profoundly thankful for what seems good in life."[13]

12. Robert Wuthnow, *After Heaven: Spirituality in America Since the 1950s* (Berkeley: University of California Press, 1998), pp. 7-8.
13. E. Griffith Jones, *Providence, Divine and Human* (London: Hodder and Stoughton, 1925), quoted in Leslie D. Weatherhead, *The Christian Agnostic* (Nashville: Abingdon, 1965), p. 207.

Both Wuthnow and Weatherhead remind me of another story I wrote about faith; this one is not about dreaming of far shores, but about the cost of discipleship. It works better than my "Dreamers" story.

The experience of Mr. and Mrs. Viand, who owned a small grocery store in Bethlehem, Ontario, during the Depression of the 1930s was one that was repeated countless times all over Canada. Their story went like this.

The Viands' grocery store was a sort of community meeting place. Community people did more than shop for their groceries there: retired men would stand around smoking their pipes, teenagers would sit at the counter and order sodas, and everyone used Mrs. Viand as a sort of living grapevine of community news.

Then the Depression hit. There wasn't much work anymore — and less money. The soda counter was shut down. The Viands moved one of the meat coolers out to make way for more bins of raw, uncooked beans and unbleached flour. Neighborhood people, perhaps ashamed of the fact that they were out of work and had time to burn, did not hang around nearly as much. The Depression was tough on everyone.

The Viands did everything they possibly could to help keep food on their neighbors' tables. They extended credit to all who needed it, especially during the Christmas season. They hired kids to stock, unstock, and stock again the same basement storage shelves, day in and day out. They slipped candy canes into children's pockets. Mrs. Viand made up Christmas food baskets for neighbors who were too ashamed to ask for more credit.

It wasn't as if the Viands were wealthy. In fact, they only just barely kept their own heads above water through the Depression. But the Viands loved their neighbors. And so it was with joy that after a few years they noticed that things were turning around, people had work again, and life was returning to normal.

But then, after the war, Loblaw's came to town. It was a chain store, a cheap chain store — not a community grocery store. At first, the neighborhood people bought only their milk, eggs, and meat at Loblaw's, and patronized the Viands' store for everything else. But as time passed, people slowly but surely chose to forget the Depression and their debt of gratitude to the Viands. People chose to shop at Loblaw's instead; after all, it was so convenient and cheap — and mostly it was so modern!

So finally, one Christmas, rather than declare bankruptcy, the Viands closed up shop. The sad truth of the matter was that, even though they had once carried the whole community on their backs, the whole community refused to pay a few cents extra for their groceries to carry just the two of them.

The truth, of course, is that the Bible never promises us that our journey through this life is going to be trouble-free. Actually, the Bible speaks of the opposite: hurting people stumbling under the weight of a sin-broken, groaning world. Jesus promised us persecutions and crosses to bear. He said we would lose our lives before we found them back, and that we would live like strangers and aliens among the other people of this world. Such a life has little cash value, at least as most people value such things. But such a life does lend itself to love of God and neighbor before all else.

chapter 8

The Trouble with Doctrine, Mores, and Tribes

Introduction

In chapter 1, I related how my childhood faith resonated with the faith of enchanted Europe before the invention of the printing press. As I grew older, went to school, and interiorized the rationality of texts and doctrines, my faith came to resemble that of many literate Christians since the Reformation. Heavy on truth, institutions, and systematization, it was also not very robust. Later on, after visiting some of the world's most poverty-stricken places, including Rwanda shortly after the genocide, and after going to graduate school, where I was introduced to the postmodern critique, I began to question much of the received wisdom of my tradition. I had a crisis of faith.

Now, as I write this chapter, I've decided to pastor another church. The production of this book has spanned years, really, and has been a journey from uncritical faith to doubting faith to somewhere beyond both of these. This chapter ends at that "somewhere beyond." But to get there, I'll examine three of the most formative aspects of my faith journey. I think of these formative influences as a trinity of influential factors: the tribe, the doctrines, and the rules — mores — by which my community lived. Their complex interplay has shaped my faith and church experience.

In this chapter I will try to pull apart those three strands to reflect on each individually and in interaction with each other. As a way of introducing that, I'll do it by looking at the Christian Reformed Church (CRC), the denomination in which I grew up, in another time and place: in northwest Iowa, about eighty years ago, as it is portrayed in the humorous but wise poetry of Sietze Buning. This story could easily serve as a mirror for the stories of people from many other Christian backgrounds, from Lake Wobegon's Lutherans and Catholics, to Baptists in America's South, to Pentecostals almost anywhere else.

Purpaleanie

Sietze Buning was the pen name of my church's bard ("poet" is too formal), who was in residence until his untimely death in 1986. His real name was Stanley Wiersma, and he grew up in a Dutch Calvinist farming community in northwest Iowa in the 1930s. His poetry describes that community in down-to-earth, colloquial terms. Sietze loved those farmers, but they drove him crazy, too. His portraits describe a kind of faith that had backbone and conviction even while it also lacked . . . well, something.

One of his poems, "Calvinist Farming," describes how the Christian Reformed "business was to farm on Biblical principles. Like, let everything be done decently and in good order." Calvinist farmers imitated God's orderly design for creation by planting straight, carefully spaced rows that were easy to cultivate mechanically. After all, God commanded, "Be ye perfect."[1] The order of those cornrows also reflected the farmers' belief in the doctrine of election. The farmers reasoned, "If we were corn kernels in God's corn planter, would we want him to plant us at random?" Members of other, sloppier faiths farmed with the unpredictable contours of the land to fight erosion, and allowed their kids go to movies and square-skipping dances. Nothing good would come of that. "Contour farmers were frivolous about the

1. Sietze Buning, *Purpaleanie and Other Permutations* (Sioux Center, IA: Middleburg Press, 1978), p. 61.

doctrine of election simply by being contour farmers." Doctrine, ethnic identity, and even farming methodology were all curiously mixed.

In another poem, "Obedience," Buning relates how members of his family, even though they know a brewing storm will destroy their harvest-ready crop if they go to church instead of to the fields, go to church anyway. "God was testing us," says the father (p. 53). And everyone knows that if they had saved the crop, the guilt of disobeying the Sunday command to rest would have overwhelmed them. Obeying the community mores was more important.

In "Excommunication," Benny Ploegster, a hopeless alcoholic who can't quit drinking in spite of his very real fear of hell, stubbornly goes to his own excommunication in the hope that it might help him change course. Once he is there, the minister declares: "Since by his stubbornness Benny daily aggravates his transgression, he is to be accounted as a Gentile and a Publican. We exhort you to keep no company with him to the end that he may be ashamed" (p. 56). The power to shame and discipline kept the community in line.

What kind of faith demands of farmers — Dutch Calvinist ones in particular — that they plant corn in imitation of the doctrine of election? What kind of faith demands of farmers that they obediently go to church on Sundays to sing, "He rides on the clouds, the wings of the storm/The lightning and wind his missions perform," rather than save their crops? What kind of faith excommunicates a drunk so full of sadness at his own failure to show evidence of his election that he goes to a church ceremony to mourn his probable damnation?

I've learned from talking to people who grew up in that era and in similar communities that, even if Buning exaggerated, he got the heart of the matter exactly right. And whatever else it is, this community so shapes the inner life of its members that they can only with great effort stand apart from it in order to see it for what it is.

I grew up in a community that was similar to the one in northwest Iowa in many ways. I remember, when I was a kid, receiving visitors one Sunday afternoon, the hottest Sunday of the year. My parents were not sticklers for legalistic detail in Sabbath observance, so while many parents in our church didn't allow their kids to ride bicycles on Sunday or go to movies on weeknights, my parents didn't mind so much. On this Sunday of the pre-air-conditioning era, in fact, my dad had put on his shorts and turned on the sprinkler so we kids could run in and out of the water; indeed, he got a little wet himself. Just then the visitors drove up. They wore dark three-piece suits, hats all around, and long-sleeved dresses. It was pretty clear to me, even as a young boy, that they were shocked by our Sunday shenanigans. Well, Dad and Mom were cowed, so the hose got turned off and we kids were told to put on somewhat more decent clothes. The visitors were served tea and cookies in the shade of a tree. As it turned out, our American visitors, who hailed from our version of Jerusalem — Grand Rapids, Michigan — were camping at Niagara Falls. They had, like us, gone to church that morning. After church they had returned to their trailer in the campground, and in their dark suits in the sweltering heat had had an earlier round of refreshments. Why? I'll never forget this conversation. It was, one of them said, so that they could "witness" to their neighbors. They wanted the campground neighbors to see that they had gone to church, and that they respected the Sabbath by keeping it holy — including by the way they dressed.

However, I don't want to give the impression that it was only other Christian Reformed people that had these extreme ideas. I have other, more personal memories of beloved children feeling — justifiably — alienated for leaving the church. I remember a vacation to Mackinac Island being cancelled so that my father, a pastoral elder, could do church work rather than take his family on vacation. That church work involved sitting by the phone to be available to two church members who had run off with each other, leaving their spouses behind, just in case they should decide to call and repent. A member of my extended family was forced to sit in the balcony, with his children, away from the rest of the church because he had been put under discipline — twice: the first time for divorcing his wife, and then later, for remarrying another woman. Like Benny Ploegster, he could have gone to a Presbyterian church and been accepted with open arms. But he didn't. He was, after all, Christian Reformed. I also remember, to my own shame, my refusal as a young pastor to officiate at a wedding because the groom wasn't a regular churchgoer.

Overall, growing up in my immigrant, Dutch, Christian Reformed community was a good experience. I was loved, felt safe, and knew the rules. People looked out for each other. Besides going to church together, we went to Christian school together, to the church picnics together, and to each other's homes for coffee and cake. As in other communities, we also exercised sanctions against people who wouldn't play by the community's rules. The warmth and comfort of my church community was balanced by its power to include and exclude. Discipline of many kinds — from gossip and disapproval to excommunication — was always in play. *Doctrine, ethnicity,* and *mores* made it so. Let's examine each one in turn.

Doctrine

Given the role that the doctrine of election played when it came to planting orderly rows of corn, doctrine obviously plays an important role in the faith of Buning's Calvinist farmers. What is remarkable about his corn-planting story, though, is how he is able to show how doctrine wasn't just a set of facts to be memorized, but how at least aspects of it were part of a deeply ingrained perspective on life. Before delving too deeply into that role, though, we should be clear about exactly what we mean by doctrine and by theology. George Lindbeck's definition will serve:

> Church doctrines are communally authoritative teachings regarding beliefs and practices that are considered essential to the identity or welfare of the group in question. They may be formally stated or informally operative, but in any case they indicate what constitutes faithful adherence to a community.[2]

Lindbeck's definition recognizes that doctrine has its primary meaning in a communal context. That is, it is authoritative — with respect to both behavior and the community's "truth." Thus Lindbeck's defi-

---

2. George A. Lindbeck, *The Nature of Doctrine: Religion and Theology in a Postliberal Age* (Louisville: Westminster John Knox, 1984), p. 74.

nition does not restrict doctrine to matters publicly confessed, such as the content of the Apostles' Creed or the Heidelberg Catechism. He recognizes that doctrine can also become informally operative. It isn't just about election, but also about planting corn, or whom you may marry, or what pastimes or work are allowed on Sundays, or how you treat people who are not measuring up to community standards.

Theology, on the other hand, is a broader term. A great diversity of opinion can characterize some matters related to understanding God or Scripture. For example, when I was young, I remember hearing arguments about the order of God's decrees of election. Did God "elect" people before (supralapsarianism) or after (infralapsarianism) the Fall? Similarly, Christian Reformed people today might disagree about whether or not God should ever be referred to using feminine language or on whether or not children should receive communion. One of my seminary professors, Neal Plantinga, once speculated in class about whether there might be other persons in the Trinity than the three traditionally thought to have been revealed in Scripture, persons Scripture simply did not reveal to us.

Doctrine has always played an important role in Christianity, even if most people, at least for the first fifteen hundred years of Christianity, did not know much doctrine beyond memorizing the Apostles' Creed, the Lord's Prayer, and the Ten Commandments. Even when there was a great deal of illiteracy, some scholars and even secular rulers struggled with doctrine, often using it as a proxy for fighting other battles. For example, the adoption of the Nicene Creed, whatever its theological merits, was heavily influenced by Constantine's political judgments.

With the advent of literacy, however, regular church members' familiarity with doctrine grew by leaps and bounds. Printed materials put what they couldn't quite remember at their fingertips, as people decided that to be schooled was to be holy. However, it wasn't just theological or biblical knowledge that increased; so did the doctrinal demands that were laid on people. People were expected not just to know more, but to accept more as definitive and authoritative. After the Reformation, the Protestant churches made their disagreements with Catholicism a central concern, but also their disagreements with other Protestant sects. This was the era known as Protestant Scholasticism, which, according to Diana Butler Bass, "insisted legalistically on the acceptance of precisely worded doctrinal confessions as the basis of faith." As a result, Bass continues,

> [t]heologians pitted devotion and morality against belief, defining faith no longer as a way of life but rather as intellectual assent to certain creeds or confessions; their books were filled with "quarrelling, disputing, scolding, and reviling." Words became weapons.[3]

Growing up, and as a young pastor, studying and arguing this sort of doctrine was one of my favorite things to do. I wrote a paper once arguing that the decrees of election and reprobation were not equally ultimate in the Belgic Confession. That is, I argued that people who subscribed to the Belgic Confession had to accept the doctrine of election, but not the flip side of that doctrine, the one that said that those not elected (the reprobate) were going to hell. Since this is exactly what the writers of the Belgic Confession undoubtedly presumed, it took a bit of sleight of hand to make the case that they didn't actually say so in the confession. Meanwhile, the careful, rational massaging of the language of the confession, so that it could be read to support my view, prevented my having to deal with issues concerning God's love presented by the doctrine of predestination. Overall, my seminary education was doctrinally focused and intended to give me an understanding of the confessions and the history of the Christian Reformed Church rather than a license to do original, nonconfessional theology. So, in addition to the regular run of courses in Old and New Testament, the curriculum was heavy with courses in the creeds and confessions, the Church Order, and the Heidelberg Catechism. Systematic theology courses focused on the heroes of Calvinist theology and the errors of people like Karl Barth (only marginally Reformed, we were instructed, though he wrote a commentary on the Heidelberg Catechism!) and Roman Catholics.

---

3. Diana Butler Bass, *A People's History of Christianity: The Other Side of the Story* (New York: HarperOne, 2009), p. 204.

Doctrinal battles over issues such as hymn singing, common grace, Pentecostalism, divorce and remarriage, women in church office, and so on are some of the key defining issues in the history of the Christian Reformed Church. Doctrinal battles were central to the agenda, and eagerly joined at the denomination's annual synod. One of the earliest stories I remember in this vein is one my father proudly told. During the great synodical debate that we called "the love of God controversy," a seminary professor by the name of Harold Dekker came under withering attack for suggesting that, even though not all people were elect, God nevertheless loved all people. How God could be said to love someone whom he was damning to hell is counterintuitive, of course. Most doctrinaire Reformed people understood this, and so they wanted to say God did not, in fact, love everyone. The debate was so contentious that even after two weeks the Synod could not resolve the matter. In an unprecedented move, Synod was reconvened a few weeks later — to try again. During the debates, my father, an otherwise uneducated layperson who had read theology for pleasure all of his life, stood up to argue that God did *not* love all people, and he hung his argument on some turn of phrase in the Canons of Dordt.

One of Dekker's defenders, Henry Stob, himself a seminary professor, then rose to say that my father was making a mountain out of a molehill. To which my father responded, "Maybe, Professor Stob, but you just tripped over it." My father loved to tell the story as a riveting example of how important it was that laypeople understand doctrine; it also showed how, if we let the theologians do the intellectual work of the church for us, they would lead us down the garden path away from biblical truth and the confessions. The church needed clear doctrine, but not theological innovation.

Arguing about doctrine and morality is something the CRC has always engaged in. In fact, many in the denomination entered such debates with gusto. This was just what churches did! But such arguments often did incalculable harm to individuals on the wrong side of the fence. I know many Christian Reformed and other Protestant people so wounded by these debates that they have left the church of their birth, not in the end because the church decided they were wrong, but because of the deep trauma they experienced from personal attacks, the loss of collegiality, and the price family members had to pay. Early in my ministry, all the women of a neighboring church wrote me a letter to warn me that I was going to hell because I did not believe in a literal six-day creation. The tone of the letter completely unnerved me. A pastor who was visiting my church once stopped the whole congregation from leaving while he dressed me down, loudly and angrily, because during the Lord's Supper celebration I read about Jesus' last meal with the disciples, on a beach after his resurrection, rather than the traditional reading from 1 Corinthians.

As the editor of *The Banner*, I often received angry letters questioning my faith, or wisdom, or love because I had written an editorial that upset the correspondent. Worse, even people who should have known better engaged in these kinds of attacks with seeming relish, including — at different times — college presidents, Christian school leaders, seminary professors, and important denominational leaders, never with any apparent concern for how the attack would affect me as a person. Being right was what mattered. The combined weight of these attacks on my own spiritual life was very heavy, though I only came to realize how heavy it was afterwards, starting on my trip in the "Bananer."

Ultimately, arguments about creation and evolution, to women in church office, to whether or not gay people can live in loving relationships have been a key unifying subtext of my denomination's life together. The CRC and many other denominations often look less like churches with a mission than churches full of doctrines to guard, people with axes to grind and ramparts to man — mostly against other Christians with slightly different opinions, and rarely with much concern about the impact such criticism and conflict might have on others.

One of the more important lessons to derive from all of this is aptly summed up by Kenneth Burke in his *Rhetoric of Religion*: "[N]othing can more effectively set people at odds than the demand that they think alike."[4] There is an irony that is deep at work in all the literate church's doctrinal formulations. While the documents are pretty

---

4. Kenneth Burke, *Rhetoric of Religion: Studies in Logology* (Berkeley: University of California Press, 1961), p. v.

much written in stone, people often change their minds. Thus, when some people raise questions or offer amendments, many take up arms against them. Putting finely detailed doctrines at the center of church life institutionalizes being at odds rather than "one," conflict rather than acceptance, and schism rather than union. In northwest Iowa, doctrinal distinctives justified the separation of Dutch Calvinists from every other kind of Christian in that corner of the state — not only doctrinally, but inevitably socially as well. And arguments about doctrines they supposedly agreed on justified schismatic splinters off the branch of Dutch Calvinism into Reformed, Christian Reformed, Protestant Reformed, United Reformed, and Netherlands Reformed denominations. The history of most doctrinal formulations, from the time of the Apostles' Creed to the present, is that even as they seek to enforce unity, they are always staging areas for confrontation and even hatred.

In this situation I believe churches must reimagine life together as one where doctrine plays a much-reduced role, more like the role it played in the oral era. Doctrine should be, for the most part, a playground rather than an arena for conflict. This should be so, not only because in our secondary oral tradition very few people have the capacity for the kind of doctrinal depth presumed by doctrinal confessions — at least compared to the era of high literacy — but also because the history of dialogue, respect, and amity in confessional churches is a very short one.

Most people would agree that for faith to be authentic, it must also be personally owned rather than imposed as a set of doctrines that some institution insists must be subscribed to. Early Reformed theologians understood this, and thus they spoke of their doctrines as "confessions." The idea was that the theology at the heart of some doctrine was alive in the believer's heart and only then necessarily found expression on the lips as well — as a confession, an unforced and exuberant "yes!" And for those who wrote the confessions, and for many who first read them, the confessions must have been just that. Perhaps when Calvinists chose to farm in imitation of the doctrine of election, that doctrine was still, really, a confession. On the other hand, choosing not to harvest weather-threatened corn on Sunday because of the shame one would then be subject to, or because one believed that not harvesting was being obedient, just seems stupid.

All in all, however, assent to doctrine, at least doctrine as detailed and prescriptive as one finds in confessions like the Canons of Dordt, doesn't seem like a good candidate for being a defining element of faith. That's why, as editor of my denomination's magazine, I argued that the church should drop the Belgic Confession and the Canons of Dordt as confessional standards.[5] Now I believe that we should do the same with the Heidelberg Catechism. And other denominations should water down their distinctives. We might declare that, while these confessions have been helpful for describing what we believed in the past, they are now understood to be historical documents that inform our faith rather than prescriptive statements that determine what we must now believe. Our history of trying to accommodate these coercive confessions to our communal lives together suggests that doctrine as authoritative teaching is just too explosive and divisive, always steering Christians, who are called to love each other, into conflict and separation. To live by doctrine is to die by it. Jesus said that people in the world would know that God had sent him by their oneness, by their love for one another. He didn't mention doctrinal unity (John 17:21). And yet this is where hundreds of years of mostly useless effort, at least when it comes to love and unity, has led. Embodying Christ seems a much more crucial constituent to faith than trying to explain Christ.

But there was more to Sietze Buning's experience of faith than doctrines that lived in newly planted or lately destroyed cornfields. It was more important, actually, that the faith he describes was a Dutch immigrant faith.

Ethnicity

I don't doubt that doctrines concerning election or the nature of Jesus' presence at the Lord's Supper played a role in the CRC's self-

5. John Suk, "Let's Take Another Look at Those Confessions," *The Banner,* February 6, 1995.

identification and community regulation. A more substantive explanation for why Christian Reformed people have stuck together for
more than 150 years in North America is that the CRC is a tribe, an
ethnic church. The CRC has always been a place where Dutch (and a
few German and lately Korean) immigrants have found pleasure, or
at least security, in each other's company, much as the Norwegians
do in Lake Wobegon's Lutheran church, and the town's Catholic
folks do in the Our Lady of Perpetual Responsibility parish. These
immigrants and their children, to the third and fourth generation,
shared a narrative: their own stories of exodus and promised land, in
which they saw the hand of God at work in a very special way. This
was also true of the Dutch Boers in South Africa and the Dutch and
German Mennonites in the Ukraine or Peru or Saskatchewan. Christian Reformed people remember ancestors felling virgin pines in a
scramble for survival and shelter in the wilderness of western Michigan. They remember breaking sod on the dry plains of southern Al-
berta. They remember founding schools for their children, hospitals
for their sick, and mission enterprises for "heathens." Through it all,
they somehow managed to survive and even grow strong. They began
to think of themselves, like the Pilgrims, as God's elect people in a
foreign land, even as small, scattered colonies in a hostile new world.
Dutch Calvinists!

They created a church in that image, a Zion, a "city on a hill,"
which served as a fortress against and refuge from the strange peoples
and culture of America. One of the effects of this self-portrait was that
outsiders rarely felt welcome or at home in CRC circles. In the meantime, the CRC continued to grow through birth, through focused so-
cialization and indoctrination of their young people, through continued immigration from the "old country," but never through opening
the doors via evangelism. Even today, few traditional Christian Reformed congregations have had anything more than token success inviting others to join.

Since at least the turn of the century, doctrinal glue has, at best,
played an important supporting role to this more fundamental ethnic
bond. That is, while everyone understood that formally it was doctrine that they confessed and doctrine that was authoritative, the

truth was this: just as few outsiders joined for the doctrine, few Christian Reformed people stayed for it. When outsiders did join, it was usually a big fat Dutch wedding that soon followed. Though debate and care and concern for doctrine was often front and center in the life of the church, it was never the engine that really powered it. Again, that more central focus was tribal identification.

And in the CRC's better moments, leaders understood and admitted as much. For example, in the January 7, 1915, issue of *The Banner*, Rev. P. A. Hoekstra lamented the sorry state of Calvinist conviction in the pews, declaring that "the doctrinal emphasis is not in popular favor these days." He attributed this, in part, to the wrong use of doctrine: "Men would warm their hearts and hands by hugging it but were frozen stiff in its embrace." He hoped to remedy this problem by writing regularly in *The Banner*, in a manner that avoided "all appearance of method, as far as possible," and by "avoiding, as far as possible, unfamiliar, theological terms." He believed doctrine was important, but doubted that it had much currency in the hearts of Christian Reformed laypeople.

On the other hand, *Banner* editor Henry Beets, writing in the same issue that Hoekstra did (and quoting an editorial he had written ten years earlier), wrote that "we desire to bless [America] with the best which God entrusted to us of *Dutch blood* and Calvinistic persuasion." And in the introduction to his 1929 study of the Belgic Confession, which he preferred to call the *Netherlandic* Confession, Beets wrote that he hoped his book would "be a flag around which shall rally the scattered members of *our Reformed family of Dutch origin* in America." So while doctrine left pew-sitters in the cold, if Hoekstra is to be believed — even if doctrine was the formal occasion for being in church together — Beets fairly trumpeted the Dutch ethnicity that was really serving to keep the home fires burning. In fact, he could hardly mention doctrine without bringing ethnicity into it.

These days that ethnic glue is drying up and crumbling. The Dutch language is only a distant memory for most Christian Reformed people in the United States, and now for most Canadian ones, too. CRC members are moving away from the little colonies to big cities as opportunity and education call. As consumers of contemporary media, and as members of the churches of consumerism and professional sports, they have been assimilated into most aspects of North American popular culture. Perhaps this kind of assimilation to the majority culture is inevitable as the ties to the old ways become diluted with every passing generation.

But here is exactly where generations of doctrinal preoccupation have not helped us. Not only was doctrine not the true center of our life together; we now live in a society where the lack of doctrinal knowledge that concerned Hoekstra in his day looks like doctrinal preoccupation to many of us today. A high level of *engaged literacy* has always been a prior condition for any church to truly remain a confessional church, even when the confessions were not the real reason for being in the church in the first place. But again, in our secondary oral setting, even as the complaints about doctrinal literacy are repeated with ever-greater urgency, they can not and will not win the day with most of today's church members. Few really believe that to be schooled is holy, and fewer have the interest, inclination, or especially the intellectual skills and background to make it so. When people don't read the confessions, or take classes in them, or hear sermons about them, or understand the history that led to their being written — there is no way that the confessions can be said to live in the heart. While Christian commentators such as David Wells and secular commentators such as Susan Jacoby and the late Neil Postman bemoan the fate of reading, given the reality of today's secondary oral tradition, we are just not going to see a new day in which a majority of church members once again turn seriously to books in order to understand or explore their faith. As a hook to keep people in the faith, doctrine cannot succeed any more than tribalism can.

At the same time, I do not want to suggest that, as church leaders, we might as well ignore theology or doctrine. The truth is that the church has always had an educated and curious intellectual wing that has made the study of Scripture its main event. That is a high calling. What is more, even in the secondary oral culture of today, the future movers and shakers of society are going to be drawn more from the highly literate sector than from those who do not read. By choosing media literacy and entertainment over deep literacy, people are choosing an easier path that won't take them on nearly as many important or influential journeys. For that reason, I believe enlightened parents should do all in their power to nurture reading and refuse to cave in to popular culture's low regard for high literacy. It is a difficult path. Ironically, no one makes a better case for this path that is rarely taken than the high priestess of media indulgence, Camille Paglia:

> To me the ideal education should be rigorous and word-based — logocentric. The student must learn the logical, hierarchical system. Then TV culture allows the other part of the mind to move freely around the outside of that system. . . . I want schools to stress the highest intellectual values and ideals of the Greco-Roman and Judeo-Christian traditions. Nowadays, "logocentric" is a dirty word. It comes from France, where deconstruction is necessary to break the stranglehold of centuries of Descartes and Pascal. But to apply Lacan, Derrida, and Foucault to American culture is absolutely idiotic. We are born into an imagistic and pagan culture ruled by TV. . . . We need to reinforce the logocentric and Apollonian side of our culture in the schools. It is time for enlightened repression of the children.[6]

In any case, today people will decide on what sort of faith, and which congregation they will attend, using a whole new set of criteria other than doctrine or ethnicity. They are searching for the kind of spiritual experience that the phrase "personal relationship with Jesus" suggests. They are inclined to pick and choose what they believe on the basis of what they want to believe, or, as many sociologists of religion are pointing out, on the basis of where their friends go to church. Meanwhile, many people leave altogether, and with little notice. I heard a sermon recently in which the pastor bemoaned the fact that the time when people left the church over serious issues is long past. The most disheartening thing he had noticed was how people who had attended church and been deeply involved for all their lives were

6. Camille Paglia and Neil Postman, "She Wants Her TV! He Wants His Book!" *Harper's*, March 1991, pp. 44-55.

leaving because they just seemed tired of it all. They left by slipping away, and they didn't land anywhere else.

Looking over the congregations I have pastored and been a member of, I know that the church's retention of youth is a shadow of what it used to be. One colleague of mine says that this is partly because when teens get to college age, the thing that sitting in church most resembles, to them, is school. It may have great memories, and they may love their pastors and teachers and fellow sojourners — but they want to graduate. And so they do, and leave. My denomination has been shrinking for a long time, and neither the doctrinal confessions nor ethnicity will stem the tide.

Morality

The last element in my trinity of factors is harder to define. The mores, or rules — or morality of life together in church — also lack the power that they used to have to keep people coming to church. I have suggested that, in secondary oral culture, churches won't easily succeed and people won't find it easier to believe unless what constitutes doctrinal distinctiveness is radically simplified. I suspect that one of the ways this actually does happen is that people substitute a focus on a few black-and-white moral issues for doctrinal depth. Lindbeck, remember, noted that church doctrines were not only communally authoritative teachings regarding beliefs, but also authoritative practices. Thus the culture wars of today are not so much about biblical inerrancy or similar doctrines on the fundamentalist divide, but about gay marriage, abortion and end-of-life issues, gun control, and even socioeconomic issues like capitalism. The culture wars offer an opportunity for denominations to sharply define themselves over against "the other" in black-and-white terms, and thereby rally the troops. This is exactly what T. W. J. Morrow says has happened in most Reformation churches — across the board.

> Dogma is essentially a corollary of orthodoxy. The increasing pluralism within Reformed confessional churches and their inability

to function with objective criteria of authority have produced a growing ambivalence to the articulation of dogma. Only in *pragmatic areas of morality* do the Reformed Churches appear to speak with authority.[7]

This is faith lining up behind right behavior. In northwestern Iowa, in the thirties, right behavior meant that you went to church on Sundays rather than save your crop from an impending hailstorm. It also meant, as it still does in many churches, that you can't be the town drunk and be welcomed in church. And it involved a long list of obligations related to giving and attending classes and who you could go out with and what games you could play and so on. The rules were not, however, so much glue as they were the social conventions that people within the community followed in order to get along.

These days moral issues are waged as campaigns that divide the world into us versus them. As such, lining up on the right side of key moral issues makes you a certain kind of Christian, and bonds you to like-minded people. These days, right behavior within the CRC means that you must be against abortion in all circumstances, you must be against all gay behavior (while somehow trying to convince gays that you nevertheless love them), that you must not rock the boat with public talk about human evolution, that premarital sex or cohabitation is absolutely out, and you don't break the Ten Commandments (except, perhaps, the Fourth).

The law was given to Israel, not just as a moral code, but to identify her as a unique nation — God's nation in a sea of Gentiles. Eating only certain foods, wearing odd clothing, abstaining from certain activities on the Sabbath, and even circumcision marked you as a Jew. The moral codes that receive so much emphasis in the culture wars today do the same for some Christians. But where smoking used to be a taboo for Baptists but not for Reformed, while going out for Sunday brunch was okay for Baptists but not for Reformed, today the hot-button issues unite many conservative Christians across denomina-

7. T. W. J. Morrow, "Dogma," in *New Dictionary of Theology,* ed. Sinclair B. Ferguson and David F. Wright (Downers Grove, IL: InterVarsity, 1988), p. 203 (emphasis added).

tional divides against nonbelievers and liberal Christians. Ironically, as the religious right unites around moral issues, they also make it easier to move from one conservative denomination to another, regardless of their doctrinal distinctives. Doctrine just doesn't count for as much anymore; being on the right side of a moral crusade does.

Wise non-Christian commentators excoriate this emphasis on moral crusades. John Wyndham's *The Chrysalids,* Victor Hugo's portrait of Javert in *Les Miserables,* and Margaret Atwood's *The Handmaid's Tale* all come to mind.

Christians tend to get defensive when they encounter these kinds of reactions to their campaigns. And, without a doubt, many Christians actually do not judge others, fully in keeping with Jesus' suggestion on this score. At the same time, these kinds of attacks on Christianity are not spurious either. There is a kind of self-righteous, campaign-style Christianity that looks down its nose at everyone who doesn't heed its moral direction. From the religious right to the Eagle Forum, Promise Keepers to the Roman Catholic prohibition of birth control methods, from the refusal to hand out condoms to people at risk of AIDS to legislators who won't fund sex education in the schools or won't support Palestinian Muslims against Israeli occupation — many parachurch and church organizations have a well-deserved reputation for bigotry and moral sneering. While such campaigns "energize" the right, to put it in the popular idiom, it is difficult to understand how such behavior equates to anything like good faith or neighborly love.

Fights over moral-social issues — the "culture wars," as they are sometimes known — have become a defining feature of Christianity. In the Christian Reformed Church, I recently had a very interesting experience. While looking for a parish where I might resume my pastoral profession, I made a point of informing interested congregations what my views were on homosexuality. Though my views are more liberal on that issue than are many in the denomination, I pointed out that this was not what we called a "confessional issue" in the CRC. There are no confessions that require officebearers to adopt this or that position with respect to homosexuality. I had made this position clear in an editorial once.

But I also told the churches that interviewed me that I was not going to be a loose cannon on this issue. I would not preach about homosexuality from the pulpit in such a way as to split the church. I would not make a political issue of it. I would hold my peace. I pointed out that I had held this view for more than twenty years, and that although I had often urged the church to relax and think twice about taking hard-line stances, I had never publicly argued against the church's latest moral statement on the issue. Still, on this non-confessional issue, all but one of the churches that interviewed me cut the discussion off at that point. They could not risk hiring me because of the conflict it might cause in their congregations, they said.

Interestingly enough, however, not one of those churches where I applied asked me about even one confessional issue. This in contrast to the United Church of Canada, where the first question I was asked by a search committee was, "Who is Jesus, really?" In the CRC, no one was interested in what I thought about the nature of Jesus' presence at the Lord's Supper, predestination, infant baptism, or the extent of Jesus' atoning sacrifice. So again, the center of gravity when it comes to discussions of faith — and whether you have the right one — has shifted from doctrinal issues to moral issues. Like the Pharisees of old, modern evangelical Christians must live up to and promote a rigid code of conduct to be really counted as "in." The moral issues, however, must now function not to support a prior tribal identification, but as a substitute for both it and for confessional allegiance. And again, as more and more people in confessional churches such as the CRC see such moral crusading as a basis of unity with other fundamentalist Christians, their ties with the CRC loosen.

Summary

What I've been describing is a situation where a unique trinity — ethnicity, doctrine, and morality — have functioned together, in different degrees in different places and times as a kind of spiritual tag team that defines "true faith" for many Christians. Now even today, no one would argue that the quality of one's faith is dependent on getting doctrine exactly right. Bass's formulation (i.e., that faith was intellectual assent to certain creeds or confessions) would immediately be flagged as putting too strict a line on it. Most of my coreligionists would be happy to point out that Catholics, who believe in the bodily ascension of Mary into heaven, or Arminians, who believe that the decision to believe or not to believe is ours, or Mennonites, who do not baptize children and do not believe that a just case can be made for any war, or even liberal Christians, who think that perhaps Jesus' resurrection was a metaphor rather than a real event — most would be happy to argue that such people may nevertheless be Christians. Not good ones, perhaps, but Christians nonetheless, because they try to follow Jesus.

At the same time, the interplay of the ethnicity-doctrine-morality trinity was experienced, at some level, as constituting what faith is all about: you belong to the right community, you believe the right things, and you do the right things, all together, in the right proportion. Or, to use Lindbeck's definition of faith, certain expectations about these three elements are *informally operative* as authoritative functions in many faith communities. There may be other important features faith possesses as well (e.g., we discussed one's personal relationship with Jesus in a previous chapter); but, practically speaking, these three are central. But how do these three actually work together? Perhaps the best way to understand how they function together in denominations is by thinking of them as offering shared substance that allows people to identify with each other and thus understand and persuade each other. This notion of consubstantiality comes from Kenneth Burke.

Perhaps a bit of background will be helpful. The problem, says Burke, is that people who inhabit their own bodies are divided from each other. Today (Burke wrote the above some fifty years ago) we might say that people in their embodied state are naturally alienated from others because we don't share our bodies and consciousness. As such, people have motivations, dreams, skills, and almost every other imaginable moral or psychological inner reality that they march to, and these are not immediately available to, or sometimes even understandable to, other people. For humans, this division is both a wonderful thing because it gives us individuality and a sense of self, but also a very troublesome thing: as humans, we don't know the other — truly and deeply. We trip over each other. We compete. We seek advantage and try to climb higher in the hierarchy than others. Sometimes — perhaps often — we use power and privilege to achieve personal rather than communal ends. In fact, Burke calls this basic human tendency — which Calvinists might identify with depravity — as the "cult of the kill."

One of the great challenges that humans face is finding some basis for overcoming this division in order to benefit from goods normally associated with human community. Ever since the time of Plato, and especially Aristotle, persuasion has often been thought of as one means for overcoming such difference and creating community. Burke builds on this by suggesting that persuasion, using words, is really just a subtype of a subtler, more pervasive kind of persuasion, which he calls identification. He argues that in order to build community, we actually use many different strategies to overcome division. Most of them have to do with sharing "substances," or symbolic properties with other people so that we identify with them.[8] So, for example, two neighbors, who are otherwise quite different — a Baptist and an atheist, perhaps, or a grumpy Anglo man and a rich Hispanic woman — might share a love of golf, and hence they often golf together. Thus, in spite of the many things that divide them, they are said to be consubstantial when it comes to golf — they share substance, and thus become attached to one another — as golfers. "As two entities are united in substance through common ideas, attitudes, material possessions, or other properties, they are consubstantial."[9]

Fundamentally, identification unites what is divided. This can be used as a means to an end by, for example, a politician. The politician may seek to curry favor with a voting block by identifying with them. He may note, for example, that since he grew up on a farm, he under-

8. Burke discusses the concept of identification in several of his books. Perhaps the best shorthand description can be found in *A Rhetoric of Motives* (Berkeley: University of California Press, 1950), pp. 20-23.

9. Sonja K. Foss et al., *Kenneth Burke and Contemporary European Thought: Rhetoric in Transition* (Prospect Heights, NJ: Waveland Press, 1991), p. 174.

stands the unique and difficult circumstances that the farmers in his audience face. He is consubstantial with the farmers, and so they think (the politician hopes!) that he will likely act in their interest as one of them, and thus is worth voting for. Identification can also operate as a means of unifying people facing a common enemy. Thus, for example, when I was growing up there were only two kinds of people in the world: "us" and "the Canadians." Canadians were wrong about religion, and they were aimless, shifty, and impenetrable. Given that this is how we spoke about Canadians in my community, I was socialized to avoid them and stick close to my kind of people: honest, resourceful, and hardworking Dutch Calvinists. Perhaps the most important kind of identification is every type that functions unconsciously in our psyche. When we see an ad for a new perfume that portrays all those who use the perfume as sexually attractive and successful, we may buy the perfume because we unconsciously identify it with those characteristics. Or, again, in the case of Canadians, I was unconsciously being socialized to stick with my tribe by the negative stereotypes that were used to portray Canadians.

Both Sietze Buning's community and mine shared ethnicity and the coercive use of doctrine and mores to create stronger identification between the community's many members. The content of the doctrine isn't nearly as important as the fact that everyone in a position of authority — pastors, elders, deacons — signs a "form of subscription," in which they state agreement with the doctrines and then even promise to promote them, while laying out a very onerous — if not impossible — process for expressing disagreement with those doctrines. Thus, the body of doctrine functions as a means of identification and community solidarity rather than as something that lives in the heart and cannot help but find expression on the lips. The truth is, most of the people who sign the form of subscription today could hardly detail what the doctrines are that they are agreeing with.

In many faith communities, doctrines, morality, and ethnicity are used consciously and unconsciously to create identification within the community. All together, this identification is thought of as "the faith." I would say, however, that a feature of healthy faith is that one is able to empty herself or himself of too great an attachment to any aspect in this trinity, while seeking greater attachment to the core teaching of Jesus about love, including love in community.

Conclusion

Emptiness doesn't have much status in our culture. We like our homes to be full of stuff, our lives full of interesting adventures and things to do, and our tummies stuffed. But in Eastern cultures emptiness is actually prized. Emptiness is thought of as being charged with positive potential. The basic feature of Japanese homes, for example, is that they are empty of all but the most basic furniture. In the East, if a room is filled, it is considered used up and hence useless. Likewise, the value in a cup or a bowl is that it, too, is empty, able and ready to do the task it was made for. One of my parishioners in Ann Arbor was a Chinese high school student. One summer she went to Taiwan and returned with a painting for Irene and me. The central feature in the painting is a nightingale in a mulberry tree. But mostly, the painting is empty white space. In fact, oriental artists usually spend more time on planning the empty space than on what they fill it with. The empty space is what gives our gift painting its aesthetic punch.

In the Bible emptiness can have a positive value, too. This is nowhere so obvious as in Jesus' sacrificing of himself for our sakes. Paul says Jesus "emptied himself, taking the form of a slave, and humbled himself, and became obedient to the point of death." Christ's emptying himself of his divine prerogatives in order to become human is sometimes called the kenotic theory of the atonement (*kenos* is the Greek word for "empty").

I am told that Korean families sometimes celebrate this image of Jesus emptying himself by using bamboo plants instead of evergreen trees as a substitute for Christmas trees. Bamboo, you see, is hollow on the inside. The emptiness of the bamboo makes it different from all other trees and gives it a special significance for Asians. The emptiness of the bamboo is what makes it light yet strong. In that emptiness the Koreans see a living parable about the mystery of who Jesus is, a parable for what happened in Jesus' birth, death, and life. He emptied himself.

Calvin knows about the power of emptiness for our salvation, too. He said that faith is an empty vessel given to us so that we can be filled with grace. But if faith is an empty vessel, or at least a roomy vessel, it must not be weighed down too much by doctrine, rules, or ethnicity. To receive grace, faith must let go of an overattachment to or identification with any of these things.

But the image that speaks to me most powerfully is that of the children that Jesus says we need to imitate in order to receive the kingdom of God. It is interesting that some of the most poignant and powerful images of the faithful life in Scripture are the ones we have the hardest time embodying — or at least the easiest time dismissing. In this case, Jesus' saying that we must become like children to receive the kingdom has sparked all kinds of ideas for sermons. One is that this saying is just impossible for us to obey: it is an ideal that is beyond us, like turning the other cheek or loving our enemies. Others suggest that we need to be innocent like children, forgetting how children who don't get their way in the sandbox have no compunctions about hitting their adversaries with a plastic shovel or throwing dirt. Perhaps, say others, the key is not in children's innocence but in their trust. But again, watching a child of a certain age being left with a babysitter suggests that, while trust in Mom or Dad might be breaking, it certainly hasn't been established yet with the babysitter! Kids are not that great at trust.

The explanation I like best is this: Jesus enjoins us to be like children because children know how to receive. They hold up their empty hands to us, and they expect those hands to be filled, even when they know they don't deserve it. In a similar way, faith is not possessing — or being filled with — the right ideas or confession, or having membership in the right tribe, or doing the right thing. Instead, faith knows how to receive, especially how to receive grace, even when we know we don't deserve it.

When we are like children, there is a sense in which, doctrinally, we are like those ancient medieval and oral Christians, who hardly knew anything about the Bible or about doctrine. In some ways, things actually have not changed that much. Though we now read and have access, if we choose, to all sorts of theological views, their very variety and mutual incompatibility suggests that most of them must trade in significant error or misunderstanding. It takes a certain kind of modernist and tragic hubris to suppose that your tribe alone has somehow figured out which ones are actually best, and that you are so sure you are willing to break fellowship with those who disagree with you. Furthermore, beyond the obvious mistakes that we must be making in trying to put doctrine together, there is, in addition, the problem of our fallibility over against God's great mystery.

I remember a class in seminary that helped me think about this problem of scale when it comes to spiritual and ultimate truth. It was the first day of class in a course entitled "The Doctrine of God." I had heard that our professor, Neal Plantinga, was ill, so I figured the class would be canceled. However, Plantinga had arranged for a guest lecturer, his brother the philosopher. I had never met Alvin Plantinga before, but he was known to everyone in class by his reputation: an internationally known philosopher, he was reputed to be an eloquent teacher, and we were quite excited to have him.

Plantinga moved to the podium, looked at us, and was silent. For a long time he said nothing — for minutes, in fact. He just stood there, and we students looked down at our desks, embarrassed by his silence and unsure of what to do. Finally he spoke. To the best of my recollection, he said something like this: "Class, today we step onto holy ground. We are about to pit our small, fallible, human minds against the task of knowing God. This ought to fill us with fear and awe. After all, who can know God? So I begin with a warning. To be flippant or sloppy in speaking about God is blasphemy. Better be silent. Let's begin this class with prayer and ask our God to give us the gift of humility as we presume to speak of the one who gave us tongues." So we prayed, and I thought, "Woe is me! I am lost! For I am a man of unclean lips and I live among a people of unclean lips" (Isa. 6:3).

Plantinga's enacted parable and words pierced my complacency and deeply impressed me. Although the piety of "fear" isn't something I'm sure I know what to do with, his eloquent statement of God's transcendence has lived with me ever since. However, there is a problem: there is no universally accepted standard for "quiet awe" of transcendence and mystery. But these days I'm convinced that the confessions of the Christian Reformed Church — those Reformation statements of faith known as the Heidelberg Catechism, the Canons of Dordt, and the Belgic Confession — cross that line by demanding too much. How dare we use what we know to be fallible theories about God coercively, when they are not confessions anymore but goads to enforce unity and communal compliance? Doctrinal emptiness and worshipful awe suit us better. Or, to use Brian McLaren's phrase, what we need is "generous orthodoxy," a simpler, more basic orthodoxy along with the freedom to explore beyond.[10]

In our Western context, emptiness sounds like a negative term, and given its association with certain Zen Buddhist meditation rituals, it may be beyond redemption. When it comes to morality, for example, we wouldn't want to say that we're "empty," or are striving for "emptiness." Perhaps we should speak of a kenotic approach to doctrine and morality, one that truly strips both doctrine and morality to their bare essentials in view of our human incapacity. Thus, when it comes to morality, rather than try to fill books and study reports with complex arguments for why certain actions under certain conditions are right or wrong, we should instead strive to give people the freedom to determine what would constitute love, given their understanding of Scripture, their freedom in Christ, and their situation. We should, like the preaching orders of the oral tradition, preach *caritas,* as the priests were instructed to in the age of orality. *Caritas* is essentially love of neighbor.

Alice Munro's story "The Bear Came Over the Mountain," which inspired the film *Away From Her* (referred to in chapter 5 above), has built into its central narrative a powerful image of surprising kenotic love that trumps conventional morality. Fiona forgets who her husband, Grant, is when he moves her into a nursing home because of Alzheimer's; she even begins a relationship with another resident, Aubrey, who becomes the center of her life. Though this is very tough on Grant, he keeps on visiting and, perhaps even more remarkably, forgives his wife for her inability to return his love and for offering it to Aubrey instead. In fact, when Fiona falls into a deep depression be-

10. Brian McClaren, *A Generous Orthodoxy* (Grand Rapids: Zondervan, 2004).

cause Aubrey has left the nursing home to go home, Grant tries to convince Aubrey's wife to send Aubrey back to the nursing home so that Fiona will be happy again. At bottom, Grant loves Fiona; so he forgives her unconventional fling. This is kenotic morality: Grant's forgiveness is so complete that, even at great personal price, it seeks the best for the other rather than the self.

It goes without saying that as simple as this notion sounds, it would actually be very hard to enact in real life. People like rules and boundaries. And there is no guarantee that we would always — or even often — agree with what other people thought was the loving thing to do. However, the point would be not to concern ourselves so much with the disagreement as we would with building a loving faith community that takes seriously individual freedom in Christ as having to do with thought as well as actions.

Which leaves ethnicity. And here the truth of a kenotic approach to faith is both simplest and most difficult. It is simple because faithful Christians must find their identity, ultimately, in following or trusting Jesus; it is difficult because our ethnic identity is often the one we feel most strongly. There can be no doubt that in the New Testament we are said to be in Christ, where there is neither Jew nor Greek. We are described as strangers and aliens in the world, and citizens of a new kingdom, of which we are ambassadors. The truth is that national churches, like nationality, have been a stain on the unity of Christianity, and they are often a cause for deep division and conflict. Ethnic churches are comfortable, but not only is there is no biblical model or basis for suggesting them as a way forward, but they are actually seriously critiqued in the New Testament.

This was how faith was experienced and lived in the early church. We need to beware of imagining that, if only we could be as good or as dedicated as those in the early church were, we will have succeeded as Christians. Still, I have always been especially struck by the account of Julian the Apostate, emperor of Rome A.D. 361-363. He wrote the letter to the pagan high priest of Galatia, explaining why the sect continued to grow despite his persecution of it. He did not focus on its doctrines or rules, but its way of life. "It is Christian benevolence to strangers, their care for the graves of their dead, the holiness of their lives that have done the most to increase their religion. When these Christians support not only their own poor, but ours as well, all men see that our people lack aid from the empire."[11] That is the kind of kenotic faith I aspire to live and preach.

11. Julian, "Letter to Arsarcius, High-priest of Galatia," in *The Works of the Emperor Julian*, ed. W. C. Wright, 3 vols., Loeb Classical Library (New York: Macmillan, 1923), pp. 69, 71.

chapter 9

Greater Than My Heart

⌒*ψ*⌒

Introduction

As a young pastor, long before I studied the oral tradition or literacy, I had to preach through a part of the Heidelberg Catechism every Sunday evening. The Heidelberg Catechism was written in the mid-sixteenth century by Zacharius Ursinus and Caspar Olevianus at the request of Elector Frederick III, the ruler of the Palatinate, a small German state. Frederick wanted a winsome summary of the Protestant faith that would speak to his people in a time of great religious tumult. In my denomination, the Heidelberg Catechism was loved for its almost poetic emphasis on comfort, its description of the Christian life as one of gratitude, as well as its clarity. With medieval preaching manuals, it shared an emphasis on basic doctrine and conduct, and its three largest sections take up the Apostles' Creed, the Lord's Prayer, and the Ten Commandments. However, its fifty-two "Lord's Days," each containing several thematically related questions and answers, also bear witness to the new linearity and rationality that literacy had helped usher in for new lay readers. The atonement is described in full substitutionary dress, and the catechism pays minute attention to arguments about the nature of Jesus' presence at the Lord's Supper and infant baptism, two Reformation-era flashpoints.

One of the best loved of the question and answers is number

twenty-one: "What is true Faith?" The answer is one that I learned as a child: "True faith is not only a knowledge and conviction that everything God reveals in his Word is true; it is also a deep-rooted assurance . . . that . . . I have had my sins forgiven."[1] This definition, with its emphasis on knowledge, conviction, and assurance, brooks no dissent. It is absolute. A train ride across the prairies. When I read it now, the answer seems to demand so much of me — even as it claims that all this is a gift from the Holy Spirit — that it conjures up the very thing it seems to have no notion of — that is, doubt.

Perhaps just because this Lord's Day always had a "best-loved" tag, I had never paid too much attention to it. It was best loved because, like the emphasis on comfort in the first question and answer, the mention of assurance in this question and answer seems, at first glance, to be heartwarming. Assurance is one of the things that Calvinists, especially the more conservative types, seem to miss out on. For example, I'll never forget hearing a funeral sermon given by a pastor of a very conservative Reformed church. The deceased woman was an elderly and beloved pastor's wife who had slaved selflessly in the kitchen serving both the church and her family — never complaining. But the sermon was about how, as holy as she might have looked on the outside, we could never know the evils that lurked within this woman's heart. Not only so, but the pastor went on for an hour about this theme, warning those present over and over again that salvation was not something anyone, even a believer, should count on. Strive, pray, plead, worry — that was the Christian life. So it was our duty to be careful and repent, or else. There was not much of assurance — none, in fact — in that archetypal Calvinist funeral sermon.

My father, who for the last few years of his life was a chaplain in a retirement home built by a Dutch Reformed community, used to marvel at how often he was called to the deathbeds of stalwart members of the community, many of whom had served as elders and deacons in the church, but were now, in the final days of their lives, struggling with whether or not they were good enough, or had been chosen, to go to heaven. There is something about Calvinism's emphasis on hu-

1. Heidelberg Catechism, Lord's Day 7.

man depravity — properly understood as existential distance and alienation from God — and its doctrine of election that makes for weak knees when it comes to assurance. On the face of it, this seventh Lord's Day's mention of assurance as a characteristic of faith could be read as a promise of assurance for those who do not have it. So it comforts.

Unfortunately, this Lord's Day does not insist that we should be assured of our salvation because God loves us. Instead, it suggests that assurance is only for those whom God has decided to give it to as a gift, just as God, in the Calvinist context, chooses who shall believe. The flip side of this assertion is the inevitable conclusion that if you don't have assurance, you must not be a believer, and are surely not elect. This Lord's Day, in spite of its mention of assurance, easily inspires hyper-Calvinists toward fear and uncertainty.

I still have the sermon I came up with the first time I had to preach on Lord's Day seven. (Even though the sermon was really about a Lord's Day entry, real sermons always have to have texts, so that you are preaching from the Bible rather than something else.) So the text for the sermon was Genesis 15:6. When, in one of Abraham's visions, God promises him a son, Scripture recounts: "Abram believed the LORD, and he credited it to him as righteousness." Though I didn't mention it in my sermon, this text is referred to several times in New Testament discussions about faith (Rom. 4:3, 9, 22; Gal. 3:6; James 2:23). The Genesis passage, as quoted by Paul in Romans, is also given as one of the proof texts for the twenty-first question and answer. So making those words the basis for my sermon seemed like a no-brainer.

My plan for the sermon was to show that Abraham's faith was full of the knowledge, conviction, and assurance that the catechism said real faith should be — just as our faith could be as well. I would note that the apostle Paul thought that Abraham's faith was impressive enough to illustrate his famous argument about justification by faith (Rom. 4), and the author of Hebrews describes Abraham as one of the heroes of faith (Heb. 11:8-19).

So I sat there at my desk, as Thursday afternoon, and then evening, came and went. I wasn't too worried yet; I was still taking notes and reading commentaries. Friday morning I chewed the tips off a couple of pencils. I went through a stack of scrap paper making false starts, crumpling them up, and tossing them into the wastebasket. Friday noon came — and still nothing. I forced myself to write as I might if I faced a seminary test on true faith, in the hope that I would be able to add a few illustrations later. But it was all awful, and on Friday night things looked really bad. It looked like I was going to have to give up my Saturday.

What happened next was one of those gifts that makes you think there must be a God after all. As I looked over my notes once again, I realized that my basic problem was that Abraham didn't seem to have those things that the catechism said were the marks of true faith: he really didn't seem to have much in the way of knowledge, conviction, and assurance. As soon as I realized that, I had something to write.

Abraham lacked knowledge. He knew nothing about Jesus or God's plans for a Redeemer. He had little to go on by way of atonement theory or even God's love for justice and mercy. Not a single work of theology, not even a single Jewish Targum, sat on his shelves. But Abraham especially lacked conviction and assurance. In Genesis 15, God comes to Abraham and promises him a great reward: presumably the son and the land that he has been waiting for since Genesis 12. Abraham's answer, paraphrased, goes something like this: "I don't like to be pushy, God, but how can I found a whole nation when I can't even get started with my own family?"

In fact, Abraham goes on to point out not only that he doesn't have a son but that some distant cousin who lives all the way in Damascus is his closest heir. Abraham may be a hero of the faith, but he doesn't have much conviction here. The story goes on to say that when God takes him outside the tent and shows him the stars and repeats his promise, Abraham believes. But you might believe, too, if you had a cosmic tour personally escorted by God, even if only in a vision, and even though you might not be so sure when you woke up the next morning.

As the story unfolds, although Abraham has more personal encounters with God, he decides that he can't really trust God — or that he doesn't believe what God says — and so he takes matters into his own hands. On his wife's advice, he gets his slave girl pregnant with a view toward making that child his heir. In view of this incident, it appears it doesn't take a lot of faith to have it counted as righteousness. But God appears once more, puts the kibosh on the slave-girl plan — even though it worked as far as begetting a child is concerned — and repeats his promise that Abraham is going to have a son with Sarah. And while everyone remembers that Sarah laughed (probably because she had the decency to try to hide this affront from God), fewer people recall that Abraham laughed at God's promises, too (Gen. 17:17). Abraham laughed because, when God appeared to him in person (not in a vision this time) and promised him a son, Abraham couldn't believe it. And so he asked God to make his heir Ishmael, his child with the maid, Hagar.

Now there are ironies in all this. One is that a plausible explanation for Abraham's wavering after a period of deep conviction is that the written text of Genesis is actually woven together from several oral sources, not all of which agree about the exact nature of Abraham's reaction to God's promises. The linear, rational consistency that conservative Christians look for in the "historical" narratives really isn't there. If you look closely and objectively, you'll find art and beauty, longing and redemption, violence and fear, wishful thinking, and certainly God — but not much history. Within our rationalist paradigm of reading Scripture and using it to proof-text doctrines, we often politely overlook the aspects of the text that don't neatly support the doctrines. So when the catechism looks for a hero of the faith, someone full of knowledge, conviction, and assurance, it picks Abraham on the basis of one verse, conveniently ignoring most of the rest of the story. While I have heard many sermons on Sarah's laughing at God's promises (Gen. 18:12-15), I've never heard one about Abraham's late-life unbelieving laughter. The thing is, when I was forced to preach on this Lord's Day, I kept stumbling up against Abraham's unbelief, not the catechism's reference to his assurance and knowledge and conviction.

The bottom line is that Abraham wasn't, after all, a man of great faith. His faith was a much more fragile, iffy thing than the catechism suggests. What's more, I can't help supposing that if God had made all those personal visits to me, I wouldn't have had half the doubt

Abraham did. Hendrikus Berkhof, speaking of Abraham and early believers' existential experience of God, confirms this.

> The narrators of Genesis leave no opportunity unused to make clear how "difficult" this faith was for Abraham and his followers. For long periods they could go through life without receiving any sign of the saving nearness of their God. Their life could thus be called "a-theistic," were it not for the fact that this "emptiness" which they experienced as the hiddenness of God must have been very trying for them, so much that it could assume the form of a "contending with God"; they were able to bear it only because they remembered former saving encounters on which they could base expectations of help for the future. The biblical narrative views Abraham's whole life from this perspective. In a groping sort of way he goes from promise to fulfillment and thence again to new promises, living a life of belief that exists on the brink of unbelief.[2]

In the meantime, I realized that I couldn't write the sermon I had expected to because what I had planned to say about faith, and what the catechism said about faith, just wasn't there in the Abraham story. But then a different sermon came — and fairly easily, too. All I had to do was share with the congregation what I had discovered, taking care not to dismiss the catechism, but rather to point out that not everyone, not even Abraham, had catechism-sized faith. And God could apparently work with that. What happened, at least according to the Genesis story of Abraham, is that, despite his huge doubts, his second-guessing, and his puzzlement about a God who said one thing but then didn't seem too concerned about making it happen, Abraham also kept doing the kinds of things God wanted him to do. He chose for Hebron. He submitted to circumcision. He tried to talk God out of destroying Sodom and Gomorrah. And, not insignificantly, even though by now he was old enough to have bankrupted his pension

2. Hendrikus Berkhof, *Christian Faith: An Introduction to the Study of Faith* (Grand Rapids: Eerdmans, 1979), p. 15.

fund, he kept getting in bed with Sarah, hoping for a child. Abraham's faith wasn't head knowledge or heart conviction; it was doing the right thing, again and again, even after he'd given up hope that it would lead anywhere.

The Ritual of the Search

I heard a story from Jack Roeda that makes sense of this sort of plodding faith. I first heard the story twenty-five years ago and didn't take notes on it, but as I recall, it went like this. Jack once had a home near a lakeside forest. In the forest there was a path, but it was hemmed in by low bramble bushes and undergrowth; it wasn't really a path meant for people. Jack's neighbor told him that if he walked that path in the early morning, he would sometimes be able to see deer going up to the lake for water. So every morning Jack walked that path, looking for the deer. He did it for one month, then two, but he never saw the deer. He walked it for a year, then two, and never once did he see the deer. But now the path was part of Jack's life, and he just walked it because it seemed like the thing to do. He walked the path even though he never really expected to see the deer anymore.

Then, one morning, when he least expected it, on the hardest part of the path, Jack actually saw a doe and her fawn sipping water out of a little creek. That morning, long after he had stopped looking for one, the deer appeared. I think that is how faith was for Abraham. He had the promises, but he had long since stopped really expecting anything from them. In the meantime, though, with the help of some visions and epiphanies for encouragement, he doggedly stuck with it anyway. Faith, for Abraham, was letting his feet do the talking when his tongue was wagging with laughter.

That is how faith — including the pastoring and preaching and writing — is for me. I used to believe in the promises of God in the way a young man and woman believe they're going to have children. But now I believe in the promises of God the way I hope for a redeemed universe, have faith in a divine Son, and continue going to church even when I fear I'll be disappointed. I believe a little, with effort, and with more doubt than I can shake a stick at. In the meantime, I also keep on praying, visiting those who are sick and dying, and preaching faith, hope, and love — while even believing some. I try to keep the faith when it can't keep me.

Is that enough? Well, according to the story of Abraham, he was going to have his son, whether he believed it or not. God had promised; God would deliver. What is nice about most stories is that we know how they end. I don't know how mine will end.

The Wisdom of the Sages

After I preached that sermon about how Abraham's — and my — faith didn't have much of knowledge or conviction or assurance in it, no matter what the catechism says about "true" faith, I came across another old passage about faith, one that resonated with me more than the catechism's did. This one I found in the Canons of Dordt, mostly remembered now for its anathemas and condemnations. The Canons of Dordt are a document that most people in my tradition pay lip service to while hoping and praying that no one will actually make them pick it up and read it. But, like the deer Jack saw when he had stopped looking, I found something in the Canons that amazed and comforted me. "Responses to the Teaching of Reprobation in Article 16" says the following:

> Those who do not yet actively experience within themselves a living faith in Christ or an assured confidence of heart, peace of conscience, a zeal for childlike obedience, and a glorying in God through Christ, but who nevertheless use the means by which God has promised to work these things in us — such people ought not to be alarmed at the mention of reprobation, nor to count themselves among the reprobate; rather they ought to continue diligently in the use of the means, to desire fervently a time of more abundant grace, and to wait for it in reverence and humility.

Here there is at least some sense that not everyone who believes does so with vim and vigor. Not everyone who believes has a confident heart. What such people are supposed to do, say the Canons of Dordt, is keep on going to church, listening to sermons, and taking the sacraments. Actually, there is more. The Canons go on to say: "Those who seriously desire to turn to God, to be pleasing to him alone, and to be delivered from the body of death, but are not yet able to make such progress along the way of godliness and faith as they would like" — they should not fear, because "our merciful God has promised that he will not snuff out a smoldering wick and that he will not break a bruised reed." The promise is that, even if our faith doesn't work very well anymore, God promises not to abandon us. I knew a person who clung to that promise with all his might. It was my father.

Greater Than My Heart

My father, Rev. William Suk, was a pastor. For him, becoming a pastor was a big deal, something he had stopped hoping for because, in his late forties, he hadn't even managed to finish college, let alone seminary. Still, he was a gifted teacher and able speaker. People in the church knew this, and eventually they persuaded him to seek ordination on the basis of his special gifts. So he became a pastor, just a few years before I did. Within four years of ordination, however, my dad suffered the first of a series of heart attacks that would eventually kill him. After the first heart attack, my dad discovered what other people recovering from heart attacks sometimes discover: heart medication can have disturbing hallucinogenic side effects. Usually the doctors can adjust the medication so that the side effects can be eliminated, or at least controlled.

My father was especially prone to hallucinating when he was relaxing. He would suddenly begin to think unkind or unholy thoughts that he couldn't rid himself of. They got to be so bad that sometimes he would even feel that he wasn't saved. While it lasted, it was awful. Eventually, he told his doctors about what was happening, and they were pretty much able to set things straight. Still, in the meantime, he had his own deep and difficult struggle to believe with the kind of faith that he thought, according to the catechism, he was supposed to have — or else.

What he did, then, in the middle of his hallucinations, was try to concentrate on something else. He would pick up his Bible and read. You must imagine him for a minute: worried and upset at this turn his life had taken, full of drug-induced but very real doubts about faith and salvation, recovering from a heart attack but knowing that the damage was severe, with his Bible open on his lap. What he read was this promise: "This, then, is how we know that we belong to the truth, and how we set our hearts at rest in his presence whenever our hearts condemn us. For God is greater than our hearts, and he knows everything" (1 John 3:19-20). These were words that cut his crisis down to size, and they are words that I cling to when my doubts don't seem to leave a lot of room for the truths of the old, old story.

The bottom line, I guess, is that when it comes to faith that lacks certainty and assurance, the psalmist promised that the loving-kindness of the Lord is from eternity to eternity. Paul promised that nothing in all creation will be able to separate us from the love of God in Christ. Jesus said that he gave his sheep "eternal life, and they shall never perish, and no one shall snatch them out of my hand." And, Jesus adds, not only does he have us Christians, but he has other sheep, too. So, even as I wrestle with the historic confessions, with the way the church deals with issues like homosexuality and evolution, even with the mystery of evil in our world, with the likelihood that Jesus will come back now, after two thousand years, when he said he was coming back soon, I try to set my heart at rest. For God is "greater than our hearts," even when we doubt.

Index

Agnosticism, Christian, 6, 72

Agons: in literate culture, 32, 38-42; in oral culture, 19-21, 23; in secondary oral culture, 108-13, 124

Anselm, 143

Anti-intellectualism, 49, 96

Apocalypticism, 113, 117

Atonement, 123-24, 188, 192; oral, 18, 20; as rationalist doctrine, 39-40, 45, 122, 198

Augustine, 18, 40, 81

Authority, of doctrine, 174-75; of scripture, 63; suspicion of, 35, 74-76, 102, 103, 115

Banaue Rice Terraces, 9, 31-32, 59, 121

The Banner, 1, 3, 9, 67, 86, 178, 182

Barthes, Roland, 78, 110

Bass, Diana Butler, 44, 45, 121, 176, 189

Bauerlein, Mark, 42n.17, 89, 92

Bellah, Robert, 105, 147

Biblical interpretation. *See* Hermeneutics

Borg, Marcus, 83, 104

Brain: as human sensorium, 54, 116, 122; plasticity, 41-42, 86-91, 96

Bright, John, 161

Brueggemann, Walter, 128

Buning, Sietze, 170-72, 180, 191

Burke, Kenneth, 15, 165, 178, 189-91

Calvin, John, 38, 92

Catechesis, 92, 103

Church: as community, 114-17, 121, 153; as institution, 75, 76, 93, 113, 167; medieval, 12, 18, 24; modern, 35-36, 38, 47-48, 65; as tribe, 28, 114, 181-85, 196

Cocooning, 67, 112

Conservatism, contemporary, 16-17, 36-37, 63, 76-77, 110-11, 186-87

Creeds and confessions, 34, 44, 81, 90, 92, 106, 115, 116-17, 187, 191, 194-95; Apostles' Creed, 16, 47, 94, 175, 179; Augsburg Confession, 64; Belgic Confession, 176, 180, 182, 195; Canons of Dordt, 64, 180, 195, 205-20; Heidelberg

Catechism, 16, 175, 176, 180, 195, 198-203; Nicene Creed, 62, 175

Culture wars, 185-87

Denominations, 96, 120, 170, 189; contemporary, 49, 63, 92-93, 177; fractured, 67, 101, 114-15, 179, 185; suspicion of, 74

Doctrine, 46, 81, 128-29, 171-80; belief in, 64, 66, 83, 92-93; and literacy, 39-40, 42-43, 57; oral and medieval, 14, 19, 20; postmodern, 123; and pragmatism, 161; and secondary orality, 92, 99, 115, 117, 183; lacks warrant, 63, 72

Doubt, 3, 32, 102, 120, 135, 164, 199, 207; Abraham's, 201-4; in Canons of Dordt, 205; as cosmopolitan relativism, 61, 62; modern, 43, 46, 48, 49; moral rejection of suffering argument, 71; in Psalms, 134-35; as second look, 3-6

Eisenstein, Elizabeth, 35, 41

Election and reprobation, 36, 51, 171-79, 188, 200, 205

Enchanted worldview, 12, 26, 32-33, 43, 101-3, 121, 146

Evolution, 7-8, 63, 67, 128, 130, 178, 186

Experience, spiritual, 13, 23, 26, 44-45, 49, 64, 93, 100, 105-6, 129, 141-57, 203, 205

Faith, 125, 130, 169, 193, 204-5; of Abraham, 198-204; as Christian agnosticism, 6; as emptiness, 192-97; experiential, 49, 100, 105-6, 115, 129, 139, 142, 143-46, 147-50, 154, 156, 184; medieval, 12-27, 121; modern, 39-42, 43, 46, 47-50, 122, 161-62; postmodern, 72-78;

propositional, 25, 27, 39, 43, 48, 49, 83, 125, 128, 129, 141, 161; in Psalms, 134-36. *See also* Oral faith

Forgiveness: human, 45, 128, 195; divine, 45, 131-33, 138, 199

Fundamentalism, 48, 56, 96-97, 109, 185, 188

God, 29, 61, 69, 71, 127; absence of, 134-36, 151-52; doctrine of, 194; human impressions of, 4, 14, 72, 119, 142, 154; nature, 133, 150, 207

Grace, 4, 45n.24, 132-34, 193

Hart, Hendrik, 48

Havelock, Eric, 22, 42n.16

Health and wealth gospel, 109-10, 124, 163

Hecht, Jennifer, 43, 61, 71

Hermeneutics, 50, 57, 63, 64, 77, 80-82, 153, 155, 202

Hermeneutics of suspicion, 6

Holy Spirit, 48, 130, 137, 152-53, 199

Homosexuality, 67, 116, 187

Illiteracy, medieval, 11, 24, 25, 33, 38

Institutions, 49, 50, 55-56, 96, 116-17, 129, 140, 150, 166-67; postmodern suspicion of, 74-75, 102, 123, 150

Jacoby, Susan, 90, 95, 96, 183

James, William, 149, 161

Kuyper, Abraham, 36, 55-56, 79

Language, religious, 22, 35, 56, 141, 149-50, 152, 156, 157, 165, 189-91

Lindbeck, George, 174, 185, 189

Literacy: in church, 98-100; and confessions, 183; decline of, 85-96, 109, 124, 183-84; early growth,

33-36, 37, 38; medieval, 15, 18, 24; and rationality, 46, 84, 175, 198; restructures human consciousness, 41-43

Liturgy. *See* Rites

Love: as *caritas*, 18, 25, 26, 43, 77, 94, 125, 195; divine, 4, 30, 138, 176, 177, 195, 206; human, 18, 25, 64, 77, 81, 125, 195

Luther, Martin, 34, 38

Marsden, George, 48

Martel, Yann, 5

McClaren, Brian, 128, 195

McLuhan, Marshall, 14, 41-42, 54, 86

Media, 88, 89, 91, 93, 97, 99-100, 110, 123, 184

Modernity, 47-50, 71, 81, 84, 124, 149, 194

Mores, 185-88

Munro, Alice, 131, 195

Ong, Walter, 21, 41, 84, 93, 108

Ontological argument, 143

Oral faith, 14-16, 38; agonistic, 19, 39-40, 84; complex teaching strategies, 24-25; conservative, 16-17; memorable, 21-23; and morality, 25; simple, 17-19, 179

Oral tradition. *See* Secondary orality

Osteen, Joel, 109, 163

Pascal, Blaise, 143-44, 184

Persuasion, 65, 145, 189-91

Plantinga, Alvin, 142, 194

Plantinga, Neal, 54, 120, 175, 194

Postmodernism, 72-82, 102, 114, 122-23, 149

Pragmatism, 100, 117, 131, 161-68

Prayer, 26, 44-45, 71, 105, 164, 165

Preaching: contemporary, 98, 100,

114, 116, 130-31; health and wealth, 163; for literate audiences, 38-39; medieval, 18, 23, 97; of mendicant orders, 44, 46; and narrative, 118, 132; rationalistic, 48

Printing press, 11, 33, 34-35, 41, 84, 92, 108, 122, 175

Progress, 30, 47, 73, 122, 123, 161

Promise Keepers, 109, 116, 164, 187

Promises of God, 125, 127, 134-35, 151, 169, 200-203

Providence, 130, 151

Puritans, 45, 49, 146

Rationality, contemporary, 106-7

Reading: to children, 85-86; in contemporary society, 90, 98; difficulty, 87-88

Reason and rationality: and literacy, 41-42, 46, 47-48, 198, 202; in postmodernism, 72-73, 77; and in secondary orality, 103, 107, 112, 115, 118, 147

Reformation, 35, 45, 49-50, 175-76

Rites, 17, 24, 35, 46, 98n.15, 99, 155, 166

Roeda, Jack, 204

Rwandan genocide, 69-70, 155, 160, 169

Sacraments, 23, 25, 39, 94, 97, 98, 206

Schism, 47, 49, 114, 153, 179

Scripture, 127-29, 132, 193; clarity, 61, 63-64, 80-82; and literacy, 35, 48, 202; and orality, 18; in secondary orality, 100, 150, 157

Secondary orality, 84, 88-92, 118, 123-24, 130, 147, 166, 177, 183; and faith, 84, 92-116

Secularism, 46, 123, 147, 149, 166

Small groups, 101

Smedes, Lewis, 2, 3, 130, 137, 138

Spirituality, 26, 154; medieval, 26, 44-45; postmodern, 78, 122; and secondary orality, 101, 105-6, 112, 115, 122

Stark, Rodney, 105, 114-15

Suk, John: childhood faith, 27-30; crisis of faith, 1-7, 118; seeds of doubt, 60-72, 78-82, 120, 160; faith, 124-25, 129-30, 132-34, 157, 170, 204-6, 207; hypocrisy, 119-20; growing up literate, 35, 50-58; television, 85-87

Suk, William, 177, 206-7

Sweet, Leonard, 100, 149, 155

Sweetman, Robert, 74-75

Syncretism, 101-8, 147

Taylor, Charles, 13, 14, 15, 44, 45, 46, 147, 149

Technology, 41, 47, 73, 84, 88, 93, 122, 149, 166

Television, 29, 84, 85-88, 93, 102, 108, 184; effect on brain, 42, 88-90; and displacement, 88, 90-92, 96; reading, 91, 118

Theology, 6, 29, 65, 94, 174-80, 182; in literate society, 35, 39-40, 46, 47-48, 57; in oral society, 14, 18, 40; and pragmatism, 161; postmodern, 76; in secondary oral society, 115, 150

Values, 49, 76, 77, 79, 90, 123, 184, 185-88

Visser, Margaret, 21n.14, 24-25

Weatherhead, Leslie, 6, 129, 167

Wells, David, 49, 91n.7, 150, 183

Wiersma, Stan. *See* Buning, Sietze

Witten, Marsha, 149-50, 166

Wolfe, Alan, 163-64

Wuthnow, Robert, 105, 166

Yancey, Philip, 142-43, 152